# Police Work and Identity

This is a book about the men and women who police contemporary South Africa. Drawing on rich, original ethnographical data, it considers how officers make sense of their jobs and how they find meaning in their duties. It demonstrates that the dynamics that lead to police abuses and scandals in transitional and neo-liberalising regimes such as South Africa can be traced to the day-to-day experiences and ambitions of the average police officer. It is about the stories they tell themselves about themselves and their social worlds, and how these shape the order they produce through their work.

By focusing on police officers, this book positions the individual in primacy over the organisation, asking what policing looks like when motivated by the pursuit of ontological security in precarious contexts. It acknowledges but downplays the importance of police culture in determining officers' attitudes and behaviour, and reminds readers that most officers' lives are entangled in, and shaped by, a range of social, political, and cultural forces. It suggests that a job in the South African Police Service (SAPS) is primarily just that: a job. Most officers join the organisation after other dreams have slipped beyond reach, their presence in the Service being almost accidental. But once employed, they re-write their self-narratives and enact carefully choreographed performances to ease managerial and public pressure, and to rationalise their coercive practices.

In an era where 'evidence' and 'what works' reigns supreme, and where 'cop culture' is often deemed a primary socialising force, this book emphasises how officers' personal histories, ambitions, and vulnerabilities remain central to how policing unfolds on the street.

**Andrew Faull** is a Senior Researcher at the Institute for Safety Governance and Criminology, University of Cape Town, Editor of *South African Crime Quarterly*, and author of *Behind the Badge: the untold stories of South Africa's police service members*. He was previously a researcher at the Institute for Security Studies (ISS) and a police reservist (volunteer) in the South African Police Service.

## Routledge Studies in Crime, Security and Justice

Edited by
*Adam Edwards, Cardiff University*
*Gordon Hughes, Cardiff University*
*Reece Walters, Queensland University of Technology*

Contemporary social scientific scholarship is being transformed by the challenges associated with the changing nature of, and responses to, questions of crime, security and justice across the globe. Traditional disciplinary boundaries in the social sciences are being disturbed and at times broken down by the emerging scholarly analysis of both the increasing merging of issues of 'crime' and 'security' and the unsettling of traditional notions of justice, rights and due process in an international political and cultural climate seemingly saturated by, and obsessed with, fear, insecurity and risk. This series showcases contemporary research studies, edited collections and works of original intellectual synthesis that contribute to this new body of scholarship both within the field of study of criminology and beyond to its connections with debates in the social sciences more broadly.

www.routledge.com/Routledge-Studies-in-Crime-Security-and-Justice/book-series/RSCSJ

# Police Work and Identity

A South African Ethnography

Andrew Faull

R Routledge
Taylor & Francis Group

LONDON AND NEW YORK

First published 2018 by Routledge

2 Park Square, Milton Park, Abingdon, Oxfordshire OX14 4RN
52 Vanderbilt Avenue, New York, NY 10017

*Routledge is an imprint of the Taylor & Francis Group, an informa business*

First issued in paperback 2019

*British Library Cataloguing in Publication Data*
A catalogue record for this book is available from the British Library

*Library of Congress Cataloging in Publication Data*
Names: Faull, Andrew, author.
Title: Police work and identity : a South African ethnography /
    Andrew Faull.
Description: Abingdon, Oxon ; New York, NY : Routledge, 2018.
    | Series: Routledge studies in crime, security and justice ; 2 |
    Includes bibliographical references and index.
Identifiers: LCCN 2017015125| ISBN 9781138233294 (hardback) |
    ISBN 9781315309859 (ebook)
Subjects: LCSH: Police—South Africa. | Group identity.
Classification: LCC HV8272.A45 S6843 2018 | DDC 363.
    20968—dc23
LC record available at https://lccn.loc.gov/2017015125


ISBN: 978-1-138-23329-4 (hbk)
ISBN: 978-0-367-22730-2 (pbk)


Typeset in Goudy
by Swales & Willis Ltd, Exeter, Devon, UK

For the men and women of the South African Police
Service and their children,
and for Kori, Lyra, and Neave.
May your futures be golden.

# Contents

# Illustrations

## Figures

## Tables

## Box

# Funding

This work is based on research supported by the South African Research Chairs Initiative of the Department of Science and Technology and National Research Foundation of South Africa (Grant Number 47303). Any opinion, finding, and conclusion or recommendation expressed in this material is that of the author and the National Research Foundation does not accept any liability in this regard.

# Preface

We are all born of and into stories. It is by telling tales about our pasts, presents, and imagined futures that we make sense of ourselves and the world around us. Where a set of stories is shared and believed to be true within a group, and where these stories shape behaviour, we call them *culture* (Geertz 1973). When we speak of culture and associate it with particular bodies, borders, and spaces, we call them *races*, *communities*, and *nations*, often contained within *countries*. All are simultaneously imaginary and real.

As individuals we make use of these stories to locate and interpret our sense of self in the social world. Through them we tell ourselves and others a story about the world, but also about ourselves, which we believe to be true. We consider this our *identity*, that is, until the story is challenged. When it is, we revise it or reaffirm our commitment to it. Despite the illusion of continuity, the stories we tell are always changing.

Here is an example of a story I told myself about myself in 2017, as I was finishing this book: When I finished high school in South Africa in the late nineties I wanted to join the South African Police Service (SAPS). Yes, the South African Police *force* (SAP) had been the coercive arm of the post-colonial and apartheid states – violently oppressing most (Black)[1] South Africans in defence of minority (White) privilege and rule – but, in the late nineties, I thought that was behind us. I was high on the euphoria of the *new* South Africa promoted by the ruling African National Congress (ANC) and the country's first African president, Nelson Mandela. That narrative framed South Africa as free of its oppressive past, and suggested that all South Africans could henceforth strive and thrive in a multicultural society, supported by the world's most progressive constitution. Yes, huge poverty and inequality remained, we were told, but what really threatened the country was *crime*. The murder rate had declined from its peak of 78 per 100,000 in 1993, but it remained at almost 60 per 100,000 when I finished high school in 1997 – a rate among the highest in the world. Leaders feared that violent crime might keep foreign investment at bay, or chase wealthy South Africans to other shores, taking their capital and skills with them. So government rallied the population to get behind the SAPS and its new human rights-respecting, service-oriented, community policing. Seduced by these narratives of hope and risk, I imagined myself contributing to the democratic order by becoming a police officer. But, I was quickly advised against it by parents and career counsellors who told a different story about the SAPS, one in which it remained tainted by its past, and so I followed the inertia of privilege and went to university instead.

Eventually, seven years later, I was drawn back to the SAPS. I was older, more critical, and more conscious of the organisation's complicated role in South Africa, but I still believed public policing could make some bad things better. In 2004 I was introduced to what at the time was a mostly American and British English language literature on police organisational culture. From the first pages I was hooked. That same year I signed up as a police reservist (volunteer) and immediately identified in the SAPS officers I met almost all the values, attitudes, and traits I had read about. So began what has been for me almost a decade and a half of research on South Africa's police, coupled with nearly 1,500 hours conducting and observing police work on the street.

Of course this book is not about me. But it is a story told by me, and therefore shaped by me and the stories that inform my world. The story above is convenient for me to believe about myself, and communicate (or *perform*) in this preface. It helps me justify the whole endeavour. Similarly, the SAPS and other police agencies, from Nairobi to New York, are tellers of tales, makers of meaning, and shapers of imagined communities. And like the story I tell myself about my past in relation to this book, so millions of police officers around the world tell themselves stories about who they are and how they came to be associated with the *police*.

This book is about the stories SAPS officers tell themselves about themselves, and how they shape their work. The subject is important because the narratives generated and enacted by SAPS officers each day literally shape South African communities. By promoting some stories and associated behaviours and negating others, policing produces culture (Loader & Mulcahy 2003; Loader 1997a, 2006).

Police work is also identity work. Police officers label and sort, legitimise and stigmatise the individuals and spaces around them. Yes, police practice is shaped by organisational culture as so much literature has attested (e.g. Loftus 2009, 2010; Cockcroft 2013; Manning 2005; Reuss-Ianni & Ianni 2005; Skolnick 2005; Muir Jr. 2005), but it also *shapes* communities, cultures, and identities, including those of the officers doing the work. This book explores the overlap and entanglement of the personal and occupational spheres of policing in early twenty-first century South Africa.

## Methodology, description, and reflection

The empirical data informing this book was gathered during eight months of ethnographic fieldwork. From August 2012 to April 2013 I shadowed police officers as they went about their work at and around four different SAPS stations. Ethnography involves participating in people's lives for an extended period of time to inform a research question (Hammersley & Atkinson 1995). The question

I hoped to answer was: *Who do South African police officers think they are and how does it shape police practice?* Answers to such questions are particularly valuable in transitioning states like South Africa. There, in response to rapid and radical shifts in social structure, law, and identity, front line SAPS officers are expected to shepherd in a new order based on a vision forged without their input (Shearing & Marks 2011). Like elsewhere (Lipsky 2010; Maynard-Moody & Musheno 2003), it is in civil servants' interpretations of South Africa's post-apartheid constitution and generally progressive legislation that their ideals are given life. This is as true for police officers as it is for teachers, social workers, and nurses. Understanding this interpretive process is key to understanding governance and the delivery of public goods.

The SAPS is a national police agency composed of almost 200,000 employees, spread across 1,140 police stations. Permission to conduct fieldwork took over a year to negotiate with its national Head Office, by which time the research question I had initially proposed had changed to the one above. When I explained this to my gatekeeper, he told me not to worry.

The memorandum of understanding (MOU) which the SAPS asked me to sign included a commitment not to leave the police stations' premises. Again, when I told my gatekeeper that I would *have to* leave the stations, I was told not to worry, that I could negotiate this at station level. Essentially, the MOU and indemnity forms were bureaucratic performances through which the SAPS absolved itself of liability for me. As I describe in Chapter 3, similar bureaucratic performances are central to SAPS officers' daily tasks. In this instance, it was a performance for which I was grateful, as it allowed me to negotiate access in the face of apparent obstacles. But, as we shall see, informality in the SAPS can be as hazardous as it can be helpful.

## Field sites

I chose my field sites based on diversity and practicality. I wanted my research sites to differ in context, community, and feel from those of the predominantly suburban stations in Cape Town, Paarl, Pretoria, and Johannesburg, where I had prior experience as a police volunteer and researcher. Between 2004 and 2011, I periodically conducted police duties as a SAPS reservist, and carried out a number of SAPS-related research projects. To the public, reservists are indistinguishable from other SAPS officers. They wear the same uniforms, carry the same weapons and have the same powers, when on duty. As a researcher, my experience as a reservist has been invaluable in helping me understand police work and police officers in South Africa. Of course I do not know what it is like *to live* as a police officer, but I have some sense. I also have a small pool of anecdotes gathered through my own police duties which, when shared with officers over the years, have helped me build rapport.

Practically, my urban sites were located in areas that I could safely reach on the two little wheels of a second hand moped, which I had purchased for the fieldwork. In this book I refer to the two Cape Town stations as Mthonjeni and Yorkton. Mthonjeni is a large township station, which I chose because it recorded some of the highest violent crime rates in the country. It is the kind of station that feeds South Africa's obsession with crime, one that is central to the SAPS' mandate, and to the imaginations of its officers. Yorkton is also a large station. Close to the inner city, its policing area includes a diversity of urban space including commercial and residential, and a thriving night time and tourist economy. It recorded high rates of property crime, fraud, and drug-related offences.

I also wanted exposure to rural policing. The Western Cape, where Cape Town is located, is the only South African province where Africans are a minority. Instead, people identifying as Coloured make up almost half the province's population, while just over a third identify as African (StatsSA 2012).

While I had hoped to work in one of the former homelands reserved for Xhosa South Africans under apartheid, and from which the majority of Africans living in Cape Town trace their heritage, initially that appeared impossible. Fortunately, three months into my fieldwork, I was invited to piggy back to the Eastern Cape with an unrelated research project. I was able to access a rural village station, which I call Gompo, and a rural town station, which I call Patterson. Between the four stations I was able to access the four most common types of populated space in South Africa: urban township, urban city (including business and suburb), rural town, and rural village.

I spent six months between the two stations in Cape Town and seven weeks at the rural stations. I divided my time in this way because the rural stations were significantly smaller, less populous, and less busy than those in the city. This meant it was easier for me to spend long hours with individuals at the rural stations than it was at the city stations. I describe the field sites in detail in Chapter 2.

This was not intended to be a comparative project, nor one that represents all police work in South Africa. The SAPS and the country are just too large. While I consciously sought to expose myself to as much diversity of police type, place, and people as possible, the work remained primarily urban-focused, and limited to four stations in two provinces.

The Western Cape and former Xhosa homelands, the Ciskei and Transkei, are connected through history, migration, identity, money, life, and death (Lee 2011, 2012). While I did not plan to write about these connections, they emerged as central to the identities of the African officers I shadowed, and so have become part of this book. The legacy of the apartheid system and its geographies of exclusion have resulted in comparable urban–rural links across the country, binding specific urban centres to particular rural regions.

## Fieldwork

It is not easy to insert oneself unobtrusively into the working lives of busy public officials. Although I posted one-page summaries of the project objective and method on bulletin boards, distributed them throughout the stations, and intro-duced myself and my work at formal briefings, few officers seemed to grasp my objectives. This was partly because of my fairly abstract research questions, but mostly because officers assumed I was there to measure their effectiveness. Most waited until they could engage me alone to probe my intentions. Understandably, some were suspicious, but there were just as many who quickly welcomed me into their routines. To all, I am deeply grateful.

I was familiar enough with the SAPS to know I would need to hang out (Marks 2004) with officers quite a bit before they trusted me. My approach at each station was to accompany officers as they went about their daily routines. This included participating in morning parades, floating between offices, holding cells and community service centres, spending days and nights on the road with patrol officers and detectives, and talking to and observing officers wherever the flow of a day took me. At each station, I split my time between the detective and uniformed officers.

Access within stations was initially negotiated through managers who would assign me to an individual or group. This was partially limiting, but, where I felt those I shadowed were unrepresentative of the demographics, functions, or work of the station, I negotiated change. In most instances I succeeded. At Mthonjeni, the townships station, I was unable to access the regular uniformed patrol shifts, but did spend considerable time patrolling with Crime Prevention officers. Similarly, because very little patrol work took place at Gompo, the vil-lage station, and because it had only one patrol car, my patrol experience there was limited. For the most part, my needs were accommodated at each station.

My general routine was to merge into the flow of a shift or squad, beginning my shifts as part of their morning or evening briefings. At times I stayed until their shifts ended, but sometimes I left early. Often, the most fruitful days were those spent with an individual or pair of officers. Whether sitting in their offices, attending crime scenes, or patrolling the streets, these were the days on which the most honest conversations took place.

The ethnographic nature of this work meant I could explore how South Africa's social and criminal justice worlds are constructed and given legitimacy in police talk (Fairclough et al. 2011). Police officers are category-makers and culture-workers (Van Maanen 1979; Loader 1997a). I sought to stay aware of officers' social and oral performances (Goffman 1959) and the work that accom-panied them. I considered these actions in relation to the narratives officers shared about their lives. Through the stories they told about themselves and their social worlds, by observing them doing police work and by asking about their self-narratives, their *personal identity* in relation to their work, I was able to gather the data required to answer my question. I had key themes in mind when I started, but allowed my questioning and focus to shift as the fieldwork unfolded, following the data rather than forcing it to fit a predefined framework or tool. Considering my own uncertainty as to how I would answer my research question, this approach was natural.

Across the four field sites, I engaged with almost 300 different SAPS officers and civilian staff. I know this because I have 298 distinct 'individual' codes in my field diary, which I analysed using the software package Nvivo 9.1. Of course the majority of these encounters were brief, even if they were repeated many times. Nevertheless, wherever possible, I made a record of them. While field notes are inevitably selective, my goal was to record as much content, in as much detail as possible at all times, fixing moments in time for later analysis and interpretation (Emerson et al. 2001). Aided by a smart phone and tablet, I was able to sketch detailed, time-specific notes throughout the day or night, as well as snap photographs and geo-tag locations to record my flow through time and space. Note-taking was easiest when at the station, or riding in the back of a detective car. It was more difficult in a patrol van with only one other officer sitting next to me, and very difficult when inside private homes or walking on the street. Where I quote police or myself in these pages, the quotes represent the words typed into my phone either as we spoke (I could type without looking at my phone) or, usually, within minutes of the conversation. While I have tried to keep these accurate they should not be considered verbatim.

But sketches made on my phone and tablet did not constitute my diary. At the end of each shift I spent two to four hours re-working my notes into a single narrative. I used the sketches as prompts, and I dictated the narrative into MS Word using the software package Dragon Naturally Speaking. It is this diary, constituting over 700,000 words, which I coded over a five-month period upon completing fieldwork. While this left me with a feast of data with which to work, it is not an approach I would recommend or repeat. Not only was it exhausting and time-consuming, but it took far longer than necessary for me to extract the data most relevant to my research question and this book.

*Who do South African police officers think they are and how does it shape police practice?* It is a question which, when I started fieldwork, I was not sure I knew how to answer. It is also a question which is not unproblematic for me to have asked.

## Ethnography and ethics

Some may question the accuracy of ethnographic research. Clearly, officers may have intentionally mislead me (e.g. Van Maanen 1979). And yet, all social interactions are selective and (mis)leading. There were many occasions where I challenged those I shadowed regarding their claims about their work and world, and the stories through which they justified them to me. I did not believe everything they told me, nor did I interpret their actions the ways they may have hoped. I am sure the same was true of their reception of me. The narrative in this book represents *my* interpretation of the officers I shadowed, of the stories they told, and of the work they performed in my presence. As police ethnographer John Van Maanen has noted of ethnography, '[f]aced with routine uncertainty and doubt [as ethnographers], the most we can do with or without the scientific method is to wait for time and fuller knowledge to explore whatever theoretical constructions we have built' (Van Maanen 1979).

Ethnography is interpretive work. I have selected what constitutes representation in this book, and so it is *my* message, *my* view of who SAPS officers think they are, which is given life in these pages. While I have tried to treat my subjects with honesty and compassion, some will disagree with my interpretation. I hope that time and critical thought will be the arbiter of its value.

My subjectivity is particularly important in the broader South African context. Yes, I share a national and partly organisational identity with those I shadowed – I was a South African and SAPS reservist, with a knowledge of South African history and social ordering shared by some officers. But in almost every other way I was a stranger, belonging to a national elite whose experience of the country and world was far removed from that of most officers. I spoke a different home language (English), had grown up in different parts of the city and country, and had lived a very different life to them. Unlike most officers, I was not married, had no children, and was part of the minority middle-class elite rather than the majority working poor.

The fact that I am English-speaking not only marked me as different from most officers, but was also my greatest limitation. While SAPS officers are required to be proficient in English, and while English is the official language of communication in the organisation, officers often communicate with each other, and with members of the public, in one of the country's other ten official languages. While I had 12 years of schooling in Afrikaans as a second language, and two years of school and nine months of university instruction in Xhosa as a second language, I remain hopeless at both. Fortunately, I was generally able to follow interactions in Afrikaans, and to note key words that helped me infer meaning when Xhosa was spoken. Where I did not understand a conversation I would often ask officers to summarise it for me afterwards. This was helpful in providing insight into the stories officers told themselves (and me) about their work. Importantly, this benefit did not apply to the public. I had few opportunities to speak to members of the public following their interactions with police. As such, my subjects were all employees of the SAPS. This limits the empirical claims I am able to make.

As I have suggested, this book is really about 800 hours divided between 300 individuals, the majority in the Western Cape, a province quite different from the rest of the country. More so, it is about my interpretation of their words and actions. At points in the book I use italicised text to summarise my interpretation of particular moments, or collections of events. To be clear, these are *my words*, not those of the officers I shadowed. They are my attempts to condense into a couple of sentences key interpretations of officers' identities and how they shaped their work.

Clifford Shearing and Monique Marks have suggested that criminological ethnography should result in suggestions for actionable change (Shearing & Marks 2011). This book will not guide the SAPS' five-year strategic plan, but I hope that it helps to explain how the implementation of such plans is more complex than we may otherwise believe. It makes visible and tries to interpret the way knowledge is produced and lives are organised in the SAPS (Smith 2005). By exploring how officers' life histories, trajectories, and worldviews feed into and off of police discourse and practice, I hope it will encourage an appreciation of the intersection between the personal and professional in policing. This is particularly important as criminology and police sociology become pre-occupied with *what works* in policing (e.g. Bayley 1994; Sherman 2013). While this is a very important and necessary line of inquiry, it threatens to reduce policing to a hard science, rather than one with an infinite gradient of contextual and human variables, built on fantasies of criminal justice efficacy (Reiner 2016; Manning 2010; Young 2011). These variables include the police officers themselves, shaped by the worlds from which they have been drawn, and those they have been asked to shape through their work. My research moves the conversation away from *the evidence* back to the fundamental experience of *being* in the world, particularly when the *being* is intimately tied to the *shaping* (Loader 1997b; Young 2011). Such inquiry is important in light of the de-linking of personal and occupational identities in the twenty-first century, the rapidly changing global employment landscape, and the implications for ontological (in)security and precarity. It is especially relevant to unequal, transitional, and post-colonial societies, like South Africa, endeavouring to implement *democratic* (e.g. Manning 2010; Loader & Walker 2001) and *evidence-based* policing, using models created in very different, developed-state contexts.

## Chapter overview

This book has been written and structured using a circular and layered, rather than linear, narrative. Key themes are repeated in most chapters to illustrate how the overlap and entanglement of personal identity, police culture, and national context (Figure 1.1) shape different elements of personal identity and police practice.

Following the introduction to the research question and methodology, Chapter 1 outlines the key concepts and the broad context in which this work is located. I have framed personal identity as the manufacture of narratives and enactment of social performances in pursuit of ontological security, and asked what policing looks like when considered through this lens. I have described South Africa as a young, violent, post-apartheid democracy, and a country of great expectations and precarity, and hinted that the SAPS is an organisation bloated with purpose – an employer and protector, and a reminder of vulnerability and risk.

Chapter 2 describes the police precincts on which this book is based, and through them the four most common types of South African space: affluent city, urban township, rural town and rural village. It describes the types of order police sought to bring about, and what constituted a good shift in each space. In so doing it explores and juxtaposes the coercion and control of poor, Black bodies in public spaces, with the protection and praise of the wealthy. It illustrates how police practices are shaped by, and perpetuate, historical inequalities across space. In so doing it begins to unpack how officers' personal identities – the stories they tell about themselves and the spaces around them – shape police practice.

Because the good shift described in Chapter 2 seldom manifests, officers present façades of accomplishment to ward off organisational and public scrutiny. Chapter 3 divides these performances into three categories of deception. It suggests that officers' performances produce a culture of suspicion in which police mistrust the public and each other. This mistrust in turn shapes their personal identities and the way they do their work. I suggest that deceptive performances spill into officers' private lives as they pursue middle-class materialism with limited finances.

Key to this work is the contexts from which policing emerges. Chapter 4 explores key themes in officers' personal narratives and emphasises the instrumentality of the job in precarious contexts. It links officers' aspirations to the themes of violence, shame and respect, touched on in earlier chapters, and describes officers' understanding of the links between the urban and rural, the respectable and criminal, and personal identity in relation to space, place and family. It emphasises the precarity from which police are drawn, and the ways in which they rewrite their self-narratives to accommodate their place in the SAPS. The chapter describes who officers think they are, aiding the interpretation of police practices described in previous and subsequent chapters.

Chapter 5 explores the intersections between police work and the violent nature of life in South Africa. Having described the order officers seek to produce, the deceptions they enact, the precarious histories they bring to the job, and their desire for upward mobility, this chapter shows how these inform the violence police deploy in their personal and professional lives. It suggests that some officers experience inadequacy and shame as they struggle to build their lives on the precarious terrain of an unequal, transitional society, in a job that requires them to do unpleasant enforcement work against the communities from which they are drawn. It links these feelings to South African masculinities, to a public thirst for coercive policing, and to police abuse of force. It connects violence and coercion to the way South Africa was governed and policed under apartheid, and links these to personal identity.

In Chapter 6 I suggest that the stories police tell themselves about themselves are of aspirant, deserving South Africans, worthy of the same privileges others enjoy, including those illegal. Thus, where streets are dirty and traffic laws ignored, police performances contribute to the disorder, and where streets are orderly, police are orderly. In this way they reproduce rather than challenge inequalities across space, their practices shaped by the stories they tell themselves about themselves and the spaces and bodies with which they work. While some of the infringements described are minor, they shape the spaces and communities in which police work. But 'carrots' as well as 'sticks' can be used to coerce change. The chapter ends by touching on the positive incentives some police introduce into their personal lives to shape the lives of their children and communities.

Chapter 7 recaps the book's central narrative and explores implications for the practice and politics of policing South Africa. It reiterates that South African police officers are individuals, primarily men, lifted from precarious contexts and placed in the relatively secure world of the SAPS. Their life trajectories often include emerging from hardship in poor rural villages or urban townships, and aspiring to shape a more secure country for themselves and their children. It reiterates that officers' personal histories, ambitions, and vulnerabilities contribute to understanding both how policing unfolds on the street, and to the three police scandals periodically discussed throughout the book.

## Note

1 In this book race is treated as a social construct. It is understood as having no biological basis. However, in South Africa, as elsewhere, race continues to have real effects on peoples' lives as individuals and groups give meaning to, and mobilise, around biological features. The labels 'Black/African', 'White', 'Coloured', and 'Indian' are still commonly used in South Africa and most South Africans identify with one of them. Affirmative action policies, including those of the SAPS, reproduce the labels to aid redress. Despite their problematic nature, meaningful engagement with South African social issues requires reference to these categories. As such, I use them where relevant. Because I don't use race descriptors for most characters, I have provided a summary of basic demographic information, together with the SAPS rank structure, in the front matter under the heading 'Summary of ranks, subject names, and demographics'.

## References

Bayley, D.H., 1994. *Police for the Future*, New York: Oxford University Press.

Cockcroft, T., 2013. *Police Culture: Themes and Concepts*, New York and London: Routledge.

Emerson, R.M., Fretz, R.I., & Shaw, L.L., 2001. Participant Observation and Fieldnotes. In P. Atkinson, A. Coffey, S. Delamont, J. Loftland & L. Loftland, eds. *Handbook of Ethnography*, London: Sage, pp. 352–368.

Fairclough, N., Mulderrig, J., & Wodak, R., 2011. Critical Discourse Analysis. In T. A. Van Dijk, ed. *Discourse Studies: A Multidisciplinary Introduction*, London: Sage, pp. 357–378.

Geertz, C., 1973. *The Interpretation of Cultures: Selected Essays*, New York: Basic Books.

Goffman, E., 1959. *The Presentation of Self in Everyday Life*, New York: Doubleday.

Hammersley, M. & Atkinson, P., 1995. *Ethnography*, London: Routledge.

Lee, R., 2011. Death 'On the Move': Funerals, Entrepreneurs and the Rural–Urban Nexus in South Africa. *Africa: The Journal of the International African Institute*, 81(2), pp. 226–247.

Lee, R., 2012. Death in Slow Motion: Funerals, Ritual Practice and Road Danger in South Africa. *African Studies*, 71(2), pp. 195–211.

Lipsky, M., 2010. *Street-Level Bureaucracy: Dilemmas of the Individual in Public Services*, New York: Russell Sage Foundation.

Loader, I., 1997a. Policing and the Social: Questions of Symbolic Power. *The British Journal of Sociology*, 48(1), pp. 1–18.

Loader, I., 1997b. Thinking Normatively About Private Security. *Journal of Law and Society*, 24(3), pp. 377–394.

Loader, I., 2006. Policing, Recognition, and Belonging. *The ANNALS of the American Academy of Political and Social Science*, 605(1), pp. 201–221.

Loader, I. & Mulcahy, A., 2003. *Policing and the Condition of England: Memory, Politics and Culture*, Oxford: Oxford University Press.

Loader, I. & Walker, N., 2001. Policing as a Public Good: Reconstituting the Connections between Policing and the State. *Theoretical Criminology*, 5(1), pp. 9–35.

Loftus, B., 2009. *Police Culture in a Changing World*, Oxford: Oxford University Press.

Loftus, B., 2010. Police Occupational Culture: Classic Themes, Altered Times. *Policing and Society*, 20(1), pp. 1–20.

Manning, P.K., 2005. The Police: Mandate, Strategies and Appearances. Reprinted in Tim Newburn, ed. *Policing: Key Readings*, Cullompton: Willan Publishing, pp. 191–214.

Manning, P.K., 2010. *Democratic Policing in a Changing World*, Boulder, CO: Paradigm Publishers.

Marks, M., 2004. Researching Police Transformation: The Ethnographic Imperative. *British Journal of Criminology*, 44(6), pp. 866–888.

Maynard-Moody, S. & Musheno, M., 2003. *Cops, Teachers, Counsellors: Stories from the Front Lines of Public Service*, Ann Arbor, MI: University of Michigan Press.

Muir Jr., W.K., 2005. The Paradox of Dispossession: Skid Row at Night. In T. Newburn, ed. *Policing: Key Readings*, Cullompton: Willan Publishing, pp. 173–190.

Reiner, R., 2016. *Crime*, Cambridge: Polity Press.

Reuss-Ianni, E. & Ianni, F., 2005. Street Cops and Management Cops: The Two Cultures of Policing. In T. Newburn, ed. *Policing: Key readings*, Cullompton: Willan Publishing, pp. 297–314.

Shearing, C. & Marks, M., 2011. Criminology's Disney World: The Ethnographer's Ride of South African Criminal Justice. In M. Bosworth & C. Hoyle, eds. *What is Criminology?* Oxford: Oxford University Press, pp. 125–140.

Sherman, L.W., 2013. The Rise of Evidence-Based Policing: Targeting, Testing, and Tracking. *Crime and Justice*, 32(1), pp. 377–451.

Skolnick, J.H., 2005. A Sketch of the Policeman's Working Personality. In T. Newburn, ed. *Policing: Key Readings*, Cullompton: Willan Publishing, pp. 264–279.

Smith, D.E., 2005. *Institutional Ethnography: A Sociology for People*, Oxford: AltaMira Press.

StatsSA, 2012. *Census 2011: Census in Brief*, Pretoria: StatsSA.

Van Maanen, J., 1979. The Fact of Fiction in Organizational Ethnography John Van Maanen. *Administrative Science Quarterly*, 24(4), pp. 539–550.

Young, J., 2011. *The Criminological Imagination*, Cambridge: Polity Press.

# Acknowledgements

This book would not have been possible without the funding, support, and cooperation of many, many people. I am indebted to the South African Police Service (SAPS) for allowing me to pursue this and previous research, and to the men and women of the SAPS who have repeatedly put up with my invasion of their occupational lives. For their assistance in negotiating and granting access, I am thankful to Lieutenant-Colonel Joubert, Major-General Mki, Colonel Gweyi, and Ms. Fundie Hoko.

I am grateful to Mark Shaw, Elrena van der Spuy, Julie Berg, Guy Lamb, Lameez Mota, and colleagues at the University of Cape Town's Institute for Safety Governance and Criminology (formerly the Centre of Criminology), and to the National Research Foundation (NRF) for hosting and resourcing me during this project.

Three anonymous reviewers were generous in thought, effort, and encouragement when I needed it most, as were Tom Sutton and Hannah Catterall throughout my engagement with Routledge. Adam Edwards provided thoughtful feedback and guidance when I'd written myself off course.

This book is builds on a doctorate which I wrote while based at the University of Oxford's Centre of Criminology. I am deeply grateful to Oppenheimer Memorial Trust, the NRF, and to Alice, Cecily, and Michael Crampin for providing the funding which made that, and so this, possible. I am similarly grateful to Jonny Steinberg, Ian Loader, Ben Bradford, Carolyn Hoyle, and Steffen Jensen, who provided guidance and feedback on various drafts of that thesis. None of them has read this book, and all errors and flaws are mine alone.

Over the past decade I have been fortunate to work with and be supported by numerous experts on crime and policing in South Africa, all of whom also happen to be plain good people. In addition to those above, they include Monique Marks, Chandre Gould, Gareth Newham, Johan Burger, Lizette Lancaster, and Hennie van Vuuren.

I am thankful to the Institute for Security Studies (ISS) for allowing me to reproduce their excellent graphs and for providing me with select data.

Phil Broster's humour and unending offers to read drafts, kept my spirits high, as did Wendy Faull's supportive feedback and careful edits in the final weeks.

Norman and Caroll Faull rescued me, as they have done so many times, in the dark of the final push.

Dave McCabe was kinder and more helpful than I could have hoped.

I could not have done this without Elona Toska who read and wrote and talked and supported me through this and dozens of other adventures along the way.

And to Kori, for reminding me that there is so much to which I am blind, and for helping me to see a little more.

# Glossary of terms

**Amapolisa**  'police' in Xhosa.

**ANC (African National Congress)**  the ruling party of South Africa since 1994. Founded in 1912, it sought to end apartheid.

**AVL (Automatic Vehicle Location system)**  vehicle tracking technology used in SAPS cars.

**Bakkie**  pickup truck.

**Bantustan**  a territory within the borders of apartheid South Africa designated for occupation by Africans; also 'reserve' or 'homeland'.

**BB gun**  a non-lethal pellet gun.

**Bishops Court**  one of the most expensive suburbs in Cape Town.

**Braai**  barbecue.

**Cape Borners**  an expression regularly used by Mthonjeni officers to describe adolescent boys whom they believed were born in Cape Town. The term inferred a lack of respect and 'rural values'.

**Cape Flats**  a flat, sandy expanse of land south-east of Cape Town's city centre. It was the area to which the apartheid state moved non-white citizens as part of its project to separate population groups. It remains poorer and more crime-ridden than the older and more affluent parts of the city.

**Cape Town Metropolitan Police Department (CTMPD)**  the city's metro police, managed and funded independently of the national SAPS, but significantly smaller.

**Car guard**  usually self-employed, often unofficial guard who 'watches cars' parked in public in return for an expected tip.

**CID (City Improvement District)**  an area in a South African city in which property owners agree to pay a levy for supplementary and complementary services intended to enhance the physical and social environment of the area; a form of private governance.

**Cluster**  a unit of administration in the SAPS. Each station belongs to a 'cluster' of stations, usually around five. One of the five is designated the 'cluster station', the accounting station for the group.

**Cockroach(es)**  a colloquial term for township taxis.

**Community Service Centre (CSC)**   the walk-in service area of police stations.

**CPUT (Cape Peninsula University of Technology)**   a university in Cape Town.

**Crime Office**   some stations have 'Crime Offices' staffed by detectives working 12-hour rotations. These detectives are tasked with helping both the public and patrol officials with urgent requests relating to investigations, or with processing arrestees for uniformed officials.

**Crime Prevention Unit (CPU)**   these are usually made up of two alternating groups of officials working disparate blocks of eight-, ten-, or 12-hour shifts beginning and ending at times that correspond with patterns of crime. These units generally only patrol and respond to urgent calls for assistance, though in rural areas they sometimes duplicate the work of regular patrol officials.

**Cubbyhole**   glove box.

**East London**   the second biggest city in the Eastern Cape province.

**FCS**   Family, Child and Sexual Offences Unit.

**FET (Further Education and Training college)**   a provider of post-school diploma courses.

**Garage**   petrol/gas station.

**Gatvol**   Afrikaans – fed up.

**Hokkie**   a small, wooden shack-like structure.

**Hoot**   to press on a car hooter or horn.

**ICD (Independent Complaints Directorate)**   government body investigating complaints against police, 1996–2012.

**IPID (Independent Police Investigative Directorate)**   government body investigating complaints against police, 2012–present.

**Jolling**   Afrikaans – partying, sleeping around.

**Klap**   Afrikaans – hit, slap, punch.

**Knobkierie**   a short club, a stick with a ball of wood at one end, a traditional weapon.

**Lang-arm**   Afrikaans – a form of dancing, a bit like waltzing.

**Lobola**   property in cash or kind, which a prospective husband or head of his family undertakes to give to the head of a prospective wife's family in consideration of a customary marriage.

**Makwere**   short for 'Makwere-kwere', a derogatory term for non-South African Africans.

**Matric**   the final year of high school.

**MEC**   Member of the Executive Council, a cabinet member in a provincial government.

**Member**   defined in the police act, 'officer' substitute.

**Moer**   to beat or hit.

**Muti**   traditional medicine or enchantment.

**Okapi knife**   a small, folding pocket knife.

**One up**   meaning a firearm is cocked, a bullet is 'up' in the chamber.

**Ontological Security**   a state in which one possesses the answers to fundamental existential questions about oneself and the world, and in which the story one tells oneself about oneself is positive and stable.

**Panga**   machete.

**Precarity**   existence without predictability or security.

**Road block**   a check-point on a road where police stop and search passing cars.

**Rondavel**   Afrikaans – a round hut of the sort traditionally found in rural southern Africa but now built with concrete and brick.

**Sangoma**   a healer and practitioner of 'traditional African medicine', which can include spiritual work.

**Serious and Violent Crime (SVC)**   a group of detectives assigned to investigate priority violent crimes in a cluster.

**Shebeen**   an illegal tavern.

**Skollie**   Afrikaans – a gangster, criminal, naughty person.

**South African Police force (SAP)**   the apartheid police force.

**Spaza shop**   tuck-shop.

**Standard (One . . . Nine)**   school years.

**Tactical Response Team (TRT)**   an elite unit within the South African Police Service (SAPS), first introduced in 2009. TRT officers are capacitated with knowledge, skills, and specialised equipment to respond to high-risk incidents such as cash-in-transit heists and bank robberies.

**Taxi rank**   taxi terminus.

**Tik**   crystal methamphetamine.

**Tracing**   follow up on the last known location of a wanted suspect in order to bring them before the court.

**Trap boy**   colloquial term for a civilian paid by police to assist with an entrapment operation (sting).

**United Democratic Front (UDF)**   a non-racial coalition of civic, religious, and workers' organisations formed in the 1980s to oppose apartheid.

**Vehicle Check Point (VCP)**   a relatively informal road block, usually lasting an hour or less and staffed by two to four officers.

**Vetkoek**   Afrikaans – fat cake, fried dough.

# Summary of ranks, subject names, and demographics

Below I list the SAPS rank structure, followed by a list of names and basic demographic information about police in this book. 'Race' and gender are indicated using language employed by the SAPS.

| SAPS rank structure |
| --- |
| National Commissioner (General) |
| Lieutenant-General |
| Major-General |
| Brigadier |
| Colonel |
| Lieutenant-Colonel |
| Captain |
| Lieutenant |
| Warrant Officer |
| Sergeant |
| Constable |
| Student Constable |

## Subject summary

| Pseudonym | Basic information | Station |
|---|---|---|
| Jacobs (Captain) | Coloured, male, mid-40s | Mthonjeni |
| Hendricks (Constable) | Coloured, male, late-20s | Yorkton |
| November (Constable) | Coloured, male, late-20s | Mthonjeni |
| Kani (Constable) | African, male, early-30s | Gompo |
| Yoyo (Constable) | African, female, late-20s | Mthonjeni |
| Magona (Constable) | African, male, mid-30s | Gompo |
| Apolles (Warrant Officers) | Coloured, male, mid-40s | Mthonjeni |
| Diedericks (Lieutenant-Colonel) | Coloured, male, early-50s | Mthonjeni |
| Bungu (Constable) | African, female, early-30s | Gompo |
| Moshoeshoe (Constable) | African, male, mid-30s | Yorkton |
| Louw (Sergeant) | White, male, mid-40s | Yorkton |
| Dlamini (Captain) | African, male, mid-40s | Gompo |
| Bhele (Constable) | African, male, late-30s | Yorkton |
| Januarie (Captain) | Coloured, male, mid-40s | Yorkton |
| Jali (Constable) | African, male, mid-30s | Yorkton |
| Ndungwane (Constable) | African, male, early-30s | Mthonjeni |
| Carelse (Student Constable) | Coloured, female, mid-20s | Yorkton |
| Nxuba (Constable) | African, male, early-30s | Gompo |
| Nkomo (Lieutenant) | African, male, mid-40s | Gompo |
| Thangana (Captain) | African, male, mid-40s | Mthonjeni |
| Jiyana (Warrant Officers) | African, male, late-30s | Mthonjeni |
| Mxenge (Constable) | African, male, mid-30s | Mthonjeni |
| Deyi (Constable) | African, male, early-30s | Mthonjeni |
| Mashile (Constable) | African, male, mid-30s | Gompo |
| Nzo (Constable) | African, male, late-20s | Mthonjeni |
| Mmaya (Student Constable) | African, male, early-30s | Gompo |
| Debeza (Constable) | African, female, early-30s | Mthonjeni |
| Cethe (Student Constable) | African, male, mid-20s | Gompo |
| Cruz (Colonel) | White, male, mid-40s | Yorkton |
| Skrikker (Warrant Officer) | Coloured, male, late-40s | Mthonjeni |
| Qoboza (Constable) | African, male, late-30s | Mthonjeni |
| Kriel (Warrant Officer) | White, male, late-40s | Yorkton |
| Mbelani (Constable) | African, male, late-20s | Gompo |
| Jonker (Sergeant) | Coloured, male, early-30s | Yorkton |
| Mqhayi (Constable) | African, male, late-20s | Mthonjeni |

# Chapter 1

# Police work, personal identity, and context[1]

## Stories

This is a book about stories – stories about people, stories about places, stories about people in places, people striving to be in places, and people ordering places. Stories are central to police work. When officers respond to calls for service, they respond to stories. When they take statements, they record stories. When detectives investigate cases, they do so in search of stories. And when testifying in court, police commit stories to record and hope that they are judged to be true. Police officers tell and re-tell stories to themselves, to each other, and to the public, daily. Each story is shaped by those that came before it, and each shapes those that come after. These in turn shape police practice, which shapes identities and communities. These stories are important sites of inquiry.

While a significant body of work has examined police stories through the lens of occupational culture, this book adopts a slightly different approach. With the South African Police Service (SAPS) as its subject, it explores officers' *personal identities*, or the stories they tell themselves about themselves, in relation to their pursuit of *ontological security* in contexts of *precarity*. It describes the *performances* officers enact, how these relate to, *shape*, and are *shaped by* SAPS and South African history and culture, and the contexts and forces in which officers' lives are *entangled*. In so doing it is guided by the question: *Who do South African police officers think they are and how does this shape their work?*

At a time when 'the evidence' and 'what works' in policing reigns supreme, and in the wake of decades of police sociology that positioned 'cop culture' as the primary force guiding officers' actions, this book shows that individuals' personal histories, ambitions, and vulnerabilities also impact the way the work is done. It is an examination of policing in South Africa forged through the overlap of personal, organisational, and national narratives, as illustrated in Figure 1.1. To interpret this overlap and entanglement, I use a cluster of concepts briefly sketched in Box 1.1 and unpacked in more detail in this and subsequent chapters.

- Characterised by *precarity*, life without predictability (e.g. Giddens 1991; Young 1999, 2007; Butler 2009; Barchiesi 2016)
- Long history of race-based structural inequality and violence
- Wealth, education and employment remain skewed by race (StatsSA 2011)
- 46% of population lack money for adequate nutrition (StatsSA 2014c)
- 45% of those who begin school don't finish
- 27% unemployment, 40% for those aged 24 to 36 (StatsSA 2016)
- Murder rate 34:100k. High rates of interpersonal violence (e.g. StatsSA 2016; Optimus 2015)
- 69% feel unsafe walking in their area of residence after dark (StatsSA 2015)
- 81% mistrust fellow citizens (Afrobarometer 2013)
- World's highest HIV/AIDS prevalence rate
- Religious and superstitious

- Def ined as the stories we tell ourselves about ourselves, which we believe to be true, in pursuit of **ontological security** – a state in which the storyone tells oneself about oneself is positive and stable

- Crime-focused constitutional mandate
- Community (sector) policing model
- Repeatedly de-/re-militarised
- Starting salary (2010) R101,532 (£5,548) vs R60,613 (£3,312) for average 'Black African' household (StatsSA2012)
- Classic elements of 'police culture', including sense of mission, suspicion, solidarity, machismo

Personal identity

Police (SAPS) culture

South Africa

Overlap and entanglement

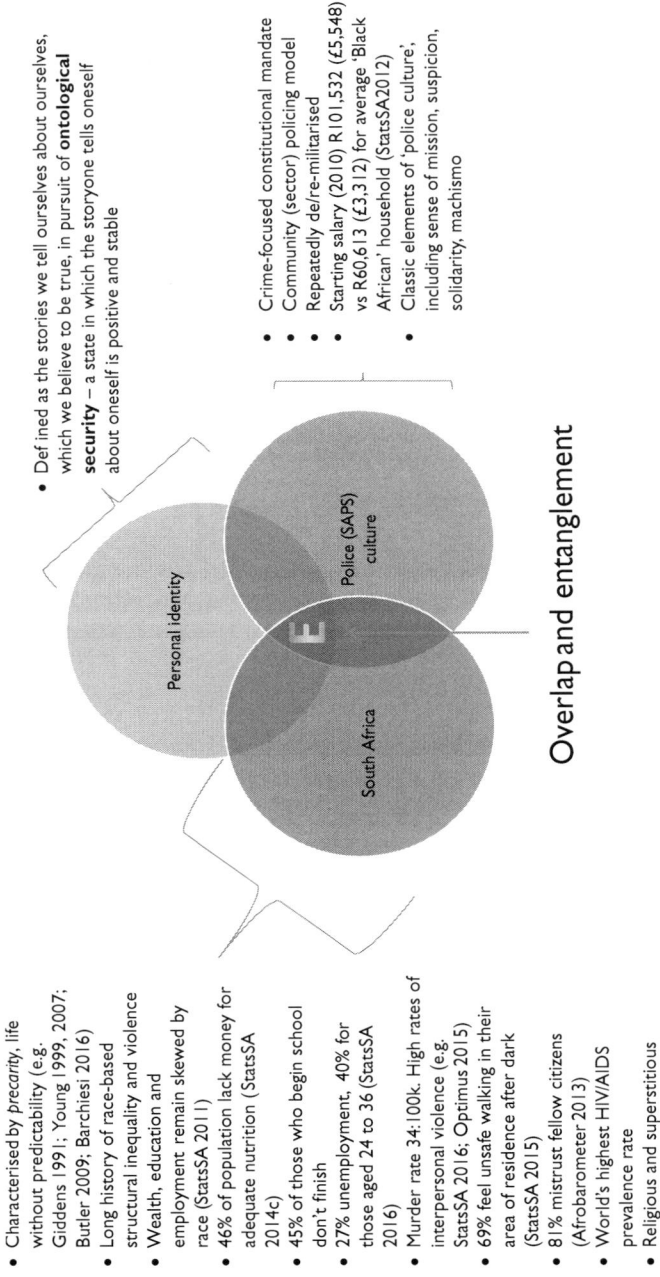

*Figure 1.1* Conceptual framework

## Box 1.1   Summary of key concepts

a) *Personal identity* – The stories we tell ourselves about ourselves, which we believe to be true (e.g. Geertz 1973; Giddens 1991; Ochs & Capps 1996; Simon 1999; Kramer & Wei 1998; Jenkins 2008);

b) *Ontological security* – A state in which one possesses the answers to 'fundamental existential questions' about the self and world (Giddens 1991), and in which the story one tells oneself about oneself is positive and stable;

c) (Social-/Identity-)*Performance* – Recognising that individuals and groups *perform* (behave) differently in different contexts, and for different audiences, to achieve strategic goals. Performances can reinforce or undermine personal and organisational identities and are central to policing (e.g. Goffman 1959; Manning 1997);

d) *Precarity* – Existence without predictability or security in a context of modernity, inequality, and risk, the opposite of ontological security (Butler 2009; Barchiesi 2016; Giddens 1991; Young 1999, 2007, 2011);

e) *Police organisational culture* – Informal values, attitudes, and practices commonly associated with police organisations and personnel (Neyroud & Newburn 2013; Reiner 2010; Cockcroft 2013);

f) (Police work as) *Shaping* and *cultural work* – The ways police work shapes and orders identities and communities (e.g. Loader & Mulcahy 2003);

g) *Overlap* and *entanglement* – Terms used to draw attention to instances and products of narrative overlap, primarily between individual/personal, organisational and national/contextual narratives. Reminders that individual narratives inform organisational narratives, and vice-versa, which in turn shape and are shaped by police culture and practice;

h) *Liminality* – A state of uncertainty and ambiguity, limbo (Turner 1994).

Because this is a book about police stories authored in the comparatively under-studied Global South, it draws on a series of empirical vignettes based on ethnographic research. The first vignette introduces a SAPS detective, and through him, the organisation, country, and key concepts. But first, it is worth contextualising this inquiry in select literature on policing, police culture, and personal identity.

## Police culture and workplace socialisation

Personal identity forms through social interaction (Jenkins 2008), and is closely related to patterns of behaviour shared by groups, i.e. culture (Glaeser 2000).

Organisational environments that encourage or require social interaction and cooperation, such as police organisations, may foster organisational culture. Where individuals spend significant amounts of time in such environments, like police officers working 12-hour shifts, these cultures shape identities. This has been described as secondary (Berger & Luckmann 1991) or institutional socialisation (Harro 1996). With employment so central to modern life, it has been suggested that institutions and organisations are the primary vehicle through which people integrate and make sense of themselves in modern societies (Deetz 1992; Kersten 2000; Manning 2007; Young 2007).

A great deal of literature has examined police organisational culture and how it fosters in officers particular attitudes and behaviour (Shearing & Ericson 1991). It has described a 'sub-culture' (Waddington 1999) of shared traits that bind officers together, forging in them 'working personalities' (Skolnick 1966) and inspiring dramatic performances intended to suppress doubt over police competency and legitimacy (Manning 1997; Holdaway 1983; Young 1991). It has presented democratic policing as a liberal paradox (Waddington 1999): breaking rules (e.g. speeding, use of force, deception) in defence of rules (Brodeur 2010). That police may deploy force in the course of their duties means they threaten the very peace they are mandated to preserve (Bittner 2005; Young 1991). What's more, while the rise of the state and, through police its monopoly of force, has slashed global violence (Pinker 2011), evidence suggests police have only limited impact on general crime (Roeder et al. 2004; Frydl & Skogan 2004; Bradford 2011). As a result, theirs is an impossible mandate (Manning 1978; Burger 2006).

When police claim to be able to prevent crime they set themselves up to fail. To hide failure, they manipulate appearances, enact dramatic scripts, and publish statements and reports that deflect attention from their limits. In these performances, police work to convince others of a common-sense logic that they are indispensable. And yet, as Peter Manning puts it, (criminal) justice is an illusion, in part maintained through the 'magic' of such *performances* (Manning 2010). Even within well-resourced jurisdictions like the United Kingdom, fewer than 3 percent of criminal offences result in conviction, and less than 1 percent in incarceration (Reiner 2016). Still, ritual performances are endlessly repeated in state bureaucracies the world over, most visibly by police, to convince all that justice *can* be done. South Africa is no different.

Key attitudes and personality traits identified in the pioneering literature on police culture include a sense of mission, cynicism, pessimism, a conservative outlook, machismo, racism, sexism, pragmatism, suspicion, isolation, and solidarity (Reiner 2010; Cockcroft 2013). It has been suggested that these attitudes are hidden in interactions with the public, but embraced in the backstage, for police audiences. There, police tell stories that categorise the people and places with which they work (Van Maanen 2005; Holdaway 1983), and connect them to informal rules that guide police actions (Ericson 2005). These rules help normalise the use and abuse of force, convincing officers that certain people and behaviours fall outside a society's notion of the good citizen (Holdaway 1983).

But is police culture forged, and does it shape policing in isolation? Peter Moskos (2008), writing about Baltimore's police, suggests that the values associated with police culture are simply those of the communities from which officers are drawn. Diddier Fassin suggests something similar of Paris's anti-crime squads (Fassin 2013).

Others have expressed concern that, while many of the traits identified in the pioneering cop-culture literature persist today (Loftus 2009; Loftus 2010), policing has changed immensely (Sklansky 2007). Thus, inquiry through the cultural lens risks stifling creativity, particularly beyond the wealthy West where it was first identified and named (Marks 2005; Shearing & Marks 2011; Reiner 2010, 2015).

An alternative approach, which I adopt in this book, is to shift the focus to officers' personal identities, and to ask how they relate to police culture and practice. By exploring the resultant narrative overlap and entanglement, I simplify and tweak Janet Chan's (1996) use of Bourdieu's *habitus* (cultural dispositions) and *field* (socio-political/structural context) to examine policing in context. Through this approach, this book explores the lives of individuals, primarily men, lifted from precarious contexts and placed in the relatively secure occupational world of the SAPS. It probes their sense of self and self-worth as they strive to secure ontological security in a risk-saturated, identity-fluid context, two decades after South Africa's first democratic election. It describes their attitudes and performances of occupational identities and duties – often as forceful coercers of the poor and jealous admirers of the better-off – and locates these within individual life narratives.

## Personal identity

Framing personal identity as the stories we tell ourselves about ourselves which we believe to be true acknowledges that we are always in flux. Everything from the cells in our bodies to our memories, beliefs, and perspectives are constantly changing. Our sense of self is an illusory product of transitory brain activity (Harris 2014). And yet, in our minds and through our words we convince ourselves of our wholeness and continuity. Julian Baggini's (2012) notion of the *ego trick* illustrates this well. He compares identity to a cloud. From a distance, it has clear edges. We can point to it, describe it, and watch it move. But up close it is revealed not as a single thing but as millions of moving droplets. The cloud exists, but not as we commonly think. 'The self is like a cloud,' Baggini tells us, 'that not only looks like a single object from the outside, but feels like one from the inside' (Baggini 2012:150). We articulate and experience these feelings through narrative.

Anthony Giddens' work on identity in modernity (1991), and Jock Young's on crime, punishment, and identity in late modernity (Young 2011, 1999, 2007) provide useful conceptual foundations from which to explore identity-as-narrative in South Africa. Both Giddens and Young acknowledge that the twentieth century was the century of the self. Perhaps more than at any other time, the individual was placed at the centre of the social world, and remains there today. Identity has been sold as the vehicle through which to attain personal happiness (Elliot 2014), proposed and protected through the manufacture and emphasis of individual and human rights. In this era, contentedness is attained in part by developing and sustaining a coherent sense of self – of being ontologically secure. Giddens describes *ontological security* as a state in which one possesses the answers to 'fundamental existential questions' about the self and world (1991:47), sustained through routine.

The twentieth century also placed employment at the centre of life, and thus at the centre of the self (Giddens 1991; Young 2007). Occupation and associated income and status had unprecedented repercussions for individuals, particularly for men. In the early twentieth century, access to employment was uneven and unstable, making the creation and maintenance of coherent self-narratives difficult.

For most of humanity's past, family, tribe and community experienced and interpreted life through unchallenged common logics of culture, meaning, and magic. But life in the early twenty-first century is different. Ideas, images, and actions can be created and countered in seconds, from opposite ends of the earth. Social interaction exposes one to existential risk. In sharing one's self-narrative with others, one invites challenge (Kramer & Wei 1998). In an era of unprecedented global visibility and connectivity, beliefs and practices, ways of being in, and interpreting, the world are constantly up for renegotiation. What was once obvious is no longer, so that life can require the constant questioning, doubting, and reflexive re-writing of personal narratives and future biographies.

Both these trends, the fictions through which we understand ourselves and our worlds (e.g. Harari 2014), and the relationship between (un)employment and personal identity, are crucial to understanding post-apartheid South Africa. Apartheid intentionally kept people apart, restricted rights, censored media, banned political and ideological groups, limited domestic migration and intercultural contact, promoted Christianity, and distributed opportunities based on race. As such it sought to manufacture a society based on racialised identities, in which the physical and ontological security of Black people was sacrificed to foster that of Whites.

Young describes the citizens of Western democracies as having been shaken by the end of twentieth century cradle-to-the-grave predictability. In South Africa, only White people experienced this. For most, the end of the twentieth century meant the birth of a *new* nation, and the promise of material and ontological fulfilment. But in 2017, most South Africans' lives were more likely to be characterised by *precarity* than ontological security.

Precarity can be thought of as the opposite of ontological security, i.e. an existence without predictability. While South Africa is not a late-modern society in the developmental sense, much of Young's (1999, 2007, 2011) characterisation of such societies as saturated in risk and uncertainty, individual choice and pluralism, and profound economic and ontological precariousness is relevant to it. With its gross inequality, high rates of violent crime, HIV and tuberculosis infections, poor education, and superstition, South Africans experience the challenges of late-modernity with the added risks and fragility of an historically divided, grossly unequal country in transition.

With this conceptual scaffolding in mind, it seems appropriate to turn to a story about police work and identity in South Africa.

## Democracy, life choices, and hard work

The setting – Cape Town, late August, 2012. The small engine of the white Toyota in which I sat, hummed. Warrant Officer Skrikker was speaking, the rapid rhythm of his voice lightening the mood set by the road's winter-wet tar.

Skrikker was a detective in the SAPS based in Mthonjeni[2] where I had recently begun what would be eight months' shadowing police officers.[3] We were driving down Cape Town's N2 freeway – a 20km stretch that connects some of the city's wealthiest and most destitute neighbourhoods, returning to the police station after running various errands. We were discussing some of Skrikker's favourite topics: work, justice, life choices, and reward.

'It comes down to the decisions you make in life, Andrew,' he told me, 'They are what determine your success.'

Skrikker was a quick-talking Coloured man in his mid-40s with a police career that stretched back over 25 years. He embraced the label *Coloured*. That it had been ascribed to him and his forbearers through racist colonial and apartheid experiments in social engineering was not of great concern to him. He was an optimist who believed in looking forward, rather than back.

'I get really angry when people who murder and rape stand up in court and say that they were raped as a child or that they live in a shack, and so ask the court to go easy on them,' he told me. I disagreed. 'In South Africa, we are not all born with equal prospects,' I countered:

> Born to White parents in a country that advanced the interests of White over Black, I was delivered into a flow of privilege in which I could afford to make mistakes. Most South Africans born at the time experienced the opposite. The system held them back and quickly punished any fault they made.

Skrikker didn't agree. We had had this discussion before and would have it again in subsequent weeks. 'Andrew,' he retorted:

> I was raised by my mother and my grandfather. I love my mother more than my wife sometimes. She is amazing. She worked her whole life to give me food and clothes and to make sure I went to school. My father was always out *jolling* with other women. He had three other kids and they are all *skollies* now. My grandfather told me not to complain about the food I received but to be grateful that I was eating at all. He instilled discipline in me. He beat me with his belt. It's how I beat my children. I'm angry that it's not allowed in school anymore.

As he spoke we passed the freeway exit that led to the police station. 'I want to stop by my house,' he responded to my expression of puzzlement.

Skrikker had mentioned his home within our first two days together. It was another of his favourite topics. 'I have a nice house in Blue Downs,' he had told me, 'It has a swimming pool and three bedrooms. My two older children have their own cars.' He also loved discussing football. With a broad grin on his face and laughter in his chest, he would recount games played by his favourite English Premier League team. In years past he had watched them in bars, but since 2008 when he could first afford it, he had subscribed to South Africa's most comprehensive satellite television bouquet. In 2012, the games played by a group of men who spoke languages Skrikker may never hear, in a country he may never visit, were beamed straight into his bedroom, where he wove them into the story of his life.

Skrikker was a proud man. He had secured a job in the former South African Police force (SAP) during apartheid's final years while many of his childhood peers had remained poor or in conflict with the law. In 2012 he was earning almost R20,000 (£1,092)[4] a month before tax, an income more than double the national average.[5] But like many police officers, he complained that he deserved more.

'Andrew,' he would say, 'I do the work of an officer but I am paid the salary of a warrant officer. I don't deserve it.' Still, he was grateful for what he had and pleased with what he believed was his financial maturity. He had put two children through school and had budgeted for the third. He was saving to support his youngest, should she be accepted into university, and planned to put his next bonus aside as a wedding gift for his eldest. During one of our conversations he listed all the expenses he needed to cover in the final months of the year: a new toilet seat, bedroom curtains, clothes for him and his daughter, 'And then the money will be finished.'

We had pulled off the freeway and were making our way into Blue Downs. Skrikker changed topic:

> South Africa is a great country, Andrew. I love the South African sun and the smell of the African soil. Many White people say Africa is in their blood. All the races in the country need each other. We need the Whites with their expertise. The guy living in Bishopscourt deserves to be there because he is up at night attending meetings and working hard. We can't be jealous of him.

Bishopscourt is one of Cape Town's most affluent formerly, and still predominantly, White suburbs. Skrikker referred to it in acknowledgement of the country's stark inequality, and the anger it sparks among millions of South Africans.[6] Perhaps he wanted me to know that he did not resent White people and their relative wealth. Like many post-colonies, national discourse in South Africa remains rich with notions of the racial other (Comaroff & Comaroff 2006), often linked to simplistic stereotypes rendered increasingly visible through social media. In 2016, for example, a middle-aged White woman, Penny Sparrow, gained notoriety for writing on Facebook that Black beach goers were 'monkeys' who brought with them 'dirt and troubles and discomfort' (e.g. Wicks 2016). At the same time, politicians regularly blamed 'White minority capital' (Khoza 2016) for monopolising the country's wealth, while politicians and citizens[7] alike accused Whites of having stolen land from Africans (Staff Writer 2016). In 2015 and 2016, most major news sites removed their online comment sections, in part due to the racist vitriol they generated daily (e.g. Trench 2015).

At the Mthonjeni detective branch where Skrikker worked there were only two White officers, one being its commander. Working in an area where almost everyone was African, and living in a predominantly Coloured neighbourhood, Skrikker didn't regularly spend time with people who looked like me or had my opportunities. And, while I liked to think of myself as progressive, I too was a product of that exceptionally divided city, so that, outside work, my world remained uncomfortably, for me, White.

Skrikker went on:

> I was watching the Olympics the other day. I watched Le Clos's father wiping tears from his eyes while holding the South African flag; it was great to see a White man so proud.

Chad Le Clos is a South African swimmer who unexpectedly beat American favourite, Michael Phelps in the 200-metre butterfly at the 2012 London Olympics, which were taking place that month. Skrikker continued:

> And then to see a White and Black man standing together on the podium after winning the running … This country is so beautiful. It has so much potential. These days any child can go to the poshest school. My daughter's fiancé wants them to emigrate to New Zealand or Canada after they are married. I won't stop them. People must make their own decisions in life, but I wish they would stay and build the country.

I told Skrikker that I found his view idealistic, that as much as I wished it were different, South Africa was not a fair country. Desmond Tutu's vision of a demographically diverse and socially and economically just *rainbow nation* had become, it seemed, another dream deferred. But the conversation was on its head. It should have been Skrikker telling me that ours was not a meritocratic society. It was he and his parents whom the apartheid state had stifled so that I and mine could prosper. But he was invested in the narrative of capital and hard work promoted by the state, and so we disagreed.

## Space, place, and race

Blue Downs, where Warrant Officer Skrikker lived, is not a wealthy part of Cape Town, but nor is it poor. Our journey took us past neighbourhoods awash with the cream, brown, and ochre of Reconstruction and Development Programme (RDP) houses, peppered with the silver and rust of adjoining shacks.[8] The houses were some of the 2.8 million built by government between 1994 and 2014 (Goldman Sachs 2013), handed to those whose land had been seized by the apartheid state, or who remained trapped in the poverty it had fostered. But the shacks stood as reminders that the houses, like so much else, were not enough.

Past this relative poverty, Blue Downs' streets were lined with generously-sized homes. In 2011, when the last census was conducted, 77 percent of Blue Downs' residents identified as Coloured and 21 percent as Black African. The remainder identified as Indian/Asian, White, and 'Other' (City of Cape Town 2014). Skrikker was proud of his racial identity and of Afrikaans, his mother tongue. When I asked about his ancestry he told me he thought there was a White woman on his great grandmother's side, and a Khoi person on his father's. The Khoi are Southern Africa's oldest inhabitants, displaced through centuries of Bantu and European settlement. Coloured South Africans trace their histories to contacts between these groups, and with slaves brought from Indonesia and Madagascar in the eighteenth century.

The apartheid state used these same Census-2011 race labels – Black/African, White, Coloured, Indian/Asian – to engineer a society in which race determined access to land, movement, employment, education, and health care. Apart from those whose labour could be exploited in White cities, factories and mines, colonial and apartheid governments relegated most Black South Africans to rural reserves. Mthonjeni, where Skrikker was employed, was established in the mid-twentieth century as a dormitory town for such workers. In 2012, almost all the area's residents were Black African. South Africa's cities remain broadly race and income-segregated; Cape Town particularly so.

That 21 percent of Blue Downs' population identified as African in 2011 suggests upward mobility. Where Africans live or school in areas or institutions previously reserved for Coloureds, Indians, or Whites, it signals class migration. Because such areas and institutions previously received disproportionate state support, they remain well-located, maintained, sought-after, and relatively expensive. The same is true of Coloureds or Indians in areas or institutions previously reserved for Whites (Soudien 2004, 2010). So, when in conversation with Skrikker's African partner, Sergeant Tambo, he told me he lived in a 'Coloured neighbourhood', I thought he was signalling class ascension. However, when I probed further the opposite was true: he said he lived in a Coloured area because it was where the state had provided him a home. In his case, then, the neighbourhood and RDP house marked the precarity of his past rather than the success of his present.

Apartheid divided the country into racial enclaves. Like many Africans living in Cape Town, Sergeant Tambo saw the Eastern Cape as *home*. Born in the former Transkei – an apartheid reserve for Xhosa people – his self-narrative was wed to a place a thousand kilometres away. One of his two children lived there with his parents so that both he and his wife could work in Cape Town, though she had been unable to find any. But, he told me, Cape Town was also home. It was where he, not his father, was the man of the house. In migrating to the city, the story Tambo told himself about himself had changed.

## Aspiration, acquisition, and precarity

Pulling up outside Skrikker's house I told him I would wait in the car. He immediately objected, 'No, come inside, I want to show you around.' The first thing I noticed as we entered the house was a 42-inch flat screen television surrounded by a plush, leather lounge suite on a polished tiled floor. Everything was impeccably neat. Skrikker led me down a passageway and into three modest bedrooms, each with its own television. The TV in his room was even bigger than the one in the lounge. He pointed to pictures of his children, told me how proud he was of them, how intelligent his youngest was and how she wanted to visit Europe one day. In the backyard he showed me his swimming pool and *braai* area. There was a glow in his face as he led me through his home, as though it were a monument to his achievements. And, of course, it was.

After ten minutes, he led me back to the car. It wasn't clear that there had been any reason to visit the house. I could only conclude that he wanted to show me what he had made of his life. It was a gesture that I would come to view with increasing significance in subsequent months, and one that is central to understanding personal identity and police work in contemporary South Africa.

### *Unemployment*

Despite being a middle-income suburb, 24 percent of residents in Skrikker's neighbourhood were unemployed in 2011, only a third of adults had completed high school, and half its households earned less than R3,200 (£175) a month (City of Cape Town 2014). Compared to his neighbours, Skrikker was very well off.

Two decades after the African National Congress (ANC) won the country's first democratic election, both the absolute number of those employed and the percentage of those unemployed had increased, as job expansion was outstripped by population growth. In 2014, 26 percent of South African residents were unemployed, jumping to 28 percent among women, and 36 percent among men and women aged 15 to 34 (StatsSA 2014b). If one included those who had given up looking for work, unemployment stood at 36 percent in June 2014, and remained there in December 2016 (StatsSA 2017).

Since 1994, South Africans have consistently identified unemployment as the most important issue for government to address (Afrobarometer 2013). Despite legislation intended to promote the employment of women, people with disabilities, and anyone previously classified African, Coloured, or Indian, White South Africans remain disproportionately better employed and paid. In 2011, the national average household income was R103,204 (£5,636) a year, less than half Skrikker's income. But this average is misleading. Female-headed households earned significantly less (R67,330/£3,677) than male-headed households (R128,329/£7,009). With an average income of R365,134 (£19,942) a year, White households earned one and a half times more than Indian households, three times more than Coloured households, and six times more than African households, the latter averaging just R60,613 (£3,310) a year (StatsSA 2012). With nearly 80 percent of the country identifying as 'Black African', Skrikker earned nearly four times more than most South Africans. Working for the SAPS had paid off for him.

### Poverty, inequality, and expectation

Mthonjeni, where Skrikker worked, was characterised by relative poverty, violent crime, overcrowding, and unemployment. When I asked him what came to mind when he thought of the area, his response was empathetic:

> The high levels of serious crime, and the poverty. There are so many informal settlements, the hardship the people live in. Most are good, God-fearing, hardworking people. I think of the suffering and expectations, what they want from government, to take them out of this poverty. There are thousands of people who don't have houses. There's no service delivery. They stay in horrible circumstances, especially in the informal settlements in winter. The unemployment is a problem, HIV is a problem, and the high levels of crime. Generally, it is the circumstances that people live in that is bothering me. I think the government must come to the party and live the lives of the people.

The expectation that Skrikker referred to is key to understanding South Africa. The hope that characterised the 1990s was expectation driven. People looked forward to jobs, houses, quality education, basic services, and feeling safe, and they looked to the new government to provide these.

However, while the anti-apartheid ANC was a socialist organisation, its post-apartheid policies have been a continuation of apartheid's neo-liberalism (Bond 2004; Super 2013). The result, some have suggested, has been a continuation of apartheid's distributional regime (Seekings & Nattrass 2005; Nattrass & Seekings 2011). As a result, South African society remains divided into two clear income groups: a small wealthy 'middle class' of professionals, and the majority working and unemployed poor.

When Skrikker said the people of Mthonjeni needed *service delivery*, he conjured a phrase rich with meaning. Having lacked access to piped water, electricity, and other services before 1994, the notion of *freedom* in South Africa includes the expectation that access to these and other services will be provided by the state. And while millions still live in poverty, the ANC government has managed some impressive feats. It has doubled expenditure on healthcare, built over 2 million RDP houses, and established a welfare net that in 2013 saw 46 percent of households receiving at least one social grant (StatsSA 2014a). That year, grants were the second most common form of income, with just 65 percent of households relying first on salaries (StatsSA 2014a). Despite this expansive welfare net, in 2014, 46 percent of South Africans lacked the R620 (£34) a month required for adequate nutrition (StatsSA 2014c). With a post-training, pre-tax salary of approximately R10,000 (£562) a month in 2012,[9] plus benefits, a job in the SAPS is, at least financially, an extremely attractive prospect.

### Education, service provision, protests, and violence

Warrant Officer Skrikker described his youngest daughter as the apple of his eye. He said he would do anything to ensure she received a university education. Until 1990, schools in South Africa were racially segregated, serving as sorting mechanisms that delineated life trajectories. In most instances, this meant limited education and post-school opportunities for all but White learners.

By 2017, South Africa's education system had yet to recover from the damage wrought by apartheid. In 2013, half of those who began school in 2001 had dropped out. Among those who reached the final year of high school, just 40 percent passed their exams and only 12 percent qualified for university (Spaull 2013). Those who do manage to finish high school in South Africa often find themselves with few opportunities for further education or employment (Simkins 2011).

With education and the economy failing them, South Africans have limited means through which to improve their standing. In this context government jobs, including those in the often-derided police service, are highly prized. Employment in the SAPS offers a rare avenue from relative poverty to relative wealth. But once inside the SAPS, many officers find their salaries don't meet their ambitions. As a result, some, including Skrikker and Tambo, are constantly on the lookout for other income-earning opportunities, both within the SAPS and elsewhere.

\*

Despite the country's impressive welfare interventions, a great many South Africans live in poverty. Public protests, whether to demand housing or electricity from government, or dignified wages from employers, are a daily feature of life.

My first day with Mthonjeni's police involved protest. Riding to the station on my moped, I was stopped at a police roadblock 1 kilometre out. Behind it, residents stood behind burning tyres, singing. Re-directed by police, I arrived at the station to find it surrounded by armour-clad officers loading rubber bullets into shotguns, poised to protect the state's property should the protesters head their way. Expectation and anger fuel South Africa's public life.

According to the SAPS, in 2012/13 its officers attended 12,399 'crowd-related incidents', 1882 of which it classified 'unrest-related' (SAPS 2014:101).[10] While the Mthonjeni police station was not damaged that day, Warrant Officer Skrikker didn't escape unharmed. When, a few days after the protest I first met Skrikker, one of his fingers was bandaged. He told me that while driving into the station with Sergeant Tambo on the day of the protests, a brick had been thrown through their car window and struck his hand. When he recounted the event, his empathy for Mthonjeni's residents was absent. He said he had held his firearm between his legs and had wanted to shoot at the protesters; said he wouldn't drive into Mthonjeni at night until the protests had ended; and that his life was worth more than the job. To this, Tambo had joked, 'They should call the police from the mines to get those people who throw bricks.' Skrikker chuckled and responded, 'What can you expect? If you shoot at the police from behind a crowd of people, then you must expect the police will shoot back.'

The detectives were referring to Marikana, a mining town 100 kilometres from Pretoria where, days earlier, SAPS officers had opened fire on striking miners, killing 34 and injuring nearly a hundred others. But while the tragedy at Marikana caused national outrage, few know that from 2004 to 2013 police killed 43 people during protests (Grant 2014). So, while most protests in South Africa are peaceful, too many still result in death. South Africa is a place where people die in pursuit of better lives. The irony is that the police who kill them do so as part of their own journeys from hardship to hope, enacting organisationally scripted performances in pursuit of their own ontological and material security.

\*

Skrikker and Tambo didn't seriously condone the killing of protestors. Rather, their comments are indicative of the cynicism and dark humour that are common to police organisations. That said, violence is endemic in South Africa, and in many instances is considered to be a just and pragmatic response to perceived violations (CSVR 2010; Collins 2013; Artz et al. 2016). In 2015/16, 34 people were murdered for every 100,000 residents, four and a half times the global average. This was up from 33 per 100,000 in 2014/15, but down from 78 per 100,000 in 1993. Contrary to popular belief, Cape Town's murder rate is twice that of Johannesburg (Kriegler & Shaw 2016). Nor is crime evenly spread within cities. Half of South Africa's murders occur in just 12 percent of police precincts (Lancaster 2015), while most of Cape Town's violent crime occurs in only seven. In Mthonjeni, people were murdered at a rate of 150 per 100,000 in 2015/16. It is possible that Mthonjeni is among the most violent neighbourhoods in the world.

Between events like the Marikana Massacre, and the more than 30 murders a day, South Africans regularly turn to violence to solve problems and seek justice. At the same time, they look to the SAPS for protection from the violence of others, and as a potential employer that might protect them from the general precarity of South African life.

## From Sharpville to Marikana, and the rebirth of policing

Marikana was not the first time South African police were involved in a mass shooting. Comparable blood was shed in 1960 and 1976 during protests of apartheid laws and policies.

Apartheid required that Black African South Africans carry pass books, which had to be endorsed by the state, to travel, work, or live in White space. It was akin to a passport and visa system but for domestic use. A significant amount of police time was spent enforcing this system. In 1960, SAP officers shot and killed 69 people, and wounded 180 others protesting the pass system in Sharpville.

Similarly, in 1976, police killed an estimated 176 protestors when school children took to the streets to object to the introduction of Afrikaans as a language of instruction in schools. In the aftermath of this shooting, government suppression of anti-apartheid activities became increasingly militarised, as did the African National Congress's (ANC) campaign of armed resistance to apartheid (Lodge 2011). Longitudinal data reveals a rapid increase in murder beginning in this period and lasting until the early 1990s (Kriegler & Shaw 2016). The 1980s saw calls to make the country's townships ungovernable through civil disobedience while labour unions crippled the economy through protest action. In 1984, a partial state of emergency was declared, and, in 1988, a full state of emergency, as the government simultaneously militarised and lost control of the country. A Mass Democratic Movement in 1989 led to the widespread flouting of race-specific laws. All these changes had major repercussions for the then SAP.

As apartheid buckled in the late 1980s and negotiations towards a democratic South Africa gained momentum in the early 1990s, it became clear that a new vision for policing was necessary. A 1993 ANC discussion document accused the SAP and ten homeland police agencies of 'being unable to deliver even a minimum level of public safety and security' (Haysom 1993:3). It called for a 'break with the apartheid past [which was characterised by] exploitation of the police as a political instrument, [making it a] militaristic, secretive, unaccountable, racist, and violent institution' (Haysom 1993:1). In its place, it proposed a democratically constituted police agency, accountable and visible to local communities, focused on quality rather than quantity, prevention oriented, demographically representative, transparent, problem rather than action oriented, politically non-partisan, and focused on service (Haysom 1993:9–11). Such a police service, the ANC believed, would be welcomed by the country's African majority, and the violent crime wracking its townships would cease.

Following the ANC's resounding victory in the country's first democratic election in 1994, the SAP and homeland police agencies merged to form the SAPS in 1995. A bill of rights and new constitution reframed South Africans as individuals in a community of equals. For example, in relation to safety it states that:

National security must reflect the resolve of South Africans, as *individuals* and *as a nation*, to live as equals, to live in peace and harmony, to be free from fear and want and to seek a better life.

(Republic of South Africa 1996) [emphasis added]

The police mandate established in Chapter 11, section 205(3) of the constitution states that:

The objects of the police service are to prevent, combat and investigate crime, to maintain public order, to protect and secure the inhabitants of the Republic and their property, and to uphold and enforce the law.

(Republic of South Africa 1996)

But one cannot enforce constitutional justice in the absence of organisational justice, and the SAP had not been just to its police or the Black public. In the early 1990s, only 5 percent of African officers held managerial (commissioned) ranks. Most held positions that marked their subservience to White police (Cawthra 1993). This began to change after Nelson Mandela was released from prison, the ANC (and other anti-apartheid parties) was unbanned, and negotiations towards a multiracial democracy began. With apartheid's end in sight, the SAP had de-racialised its training facilities, hired more women and promoted Black officers. In 1995, 65 percent of SAPS officers were African, Indian, and Coloured, and 36 percent White (Bruce et al. 2007). In the years that followed, the new SAPS sought to distance itself from its abusive past by replacing its military ranks with civilian, diversifying its workforce so that it was more reflective of the national demographic, and embracing human rights.

But the ANC's belief that a legitimate government and police service would bring an end to crime proved false. The public violence that had marked apartheid's final two decades died down, but the interpersonal violence that had become a part of daily township life did not. Instead it spread, while organised crime flourished (Shaw 2002). That which was previously restricted to Black townships spilled into middle-class (formally White) neighbourhoods and confidence in the state's ability to manage crime plummeted. Rapidly, feelings of insecurity became common to almost all South Africans, threatening to entrench the precarity of life which democracy sought to dismantle.

The ANC government's first major response to crime was to develop a holistic, multi-departmental National Crime Prevention Strategy (NCPS). But as public concern over crime mounted, this was abandoned for a 1998 police-centric

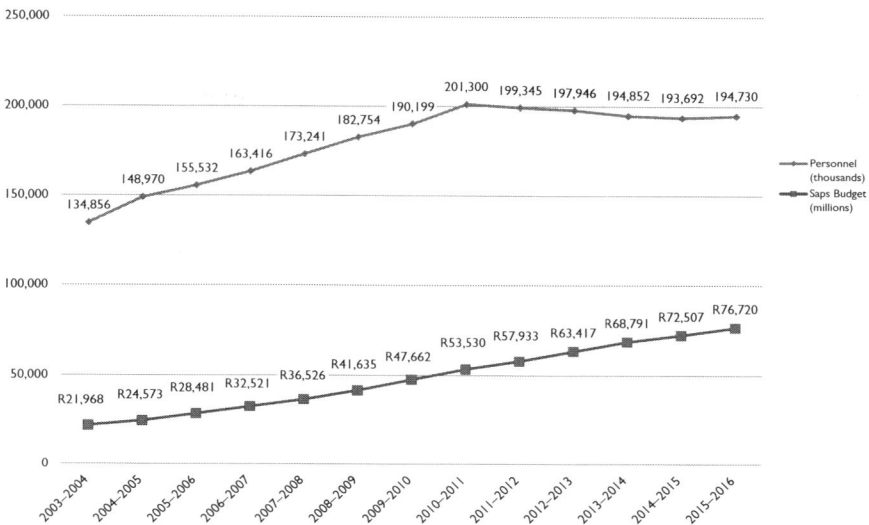

*Figure 1.2* SAPS personnel and budget 2003–2016

Source: Based on data from the Institute for Security Studies (ISS) (https://issafrica.org/crimehub)

Crime Combatting Strategy. That same year the Minister of Safety and Security, Steve Tshwete, declared that government would 'deal with criminals in the same way a dog deals with a bone' (Shaw 2002:86), pandering to a populist appetite for punishment.

Following a late-1990s moratorium on police recruitment, the SAPS received disproportionate boosts to budget and personnel for almost a decade (Figure 1.2) (ISS 2016). From 2001 to 2011 it grew from 120,000 to 200,000 officers as police were re-centred at the fore of crime-related policy. New recruits were framed as professionals for whom the job was a vocation.

The notion that police can and should prevent crime in South Africa remains central to both public and police understandings of their mandate. But the country's crime and violence is a product of a long history of exclusion and inequality. And while apartheid's police force was deeply implicated in the manufacture of this precarity, the SAPS cannot easily undo its damage.

South Africa is the quintessential divided society, fragmented along class, culture, race, linguistic, and geographic lines. It is a land increasingly characterised by streets filled by the poor and working fringe demanding housing, services, respect, and dignity. In such a context, where social consensus on what is proper becomes blurred, there is a danger that criminal law may become the basis for social control (Manning 1978). Bearing the South African context in mind, we return to August 2012.

## Ontological security, precarity, and performance

Back in the car driving down Cape Town's N2 freeway towards Mthonjeni Skrikker shared another story:

> Some years back I had a case where a father and son had returned from work to find a man breaking into their house. A scuffle ensued and they beat him to death. They were also injured by him. That man and his wife worked hard for that house and the things in it. They worked hard to send their children to school. The wife was a domestic worker.[11] She told me she would attack me if I arrested her husband and son. Those people made sacrifices to give their children things, and then these guys who sit in the sun all day in the shacks across the road come and take them. So we didn't charge the men with murder; we made it an inquest.

It was a story about other people, but also about Skrikker. It was a story in which the subtext was barely hidden. It said: '*This is how I see the world, and this is how it shapes my work.*'

A few weeks later I witnessed Skrikker's efforts to shape the world through his work. He asked me to accompany him to the station's cells where he would charge a young man, on behalf of a colleague.

The accused was a Coloured man in his early 20s. Smiling, Skrikker led him from the holding cell to a table in another room where his fingerprints would be taken. He spoke to the man in English, even though Afrikaans was each one's mother tongue. It was apparent that Skrikker was performing for me. All he needed to do was take the man's fingerprints, inform him of his rights, and complete some paperwork, but for Skrikker that was secondary. Pressing the man's fingers into the ink, Skrikker turned to me, 'Andrew,' he said, 'I like to motivate people.' Then, in gentle tones he addressed the young man:

> Why are you throwing your life away with this stuff? You don't want to go to prison. Prison is full of gangsters. Men are raped in prison. I had a relative who went to prison. He told me that even big men cry there. Life is not about tattoos and high living. I can see you are young; that this is your first time in jail. This place is like a magnet; it keeps bringing people back. That holding cell you were in is nothing. You don't want to know what prison is like. I can speak Afrikaans better than you, I can speak that gang language better than you, but that guy in prison is not your brother; you don't share a mother.
>
> I also grew up on the Cape Flats, I know what it's like for Coloured and African people in this country. It's hard. I was born into that. But one thing I always knew was that it was not going to be like that for the rest of my life. In my family, I support my children. My stepson has never been in trouble. He has just started his own business. We support each other. Maybe you don't

have that support but God gave you that voice in your head that says when something is good or bad. You must go to church, you must find God, you must not drink excessively, you must stay away from drugs.

The young man stared at the ground. 'One day you will thank me for what I have told you today,' Skrikker finished. As the man washed the ink from his hands Skrikker turned to me: 'Andrew, they should make a television programme where they show the reality of life in prison. They must scare the youngsters out of crime.' It was a thought he had shared with me before, based on a view I believe is common in South Africa: that coercion brings change; that threats, force, and punishment prevent crime. It is a belief that sustains corporal punishment in schools and homes (Artz et al. 2016), vigilante violence on townships streets (Super 2016), and community demand for ever more visible policing (O'Regan & Pikoli 2014). It is not, however, a philosophy that makes South Africa any safer.

*

Consider again the stories Skrikker shared with me in the car. Central to his sense of self was the idea that he had been raised in relative hardship, and that, through good parenting and decision making, he had avoided prison and made a success of himself. When he took me to his home, he wanted me to witness what Giddens has called the 'material manifestation of self-narrative' (1991), how his decisions had shaped his material world. Similarly, when Skrikker called me to the holding cells, he wanted me to witness his compassion. He was acting out a self-narrative, performing the story he told me about who he was, and possibly the story he had told himself about himself, too.

Goffman's (1959) work on the presentation of self is valuable here. He showed that we all manage our appearances for different audiences (including ourselves) to shape what they ought to see in us. We limit information and suggest that what we offer is who we are. Skrikker foregrounded select aspects of himself to shape my and the arrested man's view of him, and so to reinforce his own belief in his self-narrative. Giddens calls such performances 'ontological reference points' (1991:48): they embody one's sense of self, and so support ontological security.

But police performances are about much more than personal identity. When police speak, write or act in the name and iconography of the state, as Skrikker did in the police cells, they do so with an official authority. In so doing, they produce and communicate important messages about the kind of community in which they work or what it aspires to be (Loader 1997).

*

When I asked Warrant Officer Skrikker why he had joined what was at the time apartheid's South African Police force, he told me he had wanted to fight crime and make the country better. The reasons his partner, Sergeant Tambo, shared with me were less idealistic. He had joined, he told me, because he was 'just look-ing for any job'. He would have preferred to be a teacher but instead spent his days stitching together narratives that explained unnatural deaths.

On one of our last days together Tambo, Skrikker, and I attended a scene where a man had been struck and torn apart by a train. After a few minutes exam-ining the fragments of flesh scattered across the tracks, Skrikker sighed, 'This is a bad, bad thing.'

Walking back to the car I asked the detectives what they felt at such scenes. Skrikker responded first, 'What are you supposed to feel? The person has died. It is terrible. Someone is dead and you must try to identify them so that they are not an unknown on your name.' An 'unknown' would mean an unsolved case and missed performance target. Tambo added, 'You just have to take it and forget about it very quickly. You can't take it personally. It will drive you crazy.'

Both statements spoke of protecting the self, finding something stable and holding tight. Between them, I imagined other words left unspoken:

> In this job, I must be seen to be competent, but sometimes I see terrible things. They are things that threaten my sense of self and my ability to be in this place. I will do what I must do to evade sanction, but I must protect myself, too. This scene must not shape or become part of me.

As we climbed into the car Skrikker added, 'That's the worst train accident I've seen in a long time. There's nothing to look at.' Like it or not, it was character-shaping work, work their younger selves may never have imagined, would someday define them.

*

SAPS-joining narratives like Tambo's were more common than Skrikker's. Considering the romanticism of mission and vocation built into popular represen-tations of police work, this surprised me. I wasn't surprised that most SAPS officers had applied for the job out of necessity rather than vocation, but I was surprised how many admitted to it up front. I wondered if they feared I would judge them as lacking ambition if they told me they had always wanted to be police – an answer one might think more fitting of the police archetype. Rather, it seemed they wanted me to know that they were what one might think of as *accidental* police officers. They had not planned to do this work, and relatively often they did not want to be defined by it.

Whether people join police organisations in pursuit of an archetypal police identity, or because it is the only employment they can find, they generally become police officers to be part of police agencies, not to change them. As a result, police organisations have far more power to influence employees, than employees have to change organisational culture (Brodeur 2010). SAPS organisational culture shapes the lives of its officers, and through them, the contours of South African society.

## Entangled co-existence: shaping identities, communities, and culture

The more power granted to an institution or occupation, the more able it is to gain and maintain control over the meaning with which it is commonly associated (Manning 1978). Police organisations and officers also possess the ability to ascribe meaning to people and places. When SAPS officers speak, write, or act in the name and iconography of the state, the way that Skrikker did in the police cells, they do so with the appearance of official authority. As Ian Loader notes, every police stop, search, arrest, diagnosis of crime, etc., is an authoritative signal about the type of people and communities the state (dis)approves of (1997). Police help members of communities make sense of their past, present and imagined futures, and the condition of the society in which they live (Loader & Mulcahy 2003). In so doing, they contribute to individuals' ontological (in)security and personal and collective identities. An illustration of this is the manner in which, for much of the twentieth century, the SAP used pass laws to limit the presence of Black South Africans in what was considered White space. In so doing, it reminded Africans that the state did not consider them citizens. In the early twenty-first century police act out similar performances with poor, foreign Africans, signalling to them that they are different, vulnerable, and not always welcome (Steinberg 2011).

In many ways, the SAPS is a monolithic institution promoting long-standing mythologies about who police officers are and what they should do. It is a crime-focused, target-chasing organisation invested in strategic performances that connect policing with crime. The ways SAPS officers produce particular visions of order, their shaping work, can also be thought of as the manufacturing and disseminating of culture. The authoritative and cultural power of the SAPS also shapes the lives of its officers. Being part of the SAPS helps officers order their personal narratives. It shapes the stories they tell themselves about themselves and the country.

In a crime saturated country, the SAPS is one of the key institutions through which South Africans tell stories about themselves and their democracy. Still dressed in a police-blue strikingly reminiscent of the apartheid SAP, SAPS officers remain for many a reminder of an oppressive past. At the same time the SAPS is regularly conjured and appealed to to make people safe (e.g. O'Regan & Pikoli 2014). Thus, the SAPS is a reminder of its antithesis – a crime-saturated society and a government unable to provide the long-promised *better life for all*.

*

It is now generally accepted that explorations of police organisational culture must emphasise context (Chan 1996; Waddington 1999; Marks 2005; Reiner 2010). Even if most modern democratic police organisations share common origins and are comparably structured, resourced, and mandated, they exist and operate in vastly diverse environments, resulting in an array of experience and practice. The result is that the cultural, shaping influence police have on communities and individuals varies greatly. In this book I explore policing in South Africa through the overlap and entanglement of organisational, national (contextual) and personal narratives.

Warrant Officer Skrikker, for example, believed he had lived a good life, based on coercive discipline and hard work, and that he could be a role model and disciplinarian to others. But many of his colleagues, including Sergeant Tambo, continued to struggle financially, socially, and ontologically. That Skrikker's life and self-narrative was more orderly than Tambo's is not accidental, nor is my role as the author of this book. Rather, they are the outcomes apartheid had intended, of occupation and income stratified by race.

Regardless of how much the officers I shadowed had succeeded within the narrative of the *new* South Africa, all wanted more for themselves and those close to them: more money, more security, more freedom, more justice, and a more prosperous future for their children. Warrant Officer Skrikker and Sergeant Tambo were just two of the almost 200,000 men and women who make up the South African Police Service. This is a book about their stories.

## Notes

1  The analytical framework introduced in this chapter, as well as a version of Figure 1.1, were published in *Policing: a journal of policy and practice*, in April 2017 and are reproduced here with the permission of the journal. For more information, go to https://academic.oup.com/policing/article/3748209.

2  Throughout the book I use pseudonyms for the names of police stations and officers.

3  In the SAPS the title *officer* refers to the commissioned ranks of Captain and above. The correct nouns for those below this rank are *official* or *member*. However, through exposure to global media, many South Africans, including at times members of the SAPS, refer to *police officials* as *police officers*. For ease of reading in this book I use the word *officer* to describe all police men and women, regardless of rank, division, or function.

4  Based on a rate of £1 = R18.30 (August 1, 2016)

5  The 2011 national census showed the average Coloured male headed household earned R112,172 (£7,249) per annum, slightly above the national average of R103,204 (StatsSA 2012:41).

6  According to the World Bank, in 2016 South Africa was the most unequal country in the world (World Bank 2016).

7  In this book, unless otherwise specified, I use the word *citizen* to describe any long-term resident of South Africa, including non-nationals, whose status and rights, by virtue of being within South Africa's borders, are defined and protected by the country's bill of rights and constitution.

8  RDP is short for Reconstruction and Development Programme. The RDP was the first major post-apartheid socio-economic framework. It focused on addressing the widespread absence of formal housing, safe drinking water, electricity, and other services denied to millions of Black South Africans during apartheid.

9  In 2016 this had risen to R14,000 (£7,646) a year.

10 It should be noted that many have criticised the way the SAPS classifies protest action. A 2016 review of over 150,000 reported protests over five years, found that only 43 percent were protests. It also noted that actions classified as 'unrest' are determined by whether the police intervene rather than if there is violence, as the SAPS phrasing may suggest (Alexander et al. 2016).
11 'Domestic work', usually implies cleaning work and is common in South Africa. In 2014 the law required that a domestic worker employed 45 hours a week should be paid a minimum of R1,877.70 (£103) per month. Many, however, are employed part-time and/or are paid significantly less.

# References

Afrobarometer, 2013. *Summary of Results: Afrobarometer Round 5 Survey in South Africa*, Cape Town, South Africa. Available at: http://afrobarometer.org/sites/default/files/publications/Summary of results/saf_r5_sor.pdf.

Alexander, P., Runciman, C., & Maruping, B., 2016. South Africa's Incident Registration Information System (IRIS): It's Use and Abuse in Protest Analysis. *South African Crime Quarterly*, (58), pp. 9–21.

Artz, L., Burton, P., Ward, C., Leoschut, L., Phyfer, J., Loyd, S., & Kassanjee, R., 2016. *Research Bulletin: The Optimus Study on Child Abuse, Violence and Neglect in South Africa*, Cape Town: Centre for Justice and Crime Prevention. Available at: www.cjcp.org.za/uploads/2/7/8/4/27845461/cjcp_ubs_proof_18.pdf.

Baggini, J., 2012. *The Ego Trick: What Does It Mean To Be You?*, London: Granta Books.

Barchiesi, F., 2016. The Violence of Work: Revisiting South Africa's 'Labour Question' Through Precarity and Anti-Blackness. *Journal of Southern African Studies*, 42(5), pp. 875–891. Available at: http://dx.doi.org/10.1080/03057070.2016.1210290.

Berger, P.L. & Luckmann, T., 1991. *The Social Construction of Reality: A Treatise in the Sociology of Knowledge*, London: Penguin.

Bittner, E., 2005. Florence Nightingale in Pursuit of Willie Sutton: A Theory of the Police. In T. Newburn, ed., *Policing: Key Readings*. Cullompton: Willan Publishing, pp. 150–172.

Bond, P., 2004. From Racial to Class Apartheid: South Africa's Frustrating Decade of Freedom. *Monthly Review*, 55(10). Available at: http://monthlyreview.org/2004/03/01/south-africas-frustrating-decade-of-freedom-from-racial-to-class-apartheid/.

Bradford, B., 2011. Police Numbers and Crime Rates – A Rapid Evidence Review (July), pp. 1–10. Available at: http://inspectorates-dev.bang-on.net/hmic/media/police-numbers-and-crime-rates-rapid-evidence-review-20110721.pdf.

Brodeur, J.-P., 2010. *The Policing Web*, Oxford: Oxford University Press.

Bruce, D., Newham, G., & Masuku, T., 2007. In Service of the People's Democracy: An Assessment of the South African Police Service Open Society Foundation for South Africa. *The Centre for the Study of Violence and Reconciliation*. Available at: www.csvr.org.za.

Burger, F.J., 2006. Crime Combating in Perspective: A Strategic Approach to Policing and the Prevention of Crime in South Africa. *Acta Criminologica*, 19(2), pp. 105–118.

Butler, J., 2009. Performativity, Precarity and Sexual Politics. *AIBR Revista de Antropologia Iberoamericana*, 4(3), pp. i–xiii.

Cawthra, G., 1993. *Policing South Africa*, London: Zed Books

Chan, J., 1996. Changing Police Culture. *The British Journal of Criminology*, 36(1), pp. 109–134.

City of Cape Town, 2014. City of Cape Town – 2011 Census Suburb Blue Downs. Available at: www.capetown.gov.za/en/stats/2011CensusSuburbs/2011_Census_CT_ Suburb_Blue_Downs_Profile.pdf.

Cockcroft, T., 2013. *Police Culture: Themes and Concepts*, New York and London: Routledge.

Collins, A., 2013. Violence Is Not A Crime: A Broader View of Interventions for Social Safety. *South African Crime Quarterly*, 43, pp. 29–37.

Comaroff, J. & Comaroff, J.L., 2006. *Law and Disorder in the Postcolony*, Chicago, IL, and London: University of Chicago Press.

CSVR, 2010. Why South Africa Is So Violent and What Should Be Done About It: Statement by the Centre for the Study of Violence and Reconciliation, p. 5. *Centre for the Study of Violence and Reconciliation*. Available at: www.issafrica.org/crimehub/ uploads/CSVRstatement091110.pdf.

Deetz, S., 1992. *Democracy in an Age of Corporate Colonization: Developments in Communication and the Politics of Everyday Life*, Albany, NY: SUNY Press.

Elliot, A., 2014. *Concepts of the Self*, Cambridge: Polity Press.

Ericson, R.V., 2005. The Police as Reproducers of Order. In T. Newburn, ed. *Policing: Key Readings*, Cullompton: Willan Publishing, pp. 214–246.

Fassin, D., 2013. *Enforcing Order: An Ethnography of Urban Policing*, Cambridge: Polity Press.

Frydl, K. & Skogan, W., 2004. *Fairness and Effectiveness in Policing: The Evidence*, Washington, DC: National Academies Press.

Geertz, C., 1973. *The Interpretation of Cultures: Selected Essays*, New York: Basic Books, Inc.

Giddens, A., 1991. *Modernity and Self-Identity: Self and Society in the Late Modern Age*, Cambridge: Polity Press.

Glaeser, A., 2000. *Divided in Unity: Identity, Germany, and the Berlin Police*, Chicago, IL, and London: Chicago University Press.

Goffman, E., 1959. *The Presentation of Self in Everyday Life*, New York: Doubleday.

Goldman Sachs, 2013. *Two Decades of Freedom: A 20 Year Review of South Africa*, Johannesburg: Goldman Sachs. Available at: www.goldmansachs.com/our-thinking/ archive/colin-coleman-south-africa/20-yrs-of-freedom.pdf.

Grant, L., 2014. Research Shows Sharp Increase in Service Delivery Protests. *Mail & Guardian*. Available at: http://mg.co.za/article/2014-02-12-research-shows-sharp-increase-in-service-delivery-protests.

Harari, Y.N., 2014. *Sapiens: A Brief History of Humankind*, London: Penguin Random House.

Harris, S., 2014. *Waking Up: Searching for Spirituality Without Religion*, London: Penguin Random House.

Harro, B., 1996. Cycle of Socialization. In M. Adams, M. Brigha, & P. Dalpes, eds. *Diversity and Oppression: Conceptual Frameworks*, Dubuque, IO: Kendall/ Hunt, pp. 15–21.

Haysom, F., 1993. Policing the Transition: Transforming the Police, African National Congress. Available at: www.anc.org.za/content/policing-transition-transforming-police.

Holdaway, S., 1983. *Inside the British Police*, Oxford: Blackwell.

ISS, 2016. Dataset (personal communication).

Jenkins, R., 2008. *Social Identity*, 3rd edn, London and New York: Routledge.

Kersten, A., 2000. Diversity Management. *Journal of Organizational Change Management*, 13(3), pp. 235–248.

Khoza, A., 2016. Zuma Bemoans Racism, White Minority Capital. *News 24*. Available at: www.news24.com/SouthAfrica/News/zuma-bemoans-racism-white-minority-capital-20160321.

Kramer, R. & Wei, J., 1998. Social Uncertainty and the Problem of Trust in Social Groups: The Social Self in Doubt. In R.M. Tyler & T.R. Kramer, eds. *Psychology of the social self*, Mahwah, NJ: Lawrence Erlbaum Associates Publishers, pp. 357–389.

Kriegler, A. & Shaw, M., 2016. *A Citizen's Guide to Crime Statistics in South Africa*, Johannesburg and Cape Town: Jonathan Ball.

Lancaster, L., 2015. Where Murder Happens in South Africa. *Africa Check* (7 October). Available at: http://africacheck.org/2015/10/07/where-murder-happens-in-south-africa/.

Loader, I., 1997. Policing and the Social: Questions of Symbolic Power. *The British Journal of Sociology*, 48(1), pp. 1–18.

Loader, I. & Mulcahy, A., 2003. *Policing and the Condition of England: Memory, Politics and Culture*, Oxford: Oxford University Press.

Lodge, T., 2011. Resistance and Reform, 1973–1994. In R. Ross, A.K. Mager, & B. Nasson, eds. *The Cambridge History of South Africa*. Cambridge: Cambridge University Press, pp. 409–491. Available at: http://universitypublishingonline.org/ref/id/histories/CBO9780511851995A019.

Loftus, B., 2009. *Police Culture in a Changing World*, New York: Oxford University Press.

Loftus, B., 2010. Police Occupational Culture: Classic Themes, Altered Times. *Policing and Society*, 20(1), pp. 1–20.

Manning, P.K., 1978. The Police: Mandate, Strategies, and Appearances. *Policing: A view from the street*. Culver City: Goodyear Publishing Company.

Manning, P.K., 1997. *Police Work: The Social Organization of Policing*, Prospect Heights, IL: Waveland Press.

Manning, P.K., 2007. A Dialectic of Organizational and Occupational Culture. In M. O'Neil, M. Marks, & A.-M. Singh, eds. *Police Occupational Culture: New Debates and Directions*, Amsterdam: Elsevier.

Manning, P.K., 2010. *Democratic Policing in a Changing World*. Abingdon and New York: Routledge.

Marks, M., 2005. *Transforming the Robocops: Changing Police in South Africa*, Scotsville: University of KwaZulu-Natal Press.

Moskos, P., 2008. *Cop in the Hood: My Year Policing Baltimore's Eastern District*, Princeton, NJ: Princeton University Press.

Nattrass, N. & Seekings, J., 2011. The Economy and Poverty in the Twentieth Century. In R. Ross, A.K. Mager, & B. Nasson, eds. *The Cambridge History of South Africa – Vol 2*, Cambridge: Cambridge University Press.

Neyroud, P. & Newburn, T. eds, 2013. *Dictionary of Policing*, Abingdon: Routledge.

O'Regan, J.C. & Pikoli, A.V., 2014. *Towards a Safer Khayelitsha: Report of the Commission of Inquiry into Allegations Of Police Inefficiency and a Breakdown in Relations Between SAPS and the Community of Khayelitsha*, Cape Town: Khayelitsha Commission of Inquiry.

Ochs, E. & Capps, L., 1996. Narrating the Self. *Annual Review of Anthropology*, 25(1), pp. 19–43.

Pinker, S., 2011. *The Better Angels of Our Nature*, New York: Penguin Books.

Reiner, R., 2010. *The Politics of the Police*, 4th edn, Oxford: Oxford University Press.

Reiner, R., 2015. Revisiting the Classics: Three Seminal Founders of the Study of Policing: Michael Banton, Jerome Skolnick and Egon Bittner. *Policing and Society*, 25(3), pp. 308–327.

Reiner, R., 2016. *Crime*, Cambridge: Polity Press.

Republic of South Africa, 1996. Constitution of the Republic of South Africa. Available at: www.thehda.co.za/uploads/images/unpan005172.pdf.

Roeder, O., Eisen, L., & Bowling, J., 2004. *What Caused the Crime Decline?*, New York: Brennan Center for Justice at New York University School of Law.

SAPS, 2014. *Annual Report 2013/14*, Pretoria. Available at: www.gov.za/sites/www.gov.za/files/SAPS%257B_%257DAnnual%257B_%257DReport%257B_%257D2013 2014.pdf.

Seekings, J. & Nattrass, N., 2005. *Class, Race and Inequality in South Africa*, New Haven, CT: Yale University Press.

Shaw, M., 2002. *Crime and Policing in Post-Apartheid South Africa: Transforming Under Fire*, Bloomington, IN: Indiana University Press.

Shearing, C.D. & Ericson, R.V., 1991. Culture as Figurative Action. *The British Journal of Sociology*, 42(4), pp. 481–506.

Shearing, C.D. & Marks, M., 2011. Criminology's Disney World: The Ethnographer's Ride of South African Criminal Justice. In M. Bosworth & C. Hoyle, eds. *What is Criminology?*, Oxford: Oxford University Press.

Simkins, C., 2011. The Evolution of the South African Population in the Twentieth Century. In R. Ross, A.K. Mager, & B. Nasson, eds. *The Cambridge History of South Africa – Vol 2*, Cambridge: Cambridge University Press.

Simon, B., 1999. A Place in the World: Self and Social Categorizatio. In T.R. Tyler, R.M. Kramer, & O.P. John, eds. *The Psychology of the Social Self*, Mahwah, NJ: Lawrence Erlbaum Associates Publishers.

Sklansky, D., 2007. Seeing Blue: Police Reform, Occupational Culture and Cognitive Burn-In. In M. O'Neil, M. Marks, & A.-M. Singh, eds. *The Police Occupational Culture: New Debates and Directions*, Oxford: Elsevier, pp. 19–46.

Skolnick, J.H., 1966. A Sketch of the Police Officer's 'Working Personality'. In T. Newburn, ed. *Policing: Key Readings*, Cullompton: Willan Publishing, pp. 264–279.

Soudien, C., 2004. Constituting the Class: An Analysis of the Process of 'Integration' in South African Schools. In L. Chisholm, ed. *Education and Social Change in South Africa*, Pretoria: HSRC Press, pp. 89–114.

Soudien, C., 2010. The Reconstitution of Privilege: Integration in Former White Schools in South Africa. *Journal of Social Issues*, 66(2), pp. 352–366. Available at: http://doi.wiley.com/10.1111/j.1540-4560.2010.01649.x.

Spaull, N., 2013. *South Africa's Education Crisis: The Quality of Education in South Africa 1994–2011*. Available at: www.section27.org.za/wp-content/uploads/2013/10/Spaull-2013-CDE-report-South-Africas-Education-Crisis.pdf.

Staff Writer, 2016. White People Don't Own the Land – So Take It: Malema. *Business Tech*. Available at: http://businesstech.co.za/news/government/128169/white-people-dont-own-the-land-so-take-it-malema/.

StatsSA, 2012. *Statistical Release (Revised) Census 2011*, Pretoria. Available at: www.statssa.gov.za/Publications/P03014/P030142011.pdf.

StatsSA, 2014a. *General Household Survey, 2013*, Pretoria. Available at: http://beta2.statssa.gov.za/publications/P0318/P03182013.pdf.

StatsSA, 2014b. *Quarterly Labour Force Survey: Quarter 2, 2014*, Pretoria. Available at: http://beta2.statssa.gov.za/publications/P0211/P02112ndQuarter2014.pdf.

StatsSA, 2014c. *Transforming the Distributional Regime: Poverty Trends in South Africa An Examination of Absolute Poverty Between 2006 and 2011*, Pretoria. Available at: http://beta2.statssa.gov.za/publications/Report-03-10-06/Report-03-10-06March2014.pdf.

StatsSA, 2015. *Statistical release: P0341 Victims of Crime Survey 2014/15*, Pretoria.

StatsSA, 2016. *Statistical Release: PO341 Victims of Crime Survey 2015/16*, Pretoria.

StatsSA, 2017. *Statistical release P0211: Quarterly Labour Force Survey – Quarter 4 2016*, Pretoria. Available at: www.statssa.gov.za/publications/P0211/P02114thQuarter2016.pdf.

Steinberg, J., 2011. Security and Disappointment: Policing, Freedom and Xenophobia in South Africa. *British Journal of Criminology*, 52(2), pp. 345–360.

Super, G.J., 2013. *Governing through Crime in South Africa: The Politics of Race and Class in Neoliberalizing Regimes*, Oxford: Routledge.

Super, G.J., 2016. Punishment, Violence, and Grassroots Democracy in South Africa –The Politics of Populist Punitiveness. *Punishment & Society*, 18(3), pp. 325–345. Available at: http://pun.sagepub.com/cgi/doi/10.1177/1462474516645685.

Trench, A., 2015. Farewell to Comments: Why We Are Making a Change. *News 24*. Available at: www.news24.com/Columnists/AndrewTrench/Farewell-to-comments-Why-we-are-making-a-change-20150908.

Turner, V., 1994. Betwixt & Between: Patterns of Masculine and Feminine Initiation. In L.C. Mahdi, S. Foster, & M. Little, eds. *Betwixt and Between: Patterns of Masculine and Feminine Initiation*, Chicago, IL: Open Court, pp. 3–21.

Van Maanen, J., 2005. 'The Asshole'. Reprinted in T. Newburn, ed. *Policing: Key Readings*, Cullompton: Willan Publishing, pp. 280–298.

Waddington, P.A.J., 1999. Police (Canteen) Cub-Culture: An Appreciation. *British Journal of Criminology*, 39(2), pp. 287–309.

Wicks, J., 2016. 'It's Just the Facts' – Penny Sparrow Breaks Her Silence. *News 24* (1 April). Available at: www.news24.com/SouthAfrica/News/its-just-the-facts-penny-sparrow-breaks-her-silence-20160104.

World Bank, 2016. *Poverty and Shared Prosperity 2016: Taking on Inequality*. Available at: https://openknowledge.worldbank.org/bitstream/handle/10986/25078/9781464809583.pdf.

Young, J., 1999. *The Exclusive Society*, London: Sage.

Young, J., 2007. *The Vertigo of Late Modernity*, London: Sage.

Young, J., 2011. *The Criminological Imagination*, Cambridge: Polity Press.

Young, M., 1991. *An Inside Job: Policing and Police Culture in Britain*, Oxford: Oxford University Press.

# Chapter 2

# Police practice and the good shift

## Forging order across space and the good shift

South Africa is a place of contrast. A legacy of colonial and apartheid rule means that most of the country's wealthy and middle class live far removed from the majority poor. Historically, economic and spatial planning divided city, town, and countryside into racial enclaves of poverty and wealth. Railway lines, freeways, rivers, hills, and (often hundreds of) kilometres of open *veld* separated the White minority from the Black majority. Until the mid-eighties a great deal of police time was spent regulating the movement of people across space. However, since the mid-nineties, a progressive democratic constitution has compelled police to uphold the rights of all the country's inhabitants. And yet race and space continue to shape the way police officers understand themselves, the people around them, and their work.

In Chapter 1, I suggested that there is value in understanding the policing of South Africa as the product of entanglement. This allows for an exploration of how officers' personal identities shape and are shaped by the organisation and communities in which they live and work.

In this chapter I use *thick description* (Geertz 1973) to introduce the four most common forms of space in South Africa and the policing that takes place in each: township, affluent city, rural town, and rural village. I show that the four sites are connected and shaped by historical development and migration. I employ the idea of the good shift to explore the types of order officers hoped to bring about in each space. The good shift also provides an opportunity to explore officers' attempts to work through a central contradiction in democratic policing – that police must at times break rules to defend rules (Brodeur 2010). As a result, police work can be construed as illiberal or undemocratic (Holdaway 1983; Bayley 1994; Marks et al. 2009). In seeking to create particular states of order, then, the good shift reveals officers' search for ontological security through ideas of purpose at work and in the world.

But the good shift is not the same for everyone. Because police officers generally work alone or in pairs, they inevitably draw on their personal conceptions of order as they carry out their work (Manning 1978). In a country as diverse, unequal, and in flux as South Africa, personal notions of order and a good shift inevitably vary.

The narrative of a police shift is one of a world officers cannot control, and yet control is expected of them. Thus, police performances take different forms in different spaces and for different audiences. Viewed together, however, it is clear that performances are linked, even if officers don't realise it. While describing these performances, I begin unpacking how officers' personal identities are bound to their reading of race, space, and deviance, and how these shape the way they work.

## Police work as shift work

Because the SAPS never closes for business, uniformed officers, detectives, and some support staff work shifts throughout the day and night. These usually start at six or seven in the morning or evening and end 12 hours later. Most shift-bound officers staff front desks in stations' Community Service Centres (CSC), carry out sector patrols, and respond to complaints or calls for service. They are the public face of South African policing. Crime Prevention Units (CPU) are also common at station level. CPU shift patterns are based on crime pattern analysis. CPU officers are uniformed, conduct patrols, and respond to urgent calls for assistance.

Together, CPU and shift officers make up the bulk of the SAPS Visible Policing (VISPOL) programme, which is the biggest by employee count (Figure 2.1) and budget (Figure 2.2) in the organisation. VISPOL officers are responsible for the implementation of *Sector Policing*, the framework through which the SAPS provides community- and problem-oriented policing (SAPS 2015b). Sector policing requires the division of precincts into two or more *sectors*, each overseen by a sector manager and, ideally, dedicated patrollers. Sector managers are responsible for liaising with communities and coordinating crime prevention and problem solving activities in their sector.

The second largest programme in the SAPS is its Detective Service. Detectives work office hours, usually beginning their days at 7.30 in the morning and ending at 4 in the afternoon. Every evening and weekend, detectives are placed on standby to respond to crimes reported out of office hours.

With this basic structure in mind, I use the remainder of this chapter to describe the meaning which police work brought to officers' lives. I explore how it animated their visions of the country they wanted to live in, and the way they worked. I begin where I began my research, in Mthonjeni, Cape Town.

## Mthonjeni (the township)

### Meetings about murder

Murder in the Mthonjeni police precinct is common. It hangs thick in the air of the police station, clinging to its face-brick walls, echoing out from the spaces beneath doors behind which it is discussed daily with both gravity and humour.

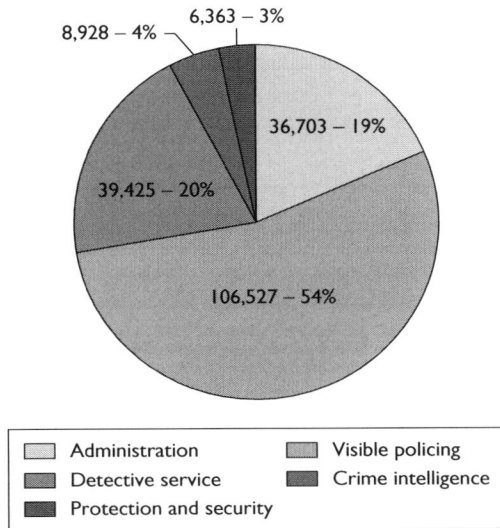

*Figure 2.1* SAPS employees by programme 2012–2013 (totals – percentage)

Source: Based on data from the Institute for Security Studies (ISS) (https://issafrica.org/crimehub)

Note: At the time of writing in May 2017, these proportions remained virtually unchanged

It was part of almost every morning meeting at the detective branch. The first murder of my time at the station was announced on my third morning, a Thursday.

The meeting began with its usual daily prayer, after which the branch commander offered his members new stationery. He had boxes of pens, paper, tape, and files with him, and pushed these down the long table as detectives shouted, laughed, stretched, and thrust their hands out to catch them. It was as if the colonel were throwing sweets to salivating children. He often treated his detectives like juveniles and, on this occasion at least, they played the part.

Whether with detectives or uniformed officers, the work spaces that struck me as most joy-filled at the four stations were those in which officers gathered before the day began. In the meeting and parade rooms, in the minutes before the weight of their work was dragged into the room, they were just South African men and women who happened to work as police. The rooms were what Goffman would call *back spaces*, places where the bearers of stigma gather with the similarly afflicted, where they could drop the pretence of being anything other than who they were (1990).

Having dispatched the stationery and allowed the murmurs of laughter to subside, the colonel announced that it was time to talk about *The Crime* – cases

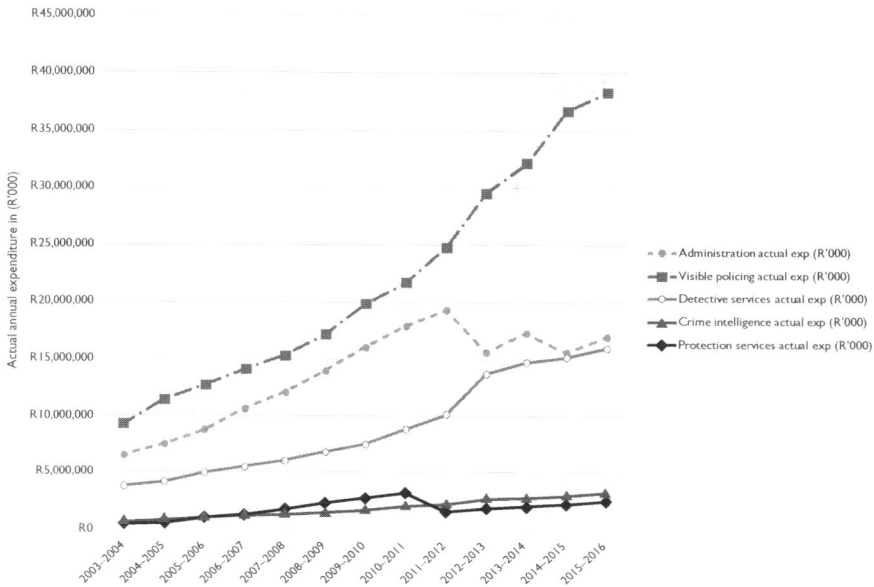

*Figure 2.2* SAPS expenditure by programme 2003–2016

Source: Based on data from the Institute for Security Studies (ISS) (https://issafrica.org/crimehub)

assigned to the branch in the 15 hours since they had left work the previous afternoon. He spoke quickly, as if running through a list: 'Last night was a heavy night for crime. While you were all sleeping at home, some of us were out there attending crime scenes.'

The first incident he described was of a man and his wife who had ventured into the cold spring night in search of paraffin with which to warm their home. While parked outside a fuel station someone had fired 15 bullets at their car, 12 had hit the man, the others the woman. The man had died. Despite what sounded like an impressive overnight investigation, detectives had failed to identify a motive for the killing. The colonel concluded that it was a taxi-related assassination gone wrong.[1] I listened, transfixed. One of the reasons I had wanted to work in Mthonjeni was that I believed the narratives of risk, loss, violence, and death that are so much a part of the popular imagination in South Africa originate in such police precincts. They flow as if from springs of dark mythology, trickling out into the streets and *veld* where they are lapped up by citizens thirsty for stories with which to make sense of their chronic insecurity.

It was with surprise that while hastily typing notes into my phone I realised there had been little change in the mood of the room. Detectives sent texts and answered mobile phones; some whispered to their colleagues while others left the room without apology. Nobody seemed particularly interested in the fact that a man had been shot 12 times. The colonel was saying, 'If we have a taxi fight going on we must know about it. We can't have a hit man running around here playing cowboys and crooks.' Another detective chimed in, 'Maybe we can call the FBI, Colonel?' It was a joke. In an occupational world that to me appeared surreal, I would find that humour was injected into these daily engagements with death, like a flimsy police cordon set up to keep contamination at bay.

The colonel moved on quickly, berating the detectives for having only closed 199 of their 400 docket target for the month. Holding up a wad of paper he boomed, 'Let's not misunderstand this: these dockets must be closed today. This is your work!'

The themes of violence, death, and performance targets dominated the detective meetings throughout my time with them. They were not always part of the good shift or day but they were part of the everyday. They smothered the early morning joviality and reminded the detectives of their heavy workloads and the performance targets that seemed impossible to meet. A good day would see them succeed against these odds so that the colonel might toss them a compliment.

At this point Sergeant Tambo, with whom I was spending the week, asked if he and I could be excused. We were due at the state mortuary where he was to stand over a chilled corpse and discuss an alleged suicide with a pathologist. As we made our way through the August rain into the city, I expressed my surprise at Tambo's colleagues' apparent disinterest in the dramatic murder. His response was one I would hear often over the months, 'These things are very, very common in Mthonjeni.'

Eleven days later the Monday morning meeting began with the colonel saying, 'We had a quiet week, a brilliant week. We only had three murders.' By the end of the meeting a fourth had been reported. In a meeting a few days later I realised that I, like the detectives, was failing to respond with particular interest when a murder was announced. My note taking was no longer hurried or as detailed, my mind wandered as the colonel filled the room with words describing lives violently ended. In just over two weeks I had become accustomed to murder as a common feature of the daily grind, the Mthonjeni police precinct and the working lives of its officers. It was a big part of where and how they worked, informing both the station's organisational culture and the personal identities of the officers entangled in it.

### Space and place

The Mthonjeni precinct, composed of a number of townships, lies roughly 30 kilometres from Cape Town's city centre on the city's Cape Flats. The term *township* was historically applied to urban areas reserved for non-White residential occupation. Many remain predominantly African, and are still called townships.

Established in the middle of the last century, Mthonjeni began as an expansion of the migrant hostels built closer to the city centre in Langa. Until the early nineties, key features of South African cities were controlled to promote White interests (Turok 2001). The movement of Africans into cities was subject to strict police regulation, including at times the provision of only temporary residency permits, and only in designated townships. In the 1980s when the SAP's control of African migration collapsed, overcrowding became common in Cape Town's townships. This led to a rapid growth in sub-letting and the erection of shacks both in the backyards of houses and on the townships' peripheries.

Since the 1980s, areas like Khayelitsha on the city's south eastern edge have replaced Mthonjeni as the first stop for new migrants. In 2011, 69 percent of residents there were born in the Eastern Cape, while almost every resident of the shack settlements was a recent arrival (O'Regan & Pikoli 2014).

Within my first weeks at Mthonjeni, a high-level commission of inquiry began work in Khayelitsha. The first of its kind in democratic South Africa, it probed and, in 2014, confirmed alarming inefficiencies in policing there, and a breakdown in relations between the community and its police. During a detective meeting in my first weeks at Mthonjeni the colonel warned his detectives that if a similar investigation were launched in their precinct, they were sure to be in trouble.[2]

Since 1994, many townships, including Khayelitsha and Mthonjeni, have been the site of government developmental intervention, predominantly in the form of small RDP houses, schools, clinics, and police stations. But apartheid's shadow is long, and by 2017 there remained few jobs in most townships, outside of new and old state facilities, or the *spaza*[3] shops, and liquor and taxi industries that emerged during apartheid.

The Mthonjeni police precinct spans less than 14 square kilometres but is home to 200,000 people. Ninety-five percent of residents self-identified as Black African in the 2011 national census, echoing the demographic distribution of apartheid. The area includes old hostels converted into state housing, new state houses, and a small number of old and new standalone private homes. Police officers called the latter *bond houses*, highlighting the exceptionalism of a bank-financed purchase in the area, and in many officers' lives, too. It is usual for those with space on their plots to build and rent out backyard shacks so that the shine and rust of corrugated iron sheeting is common. The townships of Baghdad and Mountain View, which fall under the Mthonjeni SAPS jurisdiction, are predominantly comprised of standalone shacks, tightly packed together.

Having visited Mthonjeni regularly between 1999 and 2001, I was struck during my 2012 return by the development of the area, including new houses, parks, and two shopping centres. Yet, despite these, most residents remained poor. Census data from four of the main wards in Mthonjeni show that in 2011, on average, only 31 percent of adults had completed high school; 58 percent were employed; and 21 percent earned more than R3,200 (£175) a month. Just 51 percent lived in formal housing (City of Cape Town 2013a). It is in such contexts that South Africa's violent crime incubates, and where confinement and precarity have been met with police punishment.

### The inevitable murder

Two weeks into my work at the station I spent a week with one of its ace murder investigators, Warrant Officer Apolles. Apolles often joked about murder. He said he didn't know how to investigate anything else anymore. The crime brought both meaning and disruption to his life. The meaning came through his colleagues' recognition that he was good at his job: skilled at hunting killers. But, he told me, working standby over a weekend meant never being able to relax at home; that he would inevitably be called to a murder scene before he could set foot inside his house after a long day at work. He was tired of it.

This was almost exactly how it played out that Friday. It was 5 o'clock; I had just returned home from a day at the station when I received Apolles' text: 'on my way 2 de station, dubble murder.'

Apolles arrived at the station after me. He greeted me but his usual lightness was missing. The commander of the uniformed shift casually briefed him: two men had been shot, one was dead, the other in hospital – not a double murder after all. As we climbed into his car, Apolles quipped:

> You see, what did I tell you? As soon as I get home and open the gate they call me. I don't know what's wrong with these people; they can't go a day without killing each other.

For Apolles and the other murder detectives at Mthonjeni a good weekend night was one without a single callout; one at home with the family or a stiff drink. But Apolles didn't believe this a likely probability. None of the murder detectives did.

The crime scene was little more than 700 meters from the station, on one of Mthonjeni's busier roads, so that we arrived within minutes. Apolles parked on the perimeter of the scene, which was bordered by cordons of yellow police tape. In its middle was a red VW Polo with shattered windows and bullet holes in its doors. A blue sheet covered a body in the driver's seat; cones marked the road where bullet casings lay.

Over a two-hour period Apolles inspected the scene. When he lifted the blue sheet in the car it revealed a man in his late 20s, eyes and mouth open, head tilted back, clothing soaked in blood. Bystanders had observed a hooded man walk up to the car and fire a volley of shots at it, but they shared nothing more. 'They never do,' sighed Apolles.

Over time other detectives arrived. There was Colonel Diedericks, the station's officer on standby, Sergeant Chub from the Serious and Violent Crime Task Team (SVC), and the cluster's head of Crime Intelligence. Greeting me on arrival, each commented along the lines of 'Now you see what it's like here.' Working standby over the weekend meant working with murder, shaping both the culture of the Mthonjeni SAPS, and the identities of its officers.

The Crime Intelligence officer cracked jokes, but, like Apolles, Colonel Diedericks appeared agitated. Though he often complained about an untenable workload, Diedericks was generally relaxed at the office. Not that evening though: he was unsettled. I commented that the streets were busy; that surely witnesses would provide the information they needed. He laughed sardonically, 'Nobody will have seen anything. That and the language barrier – these are the problems we face.'[4] Mthonjeni residents overwhelmingly speak Xhosa as a home language while only about half of the detective branch did. In Diedericks' good shift, information would flow seamlessly.

It was getting dark and nobody had brought spotlights to light the scene. Just over two hours after arriving, Apolles and I departed. He remained agitated. He said he did not know how much sleep he would get that night. He would need to complete his paperwork, so would save a visit to the victim in hospital for morning. But what was clear was that he feared another murder later in the evening, and more on Saturday and Sunday. For each he would need to work through the same rituals. He said he would call me in the morning so that I could accompany him on his investigation but by morning the next murder had been called in and Apolles was lost to a weekend in which four more were added to the 75 he was already investigating. It was the worst possible start to a weekend on standby, his perfect night at home left waiting at the gate.

*

Like Warrant Officer Apolles and Colonel Diedericks, Mthonjeni's other detectives felt it a near impossible task to successfully investigate the area's violent crime. They struggled to elicit leads from the community without paying for them, and, despite their best intentions, did not have the capacity to give each investigation the attention it deserved. In its place they substituted quality for organisationally scripted performances that conveyed an appearance of competence. Given the right fall of the dice, these performances led to arrest and prosecution. The *successes*, as the SAPS describes them, would give the work meaning. But in the detectives' minds this did not occur often enough. Instead they were left chasing shadows and filing paperwork.

### The death that follows police home

In 2012/13 over 250 murders were reported in the Mthonjeni area. That's 130 murders for every 100,000 residents. Across the whole of the United Kingdom only 558 murders were recorded that year, less than 1 for every 100,000 inhabitants. For every 100,000 Mthonjeni residents in 2012/13, 100 attempted murders were reported, 460 assaults with intent to do grievous bodily harm, 210 common robberies, and 200 sexual offences. It is an exceptionally violent area (see Table 2.1. for a comparison of crime rates with the other three stations).

But for many of Mthonjeni's officers, violence was not restricted to work; it was part of their personal lives, too. Casually beginning a parade briefing one

Table 2.1 Comparison of crime data across the four police precincts

| Crime type | Total reported crime and reported crime as rate per 10,000 residents in police precinct | | | | | | | | | | | | | | | |
| --- | --- | --- | --- | --- | --- | --- | --- | --- | --- | --- | --- | --- | --- | --- | --- | --- |
| | Mthonjeni | | | | Yorkton | | | | Patterson | | | | Gompo | | | |
| | 2012/13 | | 2015/16 | | 2012/13 | | 2015/16 | | 2012/13 | | 2015/16 | | 2012/13 | | 2015/16 | |
| | Total | Rate | Total | Rate | Total | Rate | Total | Rate | Total | Rate | Total | Rate | Total | Rate | Total | Rate |
| All contact crime | 3780 | 184 | 4824 | 235 | 2371 | 677 | 2348 | 671 | 260 | 108 | 229 | 95 | 73 | 107 | 49 | 72 |
| Murder | 262 | 13 | 279 | 14 | 12 | 3 | 7 | 2 | 10 | 4 | 10 | 4 | 3 | 4 | 5 | 7 |
| Assault grievous bodily harm (GBH) | 952 | 46 | 1053 | 51 | 131 | 37 | 146 | 42 | 128 | 53 | 97 | 40 | 40 | 59 | 20 | 40 |
| Aggravated robbery | 885 | 43 | 503 | 73 | 507 | 145 | 600 | 171 | 24 | 10 | 47 | 20 | 8 | 12 | 7 | 10 |
| Residential burglary | 684 | 33 | 746 | 36 | 828 | 236 | 539 | 154 | 102 | 42 | 135 | 56 | 40 | 59 | 29 | 42 |
| Drug-related crime | 1578 | 77 | 1739 | 85 | 1963 | 561 | 2712 | 775 | 11 | 5 | 33 | 18 | 7 | 10 | 10 | 15 |
| Sexual crimes | 413 | 20 | 351 | 17 | 71 | 20 | 56 | 16 | 55 | 23 | 44 | 18 | 11 | 16 | 13 | 19 |
| Theft of motor vehicle and bike | 117 | 6 | 176 | 9 | 398 | 114 | 345 | 99 | 10 | 4 | 9 | 4 | 3 | 4 | 1 | 1 |
| Stock theft | 2 | 0 | 0 | 0 | 0 | 0 | 0 | 0 | 71 | 30 | 32 | 17 | 44 | 64 | 17 | 25 |

afternoon, Captain Jacobs, the commander of a CPU, announced that there had been two murders the previous evening. Ignoring his attempt to begin the briefing, Warrant Officer Jiyana jovially asked him how he was doing. 'My friend was also shot last night,' he replied, solemnly. The room fell silent. After a pause Jiyana asked, 'Was it that guy you often drive around with?' 'Yes,' replied Jacobs, 'that one. He was only thirty.' He told a story about his friend going to a party. He, Jacobs, had also been invited but had not gone. It was while walking home that his friend had been shot:

> The gangsters shot him. I drove past his body at about ten past four this morning on my way to the station. I stopped and asked who it was and they told me it was my friend. His body was still warm.

'Sorry, Captain,' offered a constable. 'And other than that I don't have any good news,' said Jacobs.

Captain Jacobs lived in Manenberg, a part of the Cape Flats notorious for gang and drug-related crime. His story was indicative of a reality many Mthonjeni police faced: they lived in areas wracked by violent crime and they worked in an area saturated in violence. It was as if death followed them everywhere they went.

*

On another occasion while driving into the station before an evening shift, listening to the radio news, I heard that police officer at a station bordering Mthonjeni's had been killed on duty hours earlier. At the station I asked Captain Thangana, whose CPU shift I would be working with, if he had heard about the death. Having just come on duty he said he hadn't, but he had a response ready nonetheless: 'It's not nice to hear of death. No matter where they work, if they are wearing the blue they are your colleague.' I asked him what he thought should be done to address the killing of police: 'They need to change the law. They have taken away our powers. Now we are afraid to shoot.' It is a common sentiment among SAPS officers. Still, South African police kill at an alarming rate.[5]

A short while later, Captain Thangana and I joined the rest of the CPU shift for its briefing. Thangana said, 'Earlier today, Fikile passed away.' I realised he had spoken to colleagues and established that he knew the murdered officer. 'That guy was funny,' he went on. 'He always made jokes on the radio.' The other CPU officers were not surprised. Instead, a young constable responded without sympathy, 'All of our times will come, Captain.' An older warrant officer added, 'You can avoid all the routes but death will come to you,' laughing. But Captain Thangana was openly moved. He did not laugh.

Later in the evening while on patrol with Thangana and another officer, the captain asked out of nowhere, 'Oh Fikile, how can the *skollies* shoot us?'

The death was on his mind. His colleague and I remained silent but the message seemed clear: the lives of SAPS officers were not respected. It is a narrative that informs SAPS officers' identities across the country and one which adds an uncomfortable weight to any shift.

\*

The SAPS releases a comprehensive Annual Report each year, including a *Role of Honour* in its front section. This lists the names of the officers who died that year, and is usually accompanied by a photograph taken at a police funeral. Government and SAPS narratives presenting selfless police dying *in the line of a duty* are common. For much of 2015, for example, South African media was flooded with stories suggesting a sudden spike in police killings.

Of course, the murder of any police officer is heinous. But the outcry of 2015 hid as much as it revealed. As shown in Figure 2.3, in 2015/16 the killing of SAPS officers was at a near all-time low, despite the organisation having grown by 60,000 since 1994 (Figure 2.4). Three other points are notable: First, more officers are killed off duty than on. Second, more officers are killed in accidents than are killed on and off duty combined.[6] Finally, the most common cause of death for SAPS officers has been, for some years at least, suicide.[7] I suspect that SAPS suicides are partially the product of a liminality experienced by (mostly) men, accustomed to working with force and firearms, for whom ontological security appears perpetually out of reach.

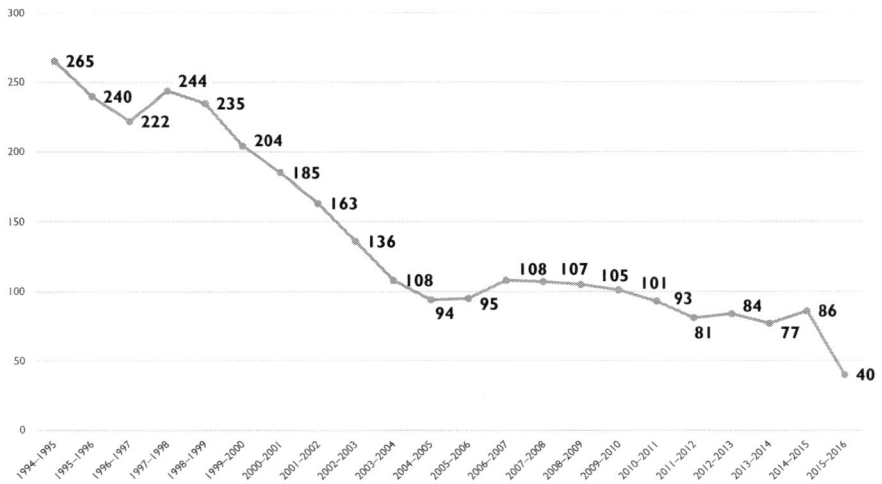

*Figure 2.3* Number of police officers killed per year in South Africa 1994–2016

Source: Based on data from the Institute for Security Studies (ISS) (https://issafrica.org/crimehub)

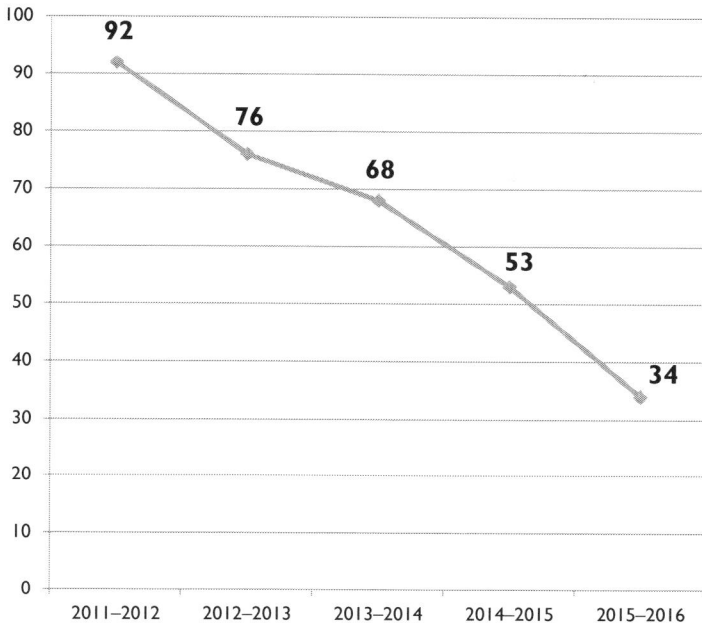

*Figure 2.4* Number of South African police deaths while on duty 2011–2016

Source: SAPS 2015a, 2016

Selective reporting about officer deaths may win public sympathy, but I propose it also leaves police feeling vulnerable, disrupting their sense of safety and, perhaps, self, possibly in very misleading ways. In 2011 Jonny Steinberg compared murder rates within the SAPS, with those of men aged 20 to 40 (the most common victims of murder) in the broader population. He showed that police were 40 percent *less likely* to be murdered than the average young South African man (Steinberg 2011).

My view is that it is where and how many officers live, rather than the simple fact that they are police officers, which puts them at risk. Many SAPS officers are recruited from, and often remain residents of, some of South Africa's most violent and precarious communities. Some are raised with violence, and surrounded by it for much of their lives. Early exposure to and use of violence plays as much a part in officers' violent deaths as does their occupation.

### Crime prevention, stop and search, and street cleaning

It was murder that set the backdrop to policing in Mthonjeni and murder which animated CPU patrols. Whereas murder detectives were cynical enough to expect death every time they worked standby, CPU officers strove to end their shifts without a notification of murder. As long as murder did not occur on their watch, they felt they had done their job.

At all four of my field sites, almost all patrol officers defined crime prevention as visible policing (random vehicular patrol) accompanied by stop and search. This was true even in the rural Eastern Cape where sparsely populated villages were connected by kilometres of empty dirt road. The logic was simple: offenders were rational so would not commit crime where police were visible. For example, when asked why so much of Mthonjeni's murder was concentrated in a particular informal settlement, officers would tell me it was because they could not patrol (drive on) the narrow paths between shacks. Similarly, detectives said shacks generated crime because they were not formally named or numbered, making it difficult for them to track down and arrest their resident suspects. The same claims were made by officers who testified at the Khayelitsha Commission (O'Regan & Pikoli 2014). The inference was that crime only existed in spaces the SAPS could not easily reach.

For CPU officers the good shift would see them traverse a network of seamlessly connected roads, stopping, searching, and sorting young men, the dirty from the clean. In this vision, a police presence alone would command respect for the uniform, for the law, and for life. But roads and respect were never guaranteed and crime was never absent. As a result, I believe, in describing informal settlements as impenetrable, SAPS officers abdicated responsibility for their violence. That most murders occurred in areas they could not easily reach by car confirmed to them their value as police officers and brought meaning to their nights.

*

Within hours of my first two CPU patrols in Mthonjeni, different officers joked that if they left me alone at the side of the road for five minutes, I would be killed. They enjoyed playing up the exceptionalism of the area, calling it 'The Republic of Mthonjeni' as if it were a place with its own violent laws. Such talk was particularly common after dark.

For CPU officers, daylight hours were not their concern. They did not believe much crime was committed when the sun was out and they were there to *prevent crime*. Nonetheless, they patrolled incessantly during the day; stopping and searching young men. Many stops were of teenagers, young enough to be legally obliged to attend school. Yet, despite truancy predicting violent offending in South Africa (Gould 2015), CPU officers only cared that they were not carrying weapons. Stops seldom involved requests for permission to search teens or men. Rather, seeing the police vehicle slowing or officers opening doors, teenagers and men stopped mid-step and waited for the instruction to raise their arms. Sometimes they simply assumed the positions without being asked. It was clear that for most it was a familiar routine.

It seemed clear to me that these rituals, whether intentional or not, tainted the Black urban sub-proletariat. Behind a veneer of impartiality, rituals marked young men as threatening. They reminded them of their choice between a future in prison or precarity on the periphery of the market. Such ritual encounters have a history in South Africa where sex, race, and class have long predicted who goes to prison (Glaeser 2000; Samara 2011; Super 2013).[8] Mthonjeni's CPU officers were part of that tradition.

In the course of a CPU shift, knives, sharpened screwdrivers, once even a machete, were collected as evidence of work done. No arrests or formal record of the confiscations was ever made. Rather, the implements were simply taken. To the officers, four or five confiscations were the mark of a good shift, and a shield against managerial critique.[9]

During the day the precinct's streets were busy. Men, women, and children walked and played in them, and sat in doorways and tiny front yards, generating an energy that is absent from the city's walled suburbs. Police understood – not least because many lived in comparable neighbourhoods – that many of Mthonjeni's residents was unemployed and had little reason or means to leave the area. As such, CPU officers simply patrolled the streets, chatted to familiar faces, and waited for a call for service.

It was at night that the officers' visions of order, and their understanding of their role in bringing it about, took a different form. Once darkness had fallen, but particularly from 10 o'clock onwards, officers did not want to see anyone on the street. Instead, they did their best to encourage people off them.

CPU officers expressed this vision in a variety of ways: There was the captain who celebrated rainy weekends because, he believed, criminals and victims would stay at home; the constable who called for a state curfew after which police could arrest anyone on the streets; the frequent cursing of Somali shop owners who, in keeping their shops open after dark were viewed as courting robbery; the shouting at young women, telling them they would be raped if they stayed outside in the dark; and the questioning or searching of almost every young man as if willing them off the streets. As Captain Thangana said of the empty streets late one night, 'There is nobody here anymore. Now my work is done.' In the simplest of terms this was an indicator of a good shift: empty streets without a report of serious crime meant the community had respected the officers and they had done their job.

\*

The practice of emptying city streets of Black bodies – in particular those of men – has a long history in South Africa. The pre-1994 division of city space into racial enclaves, and a police focus on domestic migration, made policing simple. Race guided action.

The narratives used to explain the rise of gangs in Soweto (Glaser 2000) – Johannesburg's largest township – between 1935 and 1970, were uncannily similar to those shared with me by police in 2012/13. Clive Glaser writes that from the mid-1930s the most common explanation for urban African juvenile criminality in Soweto was a perceived disconnect between rural and urban life (Glaser 1998). Where rural youth were deemed respectful and subservient, city youth were presented as corrupted by the crime, sex work, and media of city life.

Similarly, Mthonjeni's police regularly lamented what they called the *Cape Borners* – teen boys born in Cape Town and lacking rural values. Officers blamed the *Cape Borners* for much of the crime in the area and spoke of December and January as a period when they migrated to the rural Eastern Cape, taking their violence with them. Similarly, the rural police I later met in Gompo in the rural Eastern Cape, talked of city youth who brought crime to the countryside over school holidays.

Mthonjeni's officers frequently spoke of a need for development in the township. In the officers' minds it was underdevelopment and lack of opportunities in the area that pushed young men to crime. Not only was this sentiment almost a century old, but it echoed the narratives through which many officers described their own journey to the SAPS: they had joined because they had had few alternatives, but once recruited, the SAPS had become the foundation on which they had built their lives.

Soweto's mid-century gangsters separated themselves from society by embracing crime, rejecting work, and glorifying violence, their objectives: survival and the accumulation of status. They saw police as invaders of their territory (Glaser 2000). In twenty-first-century South Africa, young township men are still deemed lazy and criminally threatening, while slightly older men from similar, precarious backgrounds are recruited into the SAPS and offered security of income. The engagements that take place between township men and, often, township-men-turned-SAPS-officers are a continuation of old standoffs between men – some in uniform, others not – each vying for place and status in a society that offers few wage-earning opportunities and little security.

The framing of rural life as orderly and peaceful, and of cities as threatening to African social values, has a long history in South Africa. Where once apartheid's police incessantly stopped African residents to check pass books before removing many from White urban space, so Mthonjeni's police worked to empty township streets of their presence. They called to them, shouted at them, searched them, threatened them, and sometimes joked with them. The interactions labelled, classified and stratified, marking the men as pollutants to the imagined order (Douglas 1966), and so manufacturing culture.

If, as Tom Tyler has suggested, every police–citizen encounter is a 'teachable moment' through which police communicate meaning about the nature of the social world (2011) then the message Mthonjeni's CPU officers communicated seemed to be: '*You look like us but you are not like us. You lack our values. We, the police, have conformed, but you have not. We know your kind. These streets are ours. If you don't behave, one day we will get you.*' Through this message and its associated performances, officers manufactured the threatening *skollie* against which their personal narratives were a little more ontologically secure.

*

Mthonjeni's CPU officers' framed their prevention work as based on performance targets and managerial pressure. But it was no doubt also informed by the fact that many of the young men whom they believed caused the area's violence, were very much like the police officers themselves. Through their work, officers sought to deflect these young men – who were too much like themselves for comfort – from potential paths of criminality, and to punish them – sometimes pre-emptively – for their indiscretions. In so doing they both reproved them for failing to thrive in South Africa's marketplace, and goaded them to adapt, conform, and assume a *legitimate* place in the social and economic hierarchy. If Mthonjeni's crime was unaffected by their work, it might mean the crime in their own neighbourhoods might be resistant to SAPS intervention. This in turn challenged the idea that police work was important and worthy of respect, and that the future would be more secure than the present. The prevalence of crime in the face of police saturation simultaneously motivated in officers not only the need for more police resources and harsher laws, but also the development of the area. Shifts that promoted a sense of police competence, value, and respect, and were absent of reported crime, were good shifts.

## Yorkton (the affluent city)

The Yorkton police station is one of Cape Town's largest and oldest. Its precinct encompasses a large, leafy section of the city's mountainside suburbs, and a large business and commercial zone, bustling with boutique shops and restaurants, bars, clubs, and theatres. During the day it hosts workers from all over the city, while at night the city's wealthier residents and tourists enjoy its more luxurious offerings of food, drink, and music.

The precinct covers almost 25 square kilometres of city space, twice that of Mthonjeni, and yet its population is a sixth the size of the township station. In the 2011 census, 53 percent of residents identified as White, 25 percent as Black African and 17 percent as Coloured. Almost the entire precinct falls within a single council ward, the data from which illustrates the overlap between race and class in the city: In 2011, 85 percent of its residents had completed high school; 94 percent were employed; 82 percent earned more than R3,200 (£175) a month. Ninety-nine percent lived in formal dwellings with access to piped water, flush toilets, and electricity (City of Cape Town 2013b). As is common to South African cities, Yorkton was a different world to the townships of Mthonjeni, just a short drive away.

### The wonderful weekend

While the good night in Mthonjeni focused on emptying streets, in Yorkton, busy streets were celebrated. The area is home to some of the city's most concentrated night life and attracts thousands of revellers on summer evenings. I spent a number of these evenings with Constable Hendricks, a sector patroller.

Hendricks liked to drive the largest of the police vans in the lot. Although the headlights did not work, he told me he preferred it to the newer vans because of its size; he believed it commanded respect. Apart from attending to three property-related crime complaints, the first hours of our first shift together were spent 'cleaning' the sector, as Hendricks put it. He stopped to ask apparently homeless people and car guards whom he did not recognise to leave his sector and made friendly chit-chat with others. It seemed that with most he was popular, but those whom he did not know were warned to leave.

Another element of Hendricks' 'cleaning' involved detaining people – not always formally arresting them – in the back of the van if he thought they posed a threat to the sector or to his authority. During the course of our first night together he detained eight unrelated people. A car guard was choked and detained for not vacating the area fast enough;[10] an apparently homeless man was detained and had his walking stick broken in two because, so Hendricks claimed, he had previously been warned not to loiter in the area; a drunk man standing in the middle of the road was swiftly grabbed and pushed into the back of the van, as was another sleeping outside a corner store (the store manager rewarded Hendricks with a bag of fruit). Two young men randomly seized from a group of ten involved in an assault outside a club were detained, as was another young clubber in possession of marijuana. Despite the relative affluence of most people on the street at night, all but the last three detentions were of poor men. While the latter three were likely middle-class, they were young and Coloured, like Hendricks. Hendricks piled the men into the back of the van over a number of hours before returning to the station to process them.

After a few hours of this I asked Hendricks if he thought his work disproportionately targeted the poor. He replied that he had never thought about it but that 'research and statistics show that they are the ones who commit the crime'. He thought the statement would impress me but I knew there was no such data. He was presenting a front which he expected me to accept without challenge. Ian Loader and Neil Walker have referred to such claims as the state's 'wilful disregard of its own ignorance' (2007:117). It was a mantra which, heard enough times, Hendricks had accepted as a truth that guided his work in the city.

Despite having been assigned to a relatively quiet suburban sector, Hendricks sought out the crowds beyond its borders. Unlike Mthonjeni, this was not because he wanted to chase people away. On the contrary, he wanted to be a part of the party.

Hendricks also sought out the busy streets because they were where he could flex his muscles in front of an audience he sought to please. His decisions were quick and surgical. If stopped and asked for help, or if he spotted someone he deemed unfavourable, he simply threw the perceived threat in the back of the police van and drove on.

These events meant a *good night* for Hendricks for a number of reasons. The many arrests made him a good performer in the SAPS target-chasing performance environment. The swiftness with which he controlled and detained people saved him the potential embarrassment of resistance. It also projected an image of efficiency to onlookers. These were the young and affluent, the people with whom he liked to surround himself on his days off, and the people whose middle-class comfort he hoped to join. By seeking out the spaces in which they clustered, and in leveraging the power granted him by the state, he connected with and projected a version of himself into a future in which his life and theirs were equal.

### The policing web

That the South African state is no longer the sole provider of security is particularly evident in Yorkton. SAPS officers working there occupy a special place in a web of what Brodeur calls *police assemblages* (Brodeur 2010). In addition to the 20-odd SAPS patrol officers on duty during each shift, an array of other policing actors keep watch over the city's streets. As elsewhere in the world (Loader 1999), policing in South Africa has become a commodity that is bought and sold (Samara 2011). In addition to the SAPS, the policing web in Yorkton included: the Yorkton Improvement District (YID) – a partnership between the city, local businesses and residents; CCTV cameras managed by the city; crime prevention and traffic enforcement officers of the Cape Town Metropolitan Police Department (CTMPD); private security services hired by residents and businesses; volunteer-based neighbourhood watch groups; and a network of street-based, informal car guards.

At the top of this list of policing actors sits the SAPS. While it is possible that the various actors do not revere the SAPS – indeed their presence exposes the *police as crime preventers* narrative as fictional – it is the SAPS to whom all must turn when an arrest is made. No other actor has the authority to investigate crime. This position gives Yorkton's SAPS officers status. Even the most junior can call on or instruct a range of actors to support them in their work. But when most police working in Yorkton go home at night, it is seldom to spaces as affluent or comparably policed as Yorkton. Rather, most return to the Cape Flats and an urban fringe characterised by hardship, precarity, and violence.

### The policing of (un)familiar worlds

Not all Yorkton's police officers enjoyed the crowds like Constable Hendricks, or had the confidence or ability to function in busy affluent space, so they avoided them.

I spent a number of shifts patrolling the city with Constable Moshoeshoe. He enjoyed his job and the opportunities it had afforded him and his family. He told me he wanted to serve the community, avoid the violence and corruption he believed many of his colleagues were involved in, and make the country a better place. He did this by sticking quite rigidly to his patrol postings, alternating between long patrols on the back roads of his sector's residential neighbourhoods, and breaks, parked under trees. Unlike Hendricks, when forced to engage with the public, he often did so awkwardly. It seemed to me that he struggled to relate to and engage with the world he was being asked to police, which was very different from the one in which he had spent most of his life.

Moshoeshoe was raised in a family of ten, 1,000 kilometres from Cape Town in the rural Free State. His family had been so poor that he had had to sell fruit to pay his way through high school. His mother tongue was Sotho, not a language common to the Western Cape. Until shortly before we met he had lived in a shack on outskirts of the city, yet at work he was tasked with patrolling some of its wealthiest neighbourhoods. Its residents were mostly White and wealthy South Africans. They were people whose lives were as different from Moshoeshoe's as any could be.

In South Africa, some police officers will always be posted in communities where residents do not look or speak like them, or share their cultural values or experiences. For some, like Hendricks, this difference is appealing, it animates their imagination and work. But because Moshoeshoe was relatively unfamiliar with the language and world of those who called on him for assistance, he struggled to engage with them. Instead, he would routinely ask *me* what I thought he should do on the job. A good shift for Moshoeshoe was one in which he displayed competence and learned new skills, and was not made to look foolish.

For others working the precinct, its Whiteness and affluence were more familiar than was the rural past which had shaped Moshoeshoe's youth. Two Yorkton officers, Sergeant Louw and Warrant Officer Kriel, were comfortable amidst its affluence. Louw spent his days patrolling and drinking fine coffee, a luxury he was proud he could afford using money earned after-hours. He believed that he was in control of the spaces he patrolled; that his presence commanded respect and prevented crime. He celebrated the dramatic minority of police work – the chase and arrest – and would tell related stories whenever he could. As a White officer with an extra job on the side, Louw was comfortable in Yorkton. When he was given the chance to test and prove his skills during a shift, it made a good shift.

Similarly, Warrant Officer Kriel felt at home in middle-class space. He told me he worked for the SAPS for the enjoyment; that he earned most of his money through a construction business he owned on the side. For him, a good shift was one in which the people expressed gratitude for his work.

While on patrol one afternoon, Kriel and I stumbled across a young man running away from a screaming woman whose phone he had just stolen. Following a short Hollywood-esque chase in which Kriel ramped our van onto pavements and cut through parking lots, he apprehended the thief.[11] When the young victim finally caught up to us she burst into breathless song, 'I love South Africa! I love the South African police!' It made Kriel's day.

The brief chase and arrest may not seem like the kind of moment that should define a good shift. At face value it is an event many believe common to a police officer's day. But, as we know, popular depictions of policing are seldom true to life. It is because these archetypal actions and events are so uncommon that Louw and Kriel took so much pleasure in them. By celebrating their ability to process a rare scene, or intervene in a crime in progress, they acknowledged their relative impotence against the everyday crime in the area. In the rare experiences of chase and apprehension, they regained some agency in an occupation that seldom allows officers to glimpse the outcomes of their actions. Good shifts were made better by gratitude expressed. A shift in which the public recognised officers for their contributions was a good shift, and when that recognition came from the middle class they aspired to join, it was all the better.

Because Yorkton had such an array of policing actors working its streets, SAPS officers were able to relax more than their township peers. They could pass off certain tasks to other agencies, while carefully selecting those that they enjoyed, or which strengthened their ties to strategic groups like the middle class. The relative order of the area and the breadth of its policing web meant officers could more consciously control the structure of their shifts. But for those like Moshoeshoe, who were uncomfortable with the other-worldliness and rush of the affluent city, a good shift was one where they were not asked to do too much; where they challenged and grew as individuals and officers, but in small increments and over time. For over 300 years Moshoeshoe's forbearers were actively kept out of the Yorkton-like areas. To him, as for many, the affluent bubbles remained mostly foreign.

### Detectives defending the fortress city

Yorkton's officers saw threats to their police precinct as originating outside of its boundaries, on the Cape Flats where most police lived. As a result, most patrol work involved monitoring markers of class, and questioning those who appeared not to belong in the city after dark. But once a crime had been reported and a suspect identified, it was the detectives who took up the mantle of labelling and ordering the city's bodies. Part of this work came in the form of weekly tracing operations.

In the SAPS, *tracing* refers to the detective practice of following up on the last-known location of a wanted person in order to bring them before court. While individual detectives are free to trace during office hours, Yorkton had a dedicated tracing unit. Once or twice a week it was joined by up to ten other detectives to conduct group tracing operations. These usually took place at night from around 9 in the evening until 4 or 5 in the morning. The operations revealed another version of the good shift, and how it shapes the privilege of areas like Yorkton, and the poorer spaces of the Cape Flats.

When I arrived for my first tracing operation at the scheduled time of 9 at night, only three of the 15-odd participating detectives were present. As others arrived, I was struck by their attire. They wore comfortable, casual clothing: sweat pants and T-shirts, sneakers or working boots. Some carried hoodies and woolly hats in anticipation of temperature drops during the night. The style signature of many was reminiscent of the symbols of deviance that prompted Mthonjeni's CPU officers to stop and question young men. They stood as a reminder that *police officers* and *suspects* often come from the same communities.

Captain Januarie, the head of Yorkton's tracing unit, began the briefing by asking if everyone had their bullet-proof vests, firearms, and handcuffs, repeating the question over and over like a mantra. The inference was clear: they were heading out into the dark night and only these tools would ensure that they made it to morning unscathed.

Two young detectives arrived mid-briefing. Making her apologies, one said she had been on duty until 5 that afternoon and had then needed to collect the officers working night shift. The captain lashed out at her, chiding her for not ending her day early. He said that her sleepless state would dull her senses and limit her ability to cover her partner's back. Then, returning to his briefing, he issued an instruction:

> I want all male suspects handcuffed behind their backs; no exceptions. And if there's a wall to jump over, you had better all jump. Don't make me chase you, I brought my cane [to hit you]! And if we fight, we fight together. If you are a *sissy* and don't want to fight, go home now. Lastly, nobody is fucking left behind!

The drama was notable. Having been tracing with detectives from Mthonjeni where comparable operations lacked anything close to this urgency, the energy surprised me. While Mthonjeni's detectives regularly traced suspects wanted for murder and other violent crimes, Yorkton's generally only sought those suspected of petty thefts, traffic accidents, or fraud. Januarie's speech conveyed the age-old ability of police agencies to manufacture fear and to infuse the night with purpose. His words set the stage for the action and performances to come.

A successful tracing operation was one that resulted in the arrest of a good portion of those sought, preferably in as little time as possible, and without injury to detectives. What would become evident, however, was that for Captain Januarie a good shift included stamping his authority on the neighbourhoods that both his suspects and detectives called home. He wanted to mark the bodies of their young men as undesirable and he did so through bullying and force, encouraging others to follow his lead.

Suspects traced by Mthonjeni's detectives almost always lived in that station's police precinct. Detectives there saw Mthonjeni as a place of people at war with themselves. They would knock on the door of a shack or house within minutes of leaving the police station, and the commute to successive houses was brief. In contrast, the parts of Cape Town through which the Yorkton detectives moved on their tracing operations were very different from those of their station's area. Yorkton detectives travelled 15 to 40 kilometres out of their station area before reaching their first address. The threat to their precinct came from elsewhere, from outside.

An energy seemed to surround the convoy of cars as it made its way out into the dark. Typing notes into my phone from the back seat of one of the cars I dubbed it a *Snake of Power*. I was struck by the speed and recklessness of the procession of five unmarked vehicles.[12] We sped through the backstreets of the Cape Flats, driving through red lights and stop streets. It occurred to me that the greatest threat the detectives faced that night may be their own driving. Police in South Africa almost never wear seatbelts. Ironically, they believe them a risk to their survival should they need to leap from a car. What is more likely is that their dismissal of seatbelts is symptomatic of South Africans' general dismissal of basic laws not regularly enforced. On the one occasion that we did stop for a red light, the detective driving our car pointed out a traffic camera covering the intersection. He had been coerced to stop.

\*

Tony Samara has suggested that urban renewal in Cape Town has taken the form of crime containment (2011). He reasons that government believes socio-economic development depends on economic growth, which itself depends on a foundation of security. In this context security has become pervasive, what Loader would call the lens through which most social problems are defined and acted upon (2006). Unable to provide equal security across the city, security provision mirrors Cape Town's historical divisions. Affluent spaces and social groups are protected, while poorer spaces are regulated, and their residents disciplined. Expelled from affluent space, the poor are contained in townships like those of Mthonjeni and Khayelitsha (Samara 2011; Hannah 1997). This distribution of security is not a product of policy but rather of the distribution of wealth, and SAPS officers' interpretation of their mandate and of urban space. As townships swell with the arrival of rural migrants, the state contains the poor. Meanwhile, wealthy citizens are left to self-govern through an assortment of private security providers.

\*

The speed and recklessness of the detectives' driving was not motivated by a need to get anywhere quickly. This was clear because, rather than restricting their work to the stated task, Yorkton's Snake of Power regularly stopped in the crowded evening streets of the Cape Flats to attend to other business. Following Captain

Januarie's lead, detectives leapt from their cars, pushing young men up against walls or down on the dusty ground, particularly in the first hours of the evening, displaying group violence incomparable to what I'd seen in my two months patrolling the Yorkton police precinct, nor indeed anywhere else in my experience of the SAPS. I wondered whether the detectives felt at greater liberty to mistreat the men because there, tens of kilometres from their own police precinct and without official markers by which they might be identified, they were unlikely to be held accountable. It was also apparent from the way the detectives discussed the neighbourhoods that they saw them as soaked in deviance and criminality, in contrast to the relative cleanliness and order of the city.

The irony that most of the detectives lived in, or had grown up on, the Cape Flats was not lost on me. I was curious to what extent their violence was the acting out of frustration over the crime, violence, and damaged masculinities they saw in their own communities. I wondered if the young men were like mirrors in the night in which detectives saw themselves, their fathers, brothers, and sons. If so, it seemed they believed that state coercion and force would fashion the young men, and so the communities through which detectives told stories about themselves, into something respectable.

The desire for respect was a theme that ran throughout my engagements with police at the four stations. But if it was recognition and respect that Yorkton police sought on tracing operations, they buried their desire in silence. Whether leaping from vehicles or knocking on doors, detectives almost never identified themselves as police officers. They did not announce their presence nor produce any identification. They simply barked instructions and resorted to aggression and force when people questioned them.

At some point in the evening the Snake of Power came across four young Coloured men in the empty streets of Mthonjeni. The fact that they were Coloured in a predominantly African area signalled to the detectives that they were drug dealers. Suspected drug dealers, it seemed, deserved special treatment.

The men were forced to lie on their stomachs, aggressively searched, shouted and sworn at, walked over, hit with a metal torch, kicked and forced to eat a very small packet of marijuana allegedly found nearby. Two student constables, just months away from completing their field training, deployed much of the violence. Their actions were the embodiment of the adage: *real police work is learned not in training but on the street.*

Back in the car Constable Jali said he did not like working the way we were that night. I wondered if this was a reference to the beatings but it was not. He said he would prefer to have spent the hours preparing dockets for inspection, meeting one of his performance targets. As an afterthought he added that he did not agree with his captain's violence, either. It may not have been part of his good shift, but he was not going to complicate his life by making a fuss. Rather, he would put his head down and get on with what was expected of him.

We returned to the station at 4 o'clock the following morning. The detectives had worked hard. Five arrests had been made in six hours and muscles had been flexed in the face of resistance. It had been a good shift, at least for those of Captain Januarie's ilk.

*

Samara has suggested that in Cape Town there has been a shift in city governance from township residents as victims to township residents as problems (2011). In his view the state no longer ventures into townships but rather sticks to their peripheries, monitoring only the flow of people like the apartheid force of old. I disagree. The Mthonjeni police precinct had up to seven patrol vans on the road at any one time, while the state more broadly had invested in a court house, Home Affairs office, and clinic, not to mention all the RDP houses it had built. The state was not absent. Did it engage with township residents differently from more affluent city residents? Definitely. While Mthonjeni's police stopped and searched, labelled and sorted through their daily rituals, Yorkton's detectives took their muscle to the township streets after dark and engaged with residents in ways that were very different from their interactions in the affluent city. The threat to the Yorkton police precinct was portrayed as emanating from outside affluent space. This thinking and related police practice echoed and reproduced the apartheid-era geography of inside-safety and outside-danger. It was a discourse animated by old, lingering narratives, and characters with dark skins and meagre opportunities to whom a less forgiving policing was unofficially tailored.

*

Yorkton's largely affluent and White residents are policed very differently from those of Cape Town's poorer Black townships. While restrained city police attend to wealthy residents' needs, policing in townships targets large swathes of their populations, associating nearly all young men with crime. This confines the dispossessed to what Loic Wacquant would call penal circuits of poverty, violence, arrest, and prison. Meanwhile, like a meat eater ignorant of the slaughterhouse, the affluent are shielded from the poverty and harsh police practices on which their comfort rests (Wacquant 2013).

A good shift for Yorkton's patrol police meant being given opportunities to display skill and efficiency in front of middle-class audiences. On those occasions when the audience expressed gratitude or respect for the police, it made it all the more worthwhile. These incidents supported the idea that public policing was relevant, respected, and appreciated.

For detectives, a good tracing shift was one in which a handful of suspects were apprehended. It was also good if detectives were able to go to the Cape Flats, where many themselves lived, and to communicate – often through force – their disdain for their poor, young, male, 'criminal' community peers. In so doing, they reminded themselves of the path they had managed to avoid, and reminded communities of the power their job accorded them.

## Patterson (the rural town)

### A bridge from village to city

For the last two months of my research I moved to the Eastern Cape to shadow police at a tiny village station in Gompo, and a small-town station in Patterson. Initially I included these stations only to expose myself to the four most common forms of South African police space: the affluent city, urban township, rural town, and rural village. But, once there, the ties between the Western Cape and former Xhosa homelands – the Ciskei and Transkei – could not be ignored. The provinces are connected through history, migration, identity, money, and death. These connections are central to the identities of African police officers in Cape Town and in the Eastern Cape. While my research was limited to these provinces, comparable urban–rural links exist throughout South Africa, binding cities to the countryside.

Most African officers I met in Cape Town spoke of the Eastern Cape as 'home'. In one sense, the large rural parts of the province – particularly those that lie within the boundaries of apartheid's former homelands – are another 'outside' to the affluent 'inside' of Cape Town. However, while Yorkton's police saw the city's townships as the 'outside' threat, those in Mthonjeni saw the rural 'outside' as a space of order. But, working in the Eastern Cape, I came to believe something important was missing from rural officers' narratives. Occupying a space between the rural village and the urban fringe, I saw the rural town as a site where the imagined order of the countryside began to unravel. One might think of these different sites as three concentric circles. At the centre are the relatively rare affluent spaces in South African cities, such as Yorkton. Outside these one finds the urban periphery, townships like those of Mthonjeni and Khayelitsha, some developing, others not, most still poor. I believe the rural town also falls into this zone, while the rural village lies beyond it, where life is once again relatively orderly.

Patterson, the small town, was a space of transition much like city townships. It is the closest thing residents of surrounding villages have to an urban centre, but lacks the jobs, opportunities, and luxuries of big cities. Instead, it draws in those from the countryside who qualify for RDP houses, and introduces them to the relative anonymity and inequality of small-town life. It also introduces them to the state's sorting apparatus – its police – and the city-shaped narratives that guide their work.

*

Patterson is a town in the Indwe municipality of the Eastern Cape. It was established by British forces during their 1834–1835 war with the resident Xhosa, and later became the administrative centre for the region. In the 1960s the areas was zoned as part of the Ciskei, an apartheid Bantustan established for Xhosa South Africans. As in other homelands, the land was arid and inhospitable, and employment opportunities few, forcing residents to seek poorly paid work in exploitative factories or White cities. In 1972 the South African government declared the Ciskei a self-governing territory, and in 1982 an independent republic. The area was only restored to South African status after the 1994 elections. When I visited in 2013, it remained poor.

Patterson remains an administrative centre. The Patterson SAPS station serves as the accounting or *cluster* station for five smaller rural stations in the surrounding countryside, including Gompo where I spent most of my time in the province. Descendants of European settlers have mostly moved on, with fewer than 80 of 24,000 residents identifying as White in 2011. The vast majority identified as Black African.

The Patterson police precinct covers approximately 750 square kilometres, much of it governed by the Indwe municipality. In 2011, 40 percent of Indwe's residents were unemployed, only 6 percent had access to a flush toilet, and the average household income ranged from R9,601 (£527) to R38,200 (£2,097) per annum (Indwe Municipality 2013).The municipality's population shrank by 8 percent between 2001 and 2011, probably through out-migration to cities, including Cape Town. Many of those who were employed, and had access to indoor plumbing and decent incomes, were likely based in Patterson, where hundreds of new RDP houses had been built. Surrounding villages were even poorer than these figures suggest. The Patterson police precinct covered both the main town and several villages.

Patterson police believed that their work genuinely prevented crime. They told me that if there was a rape in two villages one month they would concentrate resources there and the next month there would be business robberies in a different village. They believed their presence prevented crime.

Against this understanding, Patterson's patrol officers employed the same logic and followed many of the same strategies as their Mthonjeni counterparts. In other words, they believed that empty streets were safe streets, and spent their weekend evenings stopping, searching, and chasing young men, work they described as *crime prevention*. But the chases in Patterson were different from those I witnessed elsewhere. Relatively often, seeing the CPU vehicle slowing to a stop, individuals and groups would take off at a sprint. Sometimes police officers gave chase; sometimes they just laughed. As in Mthonjeni, Patterson's officers could collect five or six screwdrivers and knives over the course of an evening, simply by stopping and searching (but never formally arresting or processing) young men.

As in Mthonjeni, Patterson's patrollers believed that citizen compliance with stop and search made for a good shift. While they pursued many fleeing men, they seldom caught them. On one occasion a constable sprinted into the dark, chasing a group of teens. Realising he would not catch them he stopped and fired two shots into the air. In nine years shadowing and working with police I had never witnessed a shooting. It struck me that the town was a bridge connecting countryside and cities. It was urban enough to justify random patrols but rural enough for police not to worry too much about rules. Also, the anonymity, peri-urbanism, relative underdevelopment, and scarcity of job prospects meant that in important ways the town mirrored the township.

Later that evening we spotted the group of teenagers once again. After a short pursuit, this time by car, the three constables I was with cornered one of the teens. Leaping from the car, they beat him with fists and feet, stopping after about 20 seconds. One of them retrieved a knife from the ground. Chuckling, he told the teen that next time he should just stop and hand the knife over. With it secured, the officers had their evidence of work well done and a good shift. They sent the teen running into the darkness and we departed.

\*

A good shift for Patterson's police shared elements of those in Yorkton and Mthonjeni. Patterson's officers sought to empty streets of pedestrians. While they could be aggressive with the young, they were more clearly respectful of their elders. It was as if in the rural town, police were slightly more extreme at both ends of the service spectrum: they were more respectful of those they believed deserved respect, and more punitive with those they felt needed cor-rection. It was the romanticised good of the village, with the violence of the township, in one space. If Patterson's police were sorting and ordering young men as they moved from the village, through the town, possibly on their way to life in the cities, they were teaching them that violence commanded respect. A shift in which their lessons were accepted, and their authority acknowledged, was a good shift.

## Gompo (the village)

### The romance of rural life

Gompo is a small village off a dirt road, 30 kilometres from Patterson. The Gompo SAPS station is located at its edge, bordered by dry fields. The station's solid structure and brightly coloured roof contrast with the mostly dilapidated village homes. Only the odd house is newly built or painted, likely with money sent by family working in cities.

The Gompo police precinct spans nearly 500 square kilometres and includes 14 to 19 villages (officers were unsure). In 2011 the area was home to nearly 7,000 residents, almost all of whom census data describe as Black African and Xhosa-speaking (Frith 2014).

Gompo SAPS employed just 33 staff – a tenth of Yorkton or Mthonjeni's and a quarter of Patterson's. Five were student constables who would likely leave upon completing training. All were African. Eight employees worked office hours, with the remainder divided into patrol shifts and detectives. With some officers and detectives out on investigation, attending court or meetings, or patrolling at any one time, the station was generally very quiet. Sheep, chickens, and dogs wandered onto the property to graze and scavenge. In this peaceful arena, the generally young police officers complained of boredom. It was as if they bemoaned the order of the area, as if it constrained their professional identities. Officers passed time re-playing a limited selection of pirated movies on a computer, text-chatting with friends on their phones, or sitting idly.

Very few of those based at the station had grown up in the area. Rather, they had moved there for the job, and lived in decrepit houses in the surrounding villages. As a result, they knew few local residents. The police station became both their place of work and their place of belonging and community. Amongst those who had been based at the station for many years, a great collegiality had developed, and laughter regularly spilled out through office windows as colleagues humoured one another in the midst of their quiet days. When it was time for shifts to change, some officers hung around to chat to their relief, preferring to socialise rather than head home to solitude and rest. Before Gompo, I had never witnessed anything but a rush to get home after a police shift. Gompo was different.

But at other times, the station was silent. No sounds of cars, no chatter, just birds, animals, and the wind in the large gum tree that stood in the station's front yard. Station officers who had worked in bigger towns or cities shared stories with colleagues. They described a world where things were more dangerous but also more interesting. Few had been to Cape Town, nor did many seek to visit. They had friends or family who had moved to the city for work, and knew it only as a place of crime where police were hunted and killed.

While Gompo SAPS recorded little crime compared to the city stations, it still generated data. As part of the national policing machine, it had to report its figures, just like the busy city stations. In fact, perhaps officers' greatest effort went into reporting work planned or completed, projecting an image within the bureaucracy that the station was functioning. This was coordinated by the energetic station commander, Captain Dlamini. Each morning he drove 65 kilometres from his home to bark orders at his colleagues as they arrived for, and knocked off from, their shifts. In his presence the station came to life, quietening again with his frequent departures.

Another reason that Gompo's officers lamented their idleness and boredom was, ironically, the relative respect with which they felt people treated them. It was difficult to remain completely anonymous in the surrounding villages, so that if an identified offender escaped apprehension one day, police were confident they could track them down. This reduced the anxieties more common to city police. In this environment, a good shift was one where something rather than nothing happened; something different, to challenge officers and distract them from their boredom. The case of the puppies, for example.

### Puppies, police learning, and respect

I was sitting in the Gompo CSC after another slow morning. Constable Nxuba, a stocky, relaxed officer in his early 30s walked in carrying some *vetkoek* and two litres of Stoney soda. Chewing on a *vetkoek*, Nxuba started chatting to a village resident who had walked to the station from his home two hours away. The resident, clad in an LA Galaxy football shirt, explained that he owned a dog and had agreed to mate it with a bitch belonging to a resident in a neighbouring village. In return, the owner of the bitch had said he would provide the man with two puppies from the litter. But the puppies had been born and the bitch owner was refusing to honour the agreement. Nxuba agreed to help and we drove off.

As we drove, Nxuba told me he was 'just going to talk' to the bitch owner. Once at our destination, he asked a child to call the man he sought, then respectfully engaged him, explaining why we were there. The conversation was in Xhosa so I could not follow its literal flow. However, it was clear that Nxuba wanted to keep the men calm, and to control the conversation's flow. He indicated when they could speak and when to be silent, he told them to lower their voices when they became excited and he pulled the bitch owner aside and talked to him quietly when he sensed the mediation was faltering.

The negotiation took ten minutes, after which, reluctantly, the resident retreated behind his house and returned with two tiny puppies. Nxuba looked relieved and thanked him; the complainant grabbed the puppies and tossed them into the van. Seconds later we left.

We passed through the complainant's village at 3 o'clock on the way back to the station, and dropped him off. The man had devoted most of his day to approaching the police for assistance and Constable Nxuba had met his expectations. Nxuba was pleased with himself. He had been offered a challenge and had overcome it. Rural police occupied an important position in the lives of residents in ways I had not witnessed in the city or township. In this encounter, as in others like it, I saw the respect longed for by Mthonjeni and some of Patterson and Yorkton's police, which was so central to their descriptions of rural policing.

*

Patrol might seem an odd concept in a police precinct like Gompo's, with its single patrol van and vast swathes of land between sparsely populated villages. At best, a van patrolling all day might pass through each village once, lingering for only a few minutes. And yet, the language and accompanying ideology of patrol, stop and search, and coercive deterrence, filled Gompo's officers' minds. They seemed to believe that patrol, and thus coercion, were key to a crime-free countryside. Asking me late one night what I thought of Gompo's 'crime fighting approach', a constable interrupted me before I could answer, excusing what he saw as the station's shortcomings: 'If we had a van in every village there would be no crime, but we only have this one.'

It was a logic that manifested in a number of ways. The station's Crime Analyst, Constable Xoko, presented his role as analysing crime patterns to guide police action. But because crime was relatively rare, with fewer than 20 reported cases each month, he simply recommended patrols wherever the last crime or two were reported. The fact that his post even existed in such a low-crime precinct illustrates how the station borrowed from the city and township narratives of coercive policing. Similarly, Gompo officers told me that if I drove through a particular village I would be hijacked, even though this had never occurred in the area. They inserted city narratives on crime and risk into their generally eventless shifts to make them *good*. In so doing they manufactured purpose to stave off the threat of liminality and secure their sense of self.

Gompo's police, like some of Yorkton's, felt that residents generally respected them. Theirs was not the challenge of public disdain, but of professional boredom. As such, life was predictable and ontological security within reach, though ever threatened by liminality. A shift in which their minds and skills were put to the test was a good shift.

Gompo's officers appropriated city narratives of coercion-based crime prevention. They inserted them into the imaginary of the otherwise peaceful countryside. They referred to violent crime as if common when it was not. In a crime-hyped country that couples police work with *crime fighting*, rural policing was too different from the narratives of city crime and risk that dominate national media. By inserting such narratives into their own, Gompo's police connected themselves to something bigger. They brought meaning to their shifts and so to the stories they told themselves about themselves.

## Conclusion: making meaning across place and space

This book explores how personal identity shapes police practice in South Africa. This chapter illustrates what that practice looks like in the imagined good shift, while also describing the four most common types of space in which SAPS officers work: the urban township, affluent city, rural town, and village. I have introduced the four police precincts in which this research took place, and described the key ways in which policing unfolded in each. By so doing, I have described the 'work' element of the research question, and shed more light on the contextual forces at play in officers' private and occupational lives. In these spaces, their personal narratives become entangled in the overlap of SAPS (and station) organisational culture, and the national and local contexts in which they work. In turn this shapes personal identity.

While there were differences in the ways officers interpreted and acted on their mandate across space, considered together they form the relatively neat meta-narrative, which I describe in detail shortly. This meta-narrative presents the countryside as a place of order and respect, much like the city's bubbles of middle-class wealth, and sees these as threatened by ill-socialised youth raised on the urban fringe. Often these youths' lives mirror those of SAPS officers. It is through the SAPS organisational culture in which officers are entangled that they re-write their personal narratives to distance themselves from the men with whom their work compels them to clash.

This overarching narrative also helps explain variances across space. For many, the idea of the good shift involved working through sets of rituals, box ticking, in the hope that this would lead to their desired outcomes, or at least appear to do so. In some instances, these were the absence of death, while in others they were the number of people locked up for the night, a body count indicative of their *performance*. For yet others the good shift was any respite in the managerial pressure they felt hanging over them; any distraction from the dockets needing completion and closure. Against this pressure, many officers sought out both public and institutional gratitude, indications that their work was valued. Public celebration of police action and expressions of gratitude and respect were amongst the greatest rewards officers sought. They washed away the doubt that South Africa may not want the police it has.

For some officers, it was about getting through the night without having their competence or authority challenged, while for others it was about putting their skills to test; being able to grow as a professional and avoid boredom. Ultimately it was about buying into a narrative about the place of the SAPS and its officers in the nation and community; about the experience of being a South African working in the police environment, and about the desire for respect, dignity, and ontological security. This was particularly important since much of the criminal threat that police saw it their job to subdue originated from the same neighbourhoods in which they lived. In other words, officers' private and professional lives overlapped and became entangled with the broader local and national contextual forces around them. As such, their work became a contest of legitimacy between that proposed by young men believed to be involved in crime and the men policing crime. It was a contest to define and shape the futures of both the alleged offenders and the officers and, thus, the future of the country. A shift that bolstered the narrative that the police way was the right way was a good shift.

In my experience, most African officers considered the rural Eastern Cape to be 'home'. They described it as a place of traditional authority, respect, and order. It was where they or their ancestors had lived, almost always in relative poverty, and where a portion of their monthly income was often invested. City police had moved to cities to pursue a better life, but city life was hard. Outside select affluent bubbles, cities and towns were viewed as places of anomie and disrespect, where police were hunted and killed by young men who, born and raised on the urban fringe, lacked what were considered rural values. In the township and rural town these men – young, Black, and poor – were to be stopped, searched, and questioned by police. At night they were to be chased off the streets. They were to be disciplined, taught to respect their parents, the law, and life. A shift during which officers successfully controlled the township or rural town streets was a good shift; it gave police purpose.

For police working in the affluent city, their role was to protect its order and please its middle-class residents, whom they believed respected and appreciated them. In South Africa, affluent, formerly White urban space is, like the village, remembered as part of a crime-free past. City police saw their role as being to survey interlopers from the Cape Flats – poor men from the same violent neighbourhoods to which many officers returned at night – to ensure they did not sully the city's streets. When they did, it was the detectives who left the city at night to hunt and apprehend them, meting out a coercive violence less common on the streets of their police precinct.

In the rural Eastern Cape, police sat uncomfortably between the two worlds: the peaceful countryside and the violent town and city. There, as in the city and town, they disciplined young men (and women) who strayed from their roles as respectful youth. For the most part, however, such transgressions were rare. Respected by village residents, village police were able to mediate disputes between adults, and shame or beat conformity into the young. To give meaning to often quiet days, they borrowed from urban discourses on crime and risk, reminding themselves that they were part of something bigger than the village; something important.

In summary then, I interpret these practices in the following way: The young men police targeted in their work were drawn from the same communities in which police were raised, and/or where many lived. Their alleged crimes fuelled violence and fear in their neighbourhoods, fed negative stereotypes about groups to which police belonged, and trampled beliefs in more peaceful times past. They threatened an imagined future where life was materially easier and absent of (illegitimate) violence. Through their work, officers sought to deflect these young men from potential paths of criminality, and to punish them – sometimes pre-emptively – for their indiscretions.

While SAPS officers did not necessarily long to live in the affluent city or its sterile suburbs, they wished their relative order, safety and affluence were a part of their home communities. In this way, the affluent city echoed the imagined order of the rural village while offering the material comforts promised, but not fully delivered, by the post-1994 democratic order. It was this longing for meaning, order, and material comfort in both their private and occupational lives, and in their imagined futures, which underpinned how officers interpreted and carried out their work.

## Notes

1  The South African minibus taxi industry has long been embroiled in organised crime and conflict over routes. For more see Shaw (2017 forthcoming).
2  The report provides an excellent overview of the SAPS and the challenges it faces in large city townships (O'Regan & Pikoli 2014).
3  A small shop, usually operated from a home or roadside stand/container, and common to townships.

4 Steinberg (2008) suggests that such lack of information sharing has its roots in the apartheid era when police were largely absent from townships and not trusted, and where local, non-state security assemblages were turned to for security provision.

5 South African police killed at a rate of 7.2 per million inhabitants in 2015/16. That same year American police killed at a rate of 3.5 per million, for which they were widely criticised.

6 SAPS officers almost never wear safety belts, preferring instead to clip the belts into the buckle to disable the vehicle chime that would otherwise incessantly remind them to buckle up. From 2012 to 2015 considerably more police died in vehicle (389) and other (52) accidents than were murdered (247) (SAPS 2015b). Of the 188 officers killed in 2014/15, more of those murdered were off duty (51) than on (35). Of the 102 killed in car accidents most (63) were off-duty.

7 Perkins reports that between 2012 and 2013, 115 officers killed themselves while only 29 were killed on duty in the same period (Perkins 2016). She reports that SAPS officers killed themselves at a rate of 74 per 100,000 in 2012/13. The national suicide rate in 2009 was roughly 13 per 100,000 in the general population. Perkins calculated the national suicide rate as 0.9:100,000. My calculation is based on 2009 data published by the Medical Research Council, which recorded 6,471 suicides that year, when the national population was estimated to be 50 million (Matzopoulos et al. 2013).

8 In 2014, South Africa's Black and Indian prison populations mirrored national demographics (79 percent and 1 percent respectively), while Coloured prisoners (18 percent) people were significantly overrepresented, and White prisoners (2 percent) significantly under represented (Jules-Macquet 2014).

9 The Mthonjeni station commander proudly told me that he had previously given officers confiscation quotas. He said they would end shifts with bags full of knives seized on the streets. But, when the numbers of knives on the street had begun to decline, he said his officers had started taking knives from peoples' kitchens to meet their quotas. Only then did he do away with the targets. Officers were still encouraged to stop and search, however.

10 Hendricks later told the man he had arrested him because he had embarrassed him in public. He also told me that the choke was his preferred mode of arrest because it avoided the embarrassment of being unable to control people in public.

11 In fact, it was I who had to first detain the thief, though fortunately not physically. He was on my side of the van when we caught up to him. Whether an instinct from my own policing experience, or an imagined expectation, I assumed that Kriel expected me to apprehend the man. I jumped out of the car, worried that I was going to have to physically restrain the thief. To my relief he immediately stopped running. Kriel remained in the car watching us for a few seconds, as if assessing both the thief and I. He then exited the van, walked around the car and jabbed the man in his torso with his fist.

12 'Unmarked vehicle' is the term police use to refer to police vehicles that don't carry any official police markings. Detectives tend to use these in their work.

## References

Bayley, D.H., 1994. *Police for the Future*, New York: Oxford University Press.

Brodeur, J.P., 2010. *The Policing Web*, Oxford: Oxford University Press.

City of Cape Town, 2013a. *2011 Census 'Suburb Mthonjeni'*, Cape Town.

City of Cape Town, 2013b. *2011 Census 'Suburb Yorkton'*, Cape Town.

Douglas, M., 1966. *Purity and Danger: An Analysis of the Concepts of Pollution and Taboo*, London: Routledge and Kegan Paul.

Frith, A., 2014. Census 2011. Available at: https://census2011.adrianfrith.com/.

Geertz, C., 1973. The Interpretation of Cultures: Selected Essays, New York: Basic Books.

Glaeser, A., 2000. Divided in Unity: Identity, Germany, and the Berlin Police, Chicago, IL, and London: Chicago University Press.

Glaser, C., 1998. Swines, Hazels and the Dirty Dozen: Masculinity, Territoriality and the Youth Gangs of Soweto, 1960–1976. Journal of Southern African Studies, 24(4), pp. 719–736. Available at: www.jstor.org/stable/2637471.

Glaser, C., 2000. Bo-Tsotsi: the Youth Gangs of Soweto, 1935–1976, Oxford: James Currey Ltd.

Goffman, E., 1990. Stigma: Notes on the Management of Spoiled Identity, London: Penguin.

Gould, C., 2015. Beaten Bad: The Life Stories of Violent Offenders, Pretoria: Institute for Security Studies.

Hannah, M.G., 1997. Space and the Structuring of Disciplinary Power: An Interpretive Review. Geografiska Annaler, 79(3), pp. 171–180. Available at: www.jstor.org/stable/490655.

Holdaway, S., 1983. Inside the British Police, Oxford: Basil Blackwell Publishers.

Indwe Municipality, 2013. Annual Report 2012/13. Available at: http://mfma.treasury.gov.za/Documents/06.AnnualReports/2012-13/02.Localmunicipalities/EC126Indwe/EC126IndweAnnualReport2012-13_.pdf.

Jules-Macquet, R., 2014. The State of South African Prisons. Available at: http://press.nicro.org.za/images/PDF/Public-Education-Paper-The-State-of-South-African-Prisons-2014.pdf.

Loader, I., 1999. Consumer Culture and the Commodification of Policing and Security. Sociology, 33(2), pp. 373–392.

Loader, I., 2006. Policing, Recognition, and Belonging. The Annals of the American Academy of Political and Social Science, 605(Democracy, Crime, and Justice), pp. 202–221. Available at: www.jstor.org/stable/25097805?seq=1#page_scan_tab_contents.

Loader, I. & Walker, N., 2007. Civilizing Security, Cambridge: Cambridge University Press.

Manning, P.K., 1978. The Police: Mandate, Strategies, and Appearances. Policing: A View from the Street. Culver City: Goodyear Publishing Company.

Marks, M., Shearing, C., & Wood, J., 2009. Who Should the Police Be? Finding a New Narrative for Community Policing in South Africa. Police Practice and Research, 10(2), pp. 145–155. Available at: www.tandfonline.com/doi/abs/10.1080/15614260802264560.

Matzopoulos, R., Prinsloo, M., Bradshaw, D., Pillay-van Wyk, V., Gwebushe, N., Mathews, S., Martin, L., Laubscher, R., Lombard, C., & Abrahams, N., 2013 The Injury Mortality Survey: A National Study of Injury Mortality Levels and Causes in South Africa in 2009, Cape Town: South African Medical Research Council.

O'Regan, J.C. & Pikoli, A.V., 2014. Towards a Safer Khayelitsha: Report of the Commission of Inquiry into Allegations of Police Inefficiency and a Breakdown in Relations Between SAPS and the Community of Khayelitsha, Cape Town: Khayelitsha Commission of Inquiry.

Perkins, G., 2016. Shedding Light on the Hidden Epidemic of Police Suicide in South Africa. The Conversation. Available at: https://theconversation.com/shedding-light-on-the-hidden-epidemic-of-police-suicide-in-south-africa-53318.

Samara, T.R., 2011. Cape Town After Apartheid: Crime and Governance in the Divided City, Minneapolis, MN: University of Minnesota Press.

SAPS, 2015a. 'Measures Implemented to Ensure Safety of SAPS Members and Address Unnatural Deaths', Briefing to the Portfolio Committee of Police, 28 August. Available at: http://pmg-assets.s3-website-eu-west-1.amazonaws.com/150828PoliceSafety.pdf.

SAPS, 2015b. Sector Policing Operational Guidelines, pp. 1–48. Available at: www.saps. gov.za/resource_centre/publications/sectorpolicing.php.

SAPS, 2016. 'Risk Management Strategies to Reduce Police Deaths', Briefing to the Portfolio Committee on Police, 17 February.

Shaw, M., 2017 forthcoming. *South Africa's Underworld: Organised Crime, Assassinations and the Erosion of the State*, Johannesburg: Jonathan Ball.

Steinberg, J., 2008. *Thin Blue: The Unwritten Rules of Policing South Africa*, Cape Town: Jonathan Ball.

Steinberg, J., 2011. Funeral March of a Man Who Can't Step Up to the Job. *Citizen Alert ZA*. Available at: http://citizenalertzablogspotcom-tango.blogspot.co.za/2011/08/funeral-march-of-man-who-cant-step-up.html.

Super, G., 2013. *Governing Through Crime in South Africa: The Politics of Race and Class in Neoliberalizing Regimes*, Oxford: Routledge.

Turok, I., 2001. Persistent Polarisation Post-Apartheid? Progress Towards Urban Integration in Cape Town. *Urban Studies*, 38(13), pp. 2349–2377.

Tyler, T.R., 2011. Trust and Legitimacy: Policing in the USA and Europe. *European Journal of Criminology*, 8(4), pp. 254–266.

Wacquant, L., 2013. Symbolic Power and Group-Making: On Pierre Bourdieu's Reframing of Class. *Journal of Classical Sociology*, 13(2), pp. 274–291. Available at: http://jcs.sagepub.com/cgi/doi/10.1177/1468795X12468737.

# Chapter 3

# The good shift as fiction

## Manufacturing the good shift

Much of what constituted a good shift for officers involved knowing that they were in their supervisors' good books. Often this required meeting performance targets, such as numbers of dockets ready for inspection; people stopped; or arrests made. When adequately executed, such actions, and the associated production of data, are referred to as *successes* in the SAPS. Those whom I observed failing to produce successes risked receiving poor reviews. They also risked being reprimanded; shamed for not fulfilling supervisors' interpretations of the SAPS mandate. But, at other times, pleasing or avoiding conflict with supervisors simply involved laying low or turning a blind eye. It was about maintaining a strategic front of good impressions; a kind of deception, or what Manning has called 'covering your ass' (2009) and 'magic' in support of the illusion of justice (2010).

In this chapter I explore the practices of deception and related culture of suspicion in the SAPS. I suggest that, like most police agencies (Skolnick 1966; Manning 1974, 1997, 2009, 2010; Muir 1977), the SAPS is an organisation heavily invested in the production of a fiction to justify its existence and give legitimacy to its actions. This fiction is that it is a rational, effective, evidence-based, and rule-bound organisation made up of well-trained officers engaged in common-sense activities that make South Africa safe. It is a fiction that is shaped by the South African context in at least three important ways. The first is that South Africa is a country with a historically divided population, often mistrustful of one another. The second is that, as the enforcer and protector of apartheid's racist laws, the SAPS predecessor, the SAP, was widely distrusted. While the SAPS has worked to produce an image of objective professionalism since 1995, scandals, such as the 2010 corruption conviction of its National Commissioner, Jackie Selebi; the 2012 police shooting of 112 striking mine workers at Marikana; and the 2012–2014 breakdown in the relationship between the community and police in Khayelitsha, have damaged it. Finally, the SAPS is staffed by officers whose self-narratives feed broader narratives of generations in transition. By this I mean that most police recruited since the mid-nineties are the first in their families to secure comparably stable work. Officers' personal narratives are shaped by the overlap between socio-economic and historical contextual forces with the SAPS organisational mandate and culture. It is natural that these officers do first what is required to get by. Families are their priority, as is getting ahead, securing a better future, and, thus, ontological security. The SAPS and public take priority for some only because they are the subject of income and security. As a result, shortcuts are taken to meet organisational targets. The appearance of performance gets officers ahead, bringing recognition and advancement. But where unofficial or illegal practices simulate performance, their revelation can lead to an officer's downfall. Some trust one another only to the extent that each knows the other can expose their own deception. Against this background, the SAPS fictional front seeks positively to frame a tainted profession. By participating in its manufacture, officers are forced to consider the manufacture of their own self-narratives.

## Teamwork, learning to deceive, and securing the job: Gompo

In my first week at Gompo, I was introduced to four student constables. They had already spent a year at police college and had been deployed to the village station to turn lessons into practice. But 'training' can be misleading. For three consecutive days, the students arrived in the morning, pulled table and chairs into the sun, and sat writing in their pocket books.

A pocket book is a personal diary in which officers should record every action taken during a shift. The students said their pocket books were due to be inspected; that they were getting them ready. Pocket books are meant to be completed in near real time throughout the course of a shift. But Gompo's students had all the time in the world. They could weave perfect line-by-line accounts of what they may (or may not) have accomplished in the preceding weeks. The completed entries would appear flawless, absent of the scribbles and scratches that are common to pocket books. It would be clear to any officer that they were doctored; they just looked too good. When the books were inspected and found to be in order, the inspecting officer would become complicit in a misleading performance that showed active, hard-working students out on the beat, with impeccable pocket-book-writing abilities. The students were learning that the SAPS is an organisation content with self-deception.

*

It is wishful thinking that individuals will disrupt a collective practice of deceit (Bok 1978). The students had signed up to join a police agency, not to change it (Brodeur 2010). Deception is common among those wanting to make good impressions (Keyes 2004) like SAPS students working to secure their place in the organisation.

Goffman (1959) suggested that social groupings, like police, form *teams* whose members collaborate to produce shared *fronts*. These fronts promote stereotypes such as *police catch criminals* and *police make things safe*. When a new actor, like a student constable, joins a team, they find their role pre-defined for them. As a result, the longevity and normalisation of the institutional front is extended. Through *team work*, SAPS officers suggest the organisation and its functions are obvious and rational.

In public, SAPS officers rely on each other to maintain the institutional front. As members of a *team*, each has the potential to expose the fiction behind it. Because police are bound by their shared public performances, when they are alone in offices and patrol vans – Goffman's *backstage* – they must drop their performances, because each knows it to be false. There, they can relax and tell stories that cement shared understandings of what constitutes a good performance (Shearing & Ericson 1991). A key theme to these stories is the importance being suspect, that people can't be trusted.

It has long been observed that most police socialisation and learning occurs on the street, not at training facilities. While an official version of the *front* is introduced in early training, it is unlikely to stick. Several studies have measured the effect of organisational socialisation in the SAPS (Kutnjak Ivkovich & Sauerman 2012, 2013; Steyn 2015; Steyn & Mkhize 2016). Based on a survey carried out among trainees in 2005, and repeated with the same officers in 2010, Jean Steyn and colleagues suggest that the cynicism, isolation, and solidarity identified in the broad literature on police organisational culture are present in SAPS basic training, but strengthened over time (Steyn & Mkhize 2016; Steyn 2015). Sanja Kutnjak Ivkovich and Adri Sauerman (2012, 2013) have twice replicated Klockers et al.'s (2003) famous police integrity survey among SAPS officers, finding that they adhered to a strong code of silence. Kutnjak Ivkovich and Sauerman also found that a quarter of SAPS supervisors would not report bribery and theft, and that many officers did not recognise serious corruption as a violation of rules (2012, 2013). These studies suggest that despite lack of trust between officers, most are willing to protect each other and the organisation, rather than challenge abuse. These findings help to explain the lies and cover ups exposed at the Commission of Inquiry into killings by police at Marikana (Farlam 2015).

*

While sitting with Gompo's students as they filled in their pocket books, Student Constable Mmaya, an artist turned police recruit, showed me his first SAPS training manual, titled *Basic Development Learning Programme: Module 1 – Professional conduct learner's guide* [sic]. The first page of the manual, written in all-caps, stated that it was the copyrighted property of the South African Police Service. This, I would learn, was ironic because the manual itself borrowed from other texts without proper citation and contained a number of glaring contradictions. The manual's summary of learning outcomes included: 'Conduct oneself in a professional manner'; 'Apply knowledge of Ethical principles, standards, and professional conduct'; 'Demonstrate the understanding [sic] of the Culture of the organisation'; 'Apply customer service principles'; and 'Demonstrate the ability to execute group marching activities' (SAPS 2010). It seemed from these that the first objective of SAPS training was to teach recruits to work for the *team* and to replicate the institutional script.

The first chapter began by stating that 'South Africans expect to be provided with a professional service' and that 'Non-professional behaviour [sic] by SAPS officers . . . [means] the nation experiences the SAPS as an ineffective institution and loses trust in [it]' (SAPS 2010:1). But how *professional* was the manual? Aside from its numerous grammatical errors, parts were clearly cut and pasted from elsewhere, including Wikipedia. Phrases such as 'as per new research' were made without citation, reminding me of Yorkton's Constable Hendricks' claim that *research* proved the poor committed most crime. It seemed that from their first days in training, students were taught to accept, internalise, and reproduce patterns of questionable statement and dubious fact. Outlining some of the organisation's key standing orders, the manual stated that:

> [A Constable] shall obey all orders with deference (respect) and execute them without delay ... Should an order appear to be unlawful or improper, he/she may ... afterwards complains [sic] to his/her Commander ... [A Constable] shall refrain from being overzealous or meddlesome and should, therefore, not concern him/herself unnecessarily with trifling matters.
>
> (SAPS 2010:27–28)

While one might expect a police curriculum to encourage respect for hierarchy, the events at Marikana in August 2012 (introduced in Chapter 1) are indicative of how terribly things can go when poor leadership meets unquestioning subordination.

Working through the manual while the students wrote, I found all manner of errors. I told the students that what they had been taught may not have been accurate. They seemed offended and retreated to writing in silence. Nobody wants to be told that their performance is false, let alone that they are unwittingly being taught to deceive. By doing what they were told, they hoped to secure a good job, a steady income, and a promising future. With so much at stake there was little reason for them to question authority.

The silence of writing was broken a few minutes later by the *beep-beep* of Student Constable Cethe's cell phone. Glancing at the screen, he leapt to his feet, turned his cap to the side, and started dancing: 'Life is very, very good!' he sang:

> From now on I will eat whatever I want to eat. My phone will be singing! I must buy some red wine from Robertson. Each and every time that I'm craving wine I will just pour!

The others chuckled. I asked who the message was from. Student Constable Debeza answered knowingly, 'He's getting his back pay' – outstanding money owed by the SAPS. At the end of the day that is what these performances were about for the students. It did not matter if they were being taught incorrect information, or trained to present false pocket books to superiors who would pretend they were authentic. As long as a secure job with good, steady income remained on the horizon, they would learn what they were told to learn, write what they were told to write, and dance when the money came in.

## Teamwork, learning to deceive, and securing the job: Yorkton

Lessons in deception were not limited to rural policing. I experienced the same in Yorkton when accompanying two student detectives to a meeting with provincial trainers. The students were due to have their portfolios of evidence inspected in the coming week, and the meeting was intended to check that they were on track.

We arrived late to the meeting and found 15 other student detectives already seated at a long table, portfolios of evidence in front of them. A large, middle-aged man was shouting instructions and questions at them, 'If there is a gap next to any mentor signature then please just get any detective to sign it at the station, otherwise there is going to be a problem!'

He asked students to raise their hands if they had not completed various tasks; many had not. He told them to list these in the *development plan* section of their portfolios. 'Here you are saying you will do them in the future. Write that your mentor explained this process to you,' he told them. The students responded with silence and the scratching of pens.

Again, students were being shepherded into a culture that dictated behaviour, including the production of fictions. Students could not graduate without having been exposed to certain tasks, or at least having been talked through them. But whether this had happened or not, they would record that it had, because that was what they were told to do.

Watching the interaction between trainer and students in Yorkton reminded me of firearm training I had received as a police reservist in 2011. At the time, all SAPS officers and reservists had to undergo new firearm competency testing in response to a change in legislation. The problem was that, with the legislative deadline looming, thousands of officers had yet to be trained, so corners were cut. While our shooting range instruction was thorough and well regulated, the theory was not. Not only were we taught incorrect information regarding when police may shoot, but we were given many of the answers to the written tests, too. We filled in and marked the multiple choice element of the tests as a class, under the guidance of the instructor, a captain. The class included at least one brigadier and two colonels, ranks senior to the captain's, yet none questioned him as he led us through an organisationally sanctioned fraud.

My training experience was published in a 2012 paper (Bruce 2012) and put to the then National Police Commissioner, Riya Phiyega, at the Farlam Commission of Inquiry into the police killings at Marikana. Phiyega's response was that she simply did not believe the claims. But the claims are true and not new. These practices followed old trends still used in the training of the 2012/13 recruits I observed. If officers were encouraged to deceive during their early training, and unquestioningly participated in group fraud during refresher (firearm) training, perhaps it is unsurprising that the National Police Commissioner reverted to immediate denial when standing on the most public of stages at the Marikana Commission. She had to play her part as the team leader and maintain the strategic, deceptive front.

## (Mis)Trust and learning to deceive: South Africa

Long before they join the SAPS, officers' personal identities are shaped by the communities in which they are raised. Social attitude surveys repeatedly show that South Africans distrust one another. In answer to the question, 'Generally speaking, would you say that most people can be trusted or that you must be very careful in dealing with people?', 81 percent answered 'must be very careful' in 2013 (Afrobarometer 2013:83). In 2009, 52 percent of South Africans were generally distrustful of one another, 22 percent were neutral, and only 26 percent generally trusting (Mmotlane et al. 2010). Trust is greatest within families and weakest between strangers (Afrobarometer 2013). Experimental research among a small sample of high school students ($n = 337$) suggests that trust is influenced by racial identity, with all South Africans least likely to trust (fellow) Black South Africans (Burns 2004). A 2008 national household survey found that less than a third of South African adults trusted their neighbours, and significantly fewer trusted strangers (Posel & Hinks 2013). A 2015 survey found significant mistrust in the President (66 percent), parliament (58 percent), the ruling political party – the ANC (56 percent), and the police (54 percent) (Afrobarometer 2016). In 2013, 53 percent of people believed 'all' or 'most' SAPS officers were corrupt, but most (73 percent) still agreed that police always have the right to make people obey the law (Afrobarometer 2013), hinting at South Africans' disciplinary bent.

There are a number of explanations for this mistrust. One of the most important factors has to do with the country's history. Until 1994, the state's nation-building project was predicated on the idea that there existed four clear population groups – Whites, Coloureds, Asians/Indians, and Africans. Each was presented as inherently different from the others and as most prosperous when kept separate. Built into this hierarchy were an unequal distribution of resources, opportunity, wealth and power, and a coercive fear of the racial other. Because these (manufactured) groups were kept relatively separate, they perpetuated untested stereotypes between South Africans: What did they eat? How did they discipline their children? What were their customs and beliefs? Can they be trusted? Where information did flow, messages communicated by government, schools, certain churches, as well as through segregated land rights and built environments, were scripted to support subjective, untested stereotypes.

Ignorance of others discourages empathy for them, promotes mistrust of them and can promote violence against them (Pinker 2011). Knowing this, partially explains social tensions within South African society, particularly at the intersection of race and wealth. It also provides insight into the ease with which citizens are able to demonise SAPS members – they know them only as the state on the street; not as people – and vice versa – the police's exposure to crime dulls their capacity to empathise and leads them to doubt victims' claims.

In limiting the potential of most South Africans, while fostering a race-based minority elite, apartheid created a society of deep inequality. In 2016, 22 years after the formal end of apartheid, South Africa remained one of the most unequal countries on earth (World Bank 2016). Survey data suggests that trust in South Africa increased with economic status (Posel & Hinks 2013) and diminished with lower living standards and education levels (Mmotlane et al. 2010). This is unsurprising when most lives are characterised by precarity, so that a scam, broken promise, or theft can have life-changing consequences. In South Africa, inequality correlates with crime, unemployment, and poverty, so that economic vulnerability leads to multiple insecurities for the country's poor majority (Elgar & Aitken 2011; Demombynes & Özler 2005; Kriegler & Shaw 2016; Lancaster & Kamman 2016).

While perhaps obvious, it has been empirically shown in the United States that groups once oppressed are less trusting than others (Alesina & La Ferrara 2002). Oppression-based mistrust can be passed on to children not directly affected by the original oppression (Posel & Hinks 2013:2). Young Black South Africans have been shown to be less trusting than their peers (Ashraf et al. 2003:24; Burns 2004:7). Other predictors of mistrust are a recent history of trauma, being 'unsuccessful' in education and finance, and living in a community with high income disparity (Posel & Hinks 2013; Ashraf et al. 2003), much of which applies to most South Africans.

Inequality is an extremely strong current running through and shaping South Africans' lives. Amongst other outcomes, it is a central driver of crime and insecurity. Research suggests that in South Africa fear of crime is both pervasive (StatsSA 2015), and erodes trust in government and police (Roberts & Gordon 2016). Believing that physical security will promote economic growth and ease precarity (The Planning Commission 2012), the government increased SAPS numbers from 135,000 in 2004 to 201,000 in 2012. Efficacy in reducing crime aside, police numbers serve an important symbolic purpose by promoting an image of a government that is responsive to citizens' needs. But behind the polish and shine of police boots and vans, most SAPS officers are recruited from the same precarious, anxiety-filled, crime-fearing communities in which most South Africans live.

A 2016 survey of 18-to-30-year-old South Africans living in informal settlements ($n = 232$) found high rates of symptomatic depression among both men (50 percent) and women (58 percent). Depression was associated with food insecurity (women) and stealing due to hunger (men), and shame (men), and stress (women) due to unemployment (Gibbs et al. 2016). A 2009 study found that 30 percent of South Africans suffer mental, mostly anxiety-related disorders at some point in their lives (Herman et al. 2009). Another, from 1997, described life for South Africa's majority poor as characterised by continuous ill health, hard work for little income, little to no social agency, and high levels of anxiety and stress (May & Norton 1997).

Denied a strong education, or financial support for further study, many of those who end up in the SAPS turn to it as a last resort. Although the job holds a promise of a better life, many officers remain tied to networks of the working poor and vulnerable. So, while securing the job increases police's aspirations, the weight of the vulnerable networks to which they remain wed slows their ascendance out of precarity, and fuels the distrust that accompanies it. As I describe in Chapter 5, this gap between aspiration and achievement might lead to feelings of shame (Gilligan 2000).

Two other factors that may influence (mis)trust in South Africa are superstition and jealousy. Eighty-five percent of South Africans identify as Christian (StatsSA 2014). Many incorporate aspects of traditional African belief systems into their Christianity so that Christianity's temptations of Satan are merged with beliefs in witchcraft. The daily life of many South Africans is replete with practices and beliefs framed by religious and occult superstition (Lee 2012). These are the main explanation for most individuals' successes or misfortunes, for those who are fully invested in them (Comaroff & Comaroff 2006).

In 1992, the SAP established an *occult investigation* unit to investigate conduct recognised as a crime, but based on a belief in witchcraft, Satanism, or magic. The unit interpreted the supernatural in relation to Christianity, and officers working for it had to 'strongly believe in Jesus Christ' (Keita 2014). By 2014 media reports of the unit's work suggested it focused on *muti* killings – murders where it is believed the victim is killed for the harvesting of organs and body parts for use in the production of charms and amulets. These examples provide some sense of the pervasiveness of superstition in South Africa. For believers, witchcraft can be used to gain an edge over rivals, ensure well-being, guard against attack, pass exams, or secure a job (Comaroff & Comaroff 2004). For South Africans invested in a spiritual identity that marries Christianity with traditional belief systems, life:

> Entails a continual presumption of malice. People must be constantly vigilant against occult attack [from within one's community] … Such wisdom, however, makes trust inordinately difficult.
>
> (Ashforth 2005:80)

The second factor smothers the idea that in the *new* South Africa everyone has the right to aspire to, and be granted, a better life. This is the suggestion that many South Africans become intensely jealous if their peers succeed but they do not. This has been shown among poor rural adults and urban adolescents, and has been seen in the violence meted out against foreign Africans blamed for stealing South African jobs (Bray et al. 2010; Steinberg 2008b; Africa Check 2015). Superstition and jealousy go hand in hand. For those invested in witch-craft, curses can be used to hold back those of whom one is jealous, or amulets employed to protect against the curses of others. In the aftermath of the 2012 Marikana killings, it emerged that striking miners had recruited a *sangoma* and worn amulets to protect themselves against police bullets. Commenting on this in a Mthonjeni detective meeting 12 days after the massacre, the head detective told his officers, 'We need protection, too, but not from *muti*, from our God. Our God will protect us.'

Apartheid's SAP was a staunchly Christian organisation. The oath sworn by its officers stated that the SAP 'serve[d] a nation with a Christian National Foundation'. In 1977, the Minister of Law and Order claimed that the SAP were the 'mandate holders of God' (Cawthra 1993:77). Writing in apartheid's final year, Brogden and Shearing (1993) described the SAP's culture as informed by Christian, political, and scientific discourses of white rule, which supported their recourse to brutal means in protection of white hegemony.

Christianity remains important to the SAPS in the twenty-first century. Most meetings and briefings open with a Christian prayer. Similarly, among the police I shadowed in 2012/13, at least five were Christian ministers and two *sangomas*. The former's crucifixes and the latter's beads and animal-skin armbands were reminders that many officers remain deeply invested in invisible forces which they believe shape their fortunes.

None of this is surprising when considered against South Africa's history of inequality and separateness. Not only is the country one of the most unequal in the world, but it is its poor majority who bear the brunt of the unemployment, poverty, crime (Demombynes & Özler 2005; Kriegler & Shaw 2016). The precar-ity which dominates the lives of most South Africans, then, is amplified for those whose lives are characterised by poverty, geographic seclusion, lack of quality education, and belief in supernatural threats. It is those with the least who must trust the most in strategic people, belief systems, and institutions, including the state and its police, in order to survive.

While perhaps obvious, it is seldom acknowledged that many SAPS offic-ers are recruited from the poor, disempowered, and superstitious bulk of South Africa's population. According to a SAPS recruiter whom I met while based at Yorkton, for every 200 new jobs advertised the SAPS receives 10,000 to 15,000 applications. This was not surprising. In December 2012, eight would-be traffic officers died while participating in a fitness test as part of a recruitment drive. They were part of a shortlist selected from 150,000 applications, competing for 90 posts (@CityPress 2013). Those joining the SAPS are often people scooped from contexts of precarity, and provided reprise within the institutional cocoon of the state. A job in the SAPS is something to be coveted for most recruits, even if it does not represent the life they had once hoped to live. It is perhaps unsurprising that the suspicion that pervades South African society is entangled with the kinds of police institutional suspicion found elsewhere. The result is a deeply mistrustful and misleading organisation.

\*

Simply put, a lie is a lie, or deception a deception, when the deceiver knows their statement to be false. Often, lies are told to achieve specific outcomes, including the maintenance or improvement of a self, organisational, or team image (Curtis 2003; Tyler & Feldman 2005). Not all deceit in policing is considered wrong; in fact, it is often rewarded. Many justice systems, including South Africa's, allow for entrapment through carefully planned deception, or allow detectives to deceive suspects during interviews in the hope that they implicate themselves. But SAPS officers are also expected to be trustworthy, honest, and guided by integrity (SAPS n.d.). Licence to deceive in one aspect of the job, even if in the interests of justice, opens pathways to deception in other, illegitimate areas. At times this is called 'noble cause corruption' and can include perjury in court in support of conviction, covering up abuse of force where officers deem it morally just, or the manipulation of crime data to boost police–public morale. Where otherwise-good SAPS officers believe cheating gets them ahead, they may be more likely to deceive. Where deception at a SAPS station or in a specialised unit is encouraged and/or undetected, its severity and pervasiveness may increase over time (Fleming & Zyglidopoulos 2008). The harm such lies do is cumulative and hard to reverse (Bok 1978).

What does all this have to do with personal identity and police work in the SAPS? Karl von Holdt has suggested that the South African state's aspiration to establish an effective bureaucracy stands in contradiction to its desire to rapidly develop a Black middle class (von Holdt 2010). While the former aspiration is dependent on skill and expertise, von Holdt suggests, the latter requires ambivalence towards merit. Subsequently, the state resorts to face-saving practices, asserting a public façade of competence while deflecting criticism that might expose mediocrity.

Relatedly, the *new* South African national project encourages children and young adults to construct positive images of future selves living long and successful lives marked by achievements denied their parents. But 45 percent of the *born free generation* who started school in 2002 had dropped out before completing high school in 2013 (Wilkinson 2014) and, by early 2016, 67 percent of those aged 15–24 and not engaged in formal education were unemployed. Among 24–36 year olds, this figure was 40 percent (StatsSA 2016).

Although many South Africans have succeeded in achieving qualification, employment, wealth, and status greater than their parents, hundreds of thousands have not. Many SAPS officers whom I shadowed understood their place in the organisation as signifying bigger dreams lost. But once employed by the SAPS, most worked to protect its image. Sometimes this was done through dedication to official tasks, but at other times it was achieved through deception. As such, SAPS officers' deceptions served two purposes. The first was the maintenance of an organisational façade of efficiency and effectiveness, desired by the state. The second was the safeguarding of the SAPS reputation, which was central to how officers were received in their own communities and so key to their ontological security. By deploying select social performances that promoted a positive image of the SAPS, they hoped to shape images of themselves as people deserving respect.

## Performance and deception as police practice

In Chapter 1, I noted three key aspects of policing. The first is that because police are authorised to break rules and deploy force in defence of rules and order, they embody the potential to do that which they must prevent. The second is that police present themselves as crime fighters while their impact on general crime is limited. Both can be thought of as deceptions that sit at the heart of policing. Due to their centrality to the police image and idea, it is important that they are borne in mind when considering the third point: that through their work police signal the (il)legitimacy of people and actions, and so shape communities. They communicate meaning regarding how crime and disorder are viewed and responded to, and reflect what a society believes and expects of itself (Loader & Mulcahy 2003; Manning 2009). Police are the creators and defenders of fictions, and the manufacturers of culture and identity.

Closely related to the SAPS shaping work is its official front stage image, supported by annual reports, official presentations to parliament, press statements, and the annual release of crime data, among other performances. The ability to deliver these performances requires the constant collection and flow of information through the SAPS bureaucracy, in the form of *performance measurement data*. This in turn is fed back into the SAPS public front in support of its crime-fighting claims. The front becomes both the SAPS' greatest asset and burden. It is an asset when it wins support for the organisation, but a burden because it commits the SAPS to an impossible crime-prevention mandate (Burger 2006; Manning 1997).

SAPS officers are the bearers of stigma. While they may be inconspicuous when off-duty, at work they are part of a very visible, tainted group. They are the object of daily news and argument concerning what they, and thus South Africa, should be and do about crime. These narratives are complicated by government's use of the SAPS to disseminate strategic narratives about South Africa and South Africans. The SAPS is thus deeply invested in the production of its own front, and that of South Africa's entire imagined community (Anderson 1991).

The management of this front resulted in two performative trends among the officers I shadowed, which in turn shaped the stories they told themselves about themselves. The first was the range of ways in which they misled, deceived, and lied to colleagues, managers, and the public in an effort to present particular

SAPS fronts, and the front of their occupational selves. The second was that this propensity to mislead contributed to a culture of suspicion in which officers believed that almost everyone was lying to them, so that the SAPS organisational culture was steeped in mistrust.

Deception in the SAPS is not limited to a set of carefully controlled or sanctioned actions, like entrapment. Recruits are hired and trained in an environment of both unintentional and purposeful deception which is, as I will demonstrate, quickly entrenched in daily practice, bolstered by a mistrust long embedded in South African society. SAPS organisational culture shapes the social performances and personal identities of officers entangled in the overlap of police culture and in the general precarity of South African life.

## Accountability, 'performance', and deception

Before illustrating common forms of deception in the SAPS, it is worth touching on the country's police oversight architecture.

Police work is shaped by how it is measured. Performance culture is pervasive in the SAPS. White boards in briefing rooms and offices list reported crime figures, targets set, met, or missed, and activities planned or carried out. Such data are both notoriously inaccurate and consistently critiqued (Eterno & Silverman 2010; Wicks 2016; Moore 2006), but remain sacred in the policing arena where, as Manning has noted, they become 'a version of the backstage that can be read off as accurate and valid in front stage presentations' (2009:452).

In the early 2000s, the SAPS launched a performance management tool styled on the New York Police Department's (NYPD's) CompStat. When patrol officers and detectives are briefed, their tasks are motivated through the Performance Chart (the Chart) (SAPS 2013b). In 2012, the RAND Corporation listed the Chart as an example of good practice in police performance management (Davis 2012:21). While it certainly is impressive, the practices it produces are not always congruent with the community-oriented narrative that the SAPS and government promote.

Little understood outside of SAPS management before 2012, the mechanics of the Chart were revealed in some detail at the Khayelitsha Commission of Inquiry, between 2012 and 2014 (Faull 2016; Faull 2014). There, SAPS managers described it as a tool to determine and assess organisational efficiency in terms of Constitutional obligations, by measuring accomplishments against targets. It is intended to assist managers to combat crime; guide corrective action at poorly performing stations; provide holistic overviews of stations' crime combating operations; and distinguish between the quantity and quality of police work. It is meant to compel managers to identify and correct underperformance promptly through targeted interventions.

All of this sounds good. A growing body of evidence suggests that targeted, evidence-based interventions that are monitored and revised as necessary are the best ways in which police can impact crime and disorder (Lawrence et al. 2009;

Skolnick 2008; Roeder et al. 2004). But CompStat-like tools are not perfect. They are unable to record what street-level police officers spend most of their time doing, such as patrol, responses to calls for assistance, and interactions with members of the public (Manning 2009:454).

Research on organisational goal setting suggests that workers perform best when given difficult but achievable goals (Grover 1993). Many of the goals given to SAPS officers are not achievable. Indeed, this is true of its Constitutional mandate to 'prevent, combat and investigate crime' (Republic of South Africa 1996).

This poses risks to professional, transparent policing. The more concerned one is about the opinion of others, the more likely one is to deceive (Keyes 2004). Because SAPS managers are concerned about what the government and public think of them, they pass performance-related anxiety on to subordinates. The result is that indicators are used as evidence of action. This front is particularly misleading when police are employed to intervene in the absence of more appropriate state apparatus, like social workers (Samara 2011). By deploying police officers in such ways, the state shapes South Africa's social narrative by suggesting that solutions to social ills are grounded in security.

The SAPS, like many public institutions, puts forward an image of itself that is rule, record, and strategy driven. And yet, for the sake of pragmatism, street-level bureaucrats from police officers to teachers do not typically perform their duties per the standards set for them. Most famously, Michael Lipsky showed that with large workloads and limited time and resources, frontline government workers develop shortcuts through which to work, while maintaining a veneer of order and formality (2010). Such informalities have been well documented in the SAPS (Altbeker 2005; Steinberg 2008a; Vigneswaran & Hornberger 2009; Hornberger 2011; Faull 2010). But police officers work hard to support the fiction that there are no informalities, while most know that they are making things up as they go (Manning 1974). Perhaps the most important SAPS system dedicated to guiding the crafting of an image of professionalism is the Chart.

Performance targets measured by the Chart fall under six broad categories: crime prevention, crime reaction, crime investigation, human resource management, vehicle management, and data integrity. From its inception the Chart included a target of 'customer satisfaction', but no means to measure this has been developed (O'Regan & Pikoli 2014; Faull 2016).

The primary object of the Chart's measurement is the police station. Annual targets are determined for each station based on its performance in the previous year. Stations must always improve. While SAPS stations are required to establish Community Policing Forums (CPFs) and Sector Forums to engage communities and ascertain their needs, such interactions are not fed into the Chart or a station's performance targets. Rather, station-level targets are set by the SAPS Head Office in Pretoria.

In 2012/13, when the Khayelitsha Commission hearings were under way, and when I was shadowing the officers described in this book, the national targets for all SAPS stations were: Crimes Dependent on Police Action +3 percent; Contact

Crimes −4 percent; Property Related Crimes −2 percent; Contact Related Crimes −2 percent; and All Other Serious Crimes −2 percent (O'Regan & Pikoli 2014). If a station's year-on-year target was below that of the national target, then the latter was adopted. For example, if contact crime at a station decreases by 5 percent in 2017, then it should decrease by more than 5 percent in 2018. But if contact crime only decreases by 2 percent in 2017, then the station must adopt the national target of 4 percent for 2018.

What was clear during the proceedings of the Khayelitsha Commission was that while the three stations under review had performed relatively well based on the Chart's measures, the residents of Khayelitsha felt that police there were hopeless (O'Regan & Pikoli 2014). This challenges the SAPS' claim that the Chart promotes effectiveness and accountability. The Chart's emphasis on nationally set crime targets means that community priorities risk being silenced.

A police organisation that is internally democratic and fair is more likely to produce democratic and fair police practice on the streets (Myhill & Bradford 2013; Stanko et al. 2012) While important, a narrow focus on particular performance outputs or achievable targets, generates data that suggests a professional police service hard at work, potentially hiding more than it reveals (Faull 2016). If operational officers and detectives are constantly being hounded to produce the appearance of efficiency, the SAPS Chart may promote an autocratic, rather than democratic workplace culture. The manipulation of data by police officers may reflect their dissatisfaction and inability to handle the pressures placed on them. Drawn away from their community orientation by crime-centric performance targets means they are unable to pursue the type of order-maintenance and lever-pulling work that may more effectively encourage community cohesion and public safety. Instead, their crime orientation promotes distrust among South Africans, each of whom must wonder if the next person they pass on the street is what the SAPS and their political overseers repeatedly label 'criminal'.

The Chart fails to reflect the realities of everyday policing in several other ways, the most obvious of which is its inability to capture routine interactions between the public and police. While the SAPS presents itself, both in speech and policy, as community focused, it does not measure or hold officers accountable for building strong community ties. For instance, sector policing, the model through which the SAPS implements community policing, describes Sector Managers as lever pullers. They are expected to liaise with local stakeholders and mobilise police and other public and private resources to address local concerns. And yet, aside from very basic measures such as 'Sector file is up to date' and 'Sector forum established' (SAPS 2015), its implementation and impact is not measured. In Khayelitsha it was found to be dysfunctional (O'Regan & Pikoli 2014). To change SAPS officers' behaviours, one would need to emphasise and measure things like community perceptions of safety or police legitimacy in a station or sector area. This would signal to officers that they are more than crime fighters, and that there are many ways to be an effective police officer.

The Chart, without any real measures outside reported crime and case processing, promotes a 'crime fighting' orientation that meets the SAPS political, practical, and symbolic interests, but which runs counter to the reforms needed in a post-apartheid democracy. What is needed is a balance between police work that effectively contributes to public safety, while fostering feelings of respect, community, and belonging. Without this balance in its performance Chart, the SAPS will continue to struggle to win the hearts and minds of the public it strives to serve.

The notion that the SAPS will make South Africa safe is a fiction. Police are important to state order (Pinker 2011) but limited in their ability to prevent crime (Frydl & Skogan 2004; Lawrence et al. 1997). Yet, recruits enter the organisation with crime framed as the object of their work. They are trained in an environment of uncritical and unquestioning acceptance, and taught early on that they are expected to maintain the SAPS façade. This is not unusual in public policing. But amidst the precarity of South African life, deception in the SAPS is central to officers' pursuit of ontological security, as individuals and for those in the networks they support. Deception becomes part of their social performances at work, and so part of the story they tell themselves about themselves which they believe to be true.

## Categories of deception

Against this background and that of the SAPS Performance Measurement Chart, four categories of deceit commonly emerge in the policing of South Africa: (1) public performance deceptions; (2) data performance deceptions; (3) internal and external deceptions; all of which lead to and are connected by a (4) culture of suspicion. Each overlaps with, or builds on the others, and all are connected by an organisational culture of deceptive team work.

### Public performance deceptions

By *public performance deception* I refer to the ways officers purposefully engage with public space, with the intention of presenting a façade of 'visible policing' or other popular notions of police work. Whether or not they are doing anything of substance, they *are seen to be doing* something. An example was the weekly 'community outreach' patrol at Mthonjeni. The stated intention of patrols was to encourage the formation of anti-crime street committees, and promote community–police cooperation. These are good intentions, but actual patrols didn't live up to this vision.

Patrols took place twice a week and involved about 15 employees. However, only about five were police officers. The majority were civilian staff who, happy to be relieved of desk work for a few hours, donned fluorescent 'POLICE'-branded bibs and hit the streets for a stroll. A marked police car would lead the group, while two walkers carried a banner reading, 'Take your street. Own your street. Fight crime.' The remaining patrollers sought out residents, or gaps in doors and fences, to offload hundreds of photocopied pamphlets of 'safety tips' and contact information.

But the pamphlets unwittingly contributed to the disorder of the streets. When patrollers accidently dropped them they seldom picked them up. Residents, too, occasionally tossed the pages into the street after glancing at them. Towards the end of patrols whole wads of pamphlets would be dropped into yards to offload stock. Patrollers didn't seem to associate dirty streets with disorder, something I return to in Chapter 6.

Some civilian staff seemed to enjoy pretending to be police officers. For instance, an administrator repeatedly admonished and threatened with arrest, a woman selling chickens at a roadside stall, accusing her of animal cruelty. The threats were aggressive but, unbeknown to the seller, without authority. In this way, patrollers drew on the SAPS authority when it suited them, but for the most part kept it packed away.

Similarly, when the wind blew, the SAPS banner was difficult to hold. On such days it would only be unfolded for photographs. Photographing the patrol, particularly interacting with residents, was central to the events. Photographs served as evidence of work done, even though they reflected little of the patrols' real substance. Instead, they were a medium through which the SAPS misled itself.

In 2012 the SAPS did not have a sophisticated social media presence. This has since changed. The SAPS Twitter and Facebook feeds post a dozen or more photographs of SAPS officers in action each day, posing with 'recovered property', 'confiscated drugs', or 'suspects arrested'. Occasionally they depict the type of outreach activity I have just described, too. The SAPS Twitter and Facebook feeds present it as an incredibly efficient and engaged organisation, playing an important role in the manufacture of its strategic front.

\*

Photographs shared on Twitter or Facebook emerge out of public performance deceptions, but become *data performance deceptions*.

South Africa has one of the worst road death rates in the world, ranking 177 out of 182 measured (WHO 2010). Easter weekends are particularly deadly as many thousands speed their way across the country. The weekend is a focus of law enforcement, with hundreds of roadblocks set up to check sobriety, vehicle road worthiness, speeding, and overloading. Whether these interventions save lives or not, there is no doubt that, through them, police are *seen to be doing something*.

On Good Friday 2013, the start of the long weekend, I accompanied Captain Dlamini, Gompo's station commander, on a cluster roadblock operation outside Patterson. Fourteen officers were assigned to the operation. At the briefing, Dlamini recorded their names and force numbers on the official attendance form.

Once finished, he asked for my SAPS appointment certificate (ID card) and copied my reservist details onto his form. Then, counting the names under his breath he muttered, 'fifteen'. He had formally booked me on duty. It was not that he wanted me to work, but every name added to the operation's record would make it appear more impressive to Dlamini's superiors.

While they have the necessary authority, the SAPS does not have a clear traffic policing mandate and officers almost never act against traffic violations. Officers are also regular transgressors of almost every traffic law, as I discuss in Chapter 6. At this roadblock, SAPS officers were accompanied by four provincial traffic officers, to aid their work. The group set up the roadblock a few kilometres outside Patterson on the national road and waited for the instruction to begin stopping cars.

What followed is important. When officers stopped cars they did so with little intent. They requested licences from drivers and confirmed that these, and car registration papers, were valid; some half-heartedly searched car boots. At face value, they were doing police work. But what they ignored is more important. Half the drivers and almost no passengers stopped wore safety belts. Only one was asked to fasten his belt before departing, and none was fined. Similarly, while his car was searched, one driver urinated next to it, while another dropped a Coke can at the feet of the officer to whom he was talking. Police seemed oblivious of these authority-challenging illegal infractions, because they were too busy recording driver names and licence information.

Driving back to Gompo after the operation, Captain Dlamini volunteered, 'It was a very successful operation: we issued lots of fines, eight or nine!' They could have issued 30 more, or simply asked people to buckle up. What was important to Dlamini, however, was a list containing the information of about 50 cars and their drivers, because it was proof of work done. Police had also been visible on a busy national road for two hours, delivering a public performance that was likely noted by all those who passed by.

*

In addition to the data-based deception which I discuss in the next section, these community-outreach and roadside performances serve an important purpose. Like most visible policing, they make mundane what might otherwise be thought invasive. They burn the memory of a police presence into the public mind so that citizens will not say they were absent, and they entrench the SAPS' right to insert itself, uninvited, into individuals' lives, when it deems fit.

If a thousand road users die, the SAPS will have the data to prove its efforts to save them; if a community protects its offenders, the SAPS can produce photographs of its attempts to reach out. With an impossible mandate and inadequate tools with which to carry it out, SAPS officers repeatedly rehearse these and related performances to defend their centrality of place in a country that expects more of them than they can ever hope to achieve.

### Data performance deceptions

*Public performance deceptions* often link to *data performance deceptions*. The latter refer to the data generated by public performances, or forged in the absence of organisationally required public performances. Captain Dlamini's record of cars stopped and fines issued is an example, as are the posed photographs taken during outreach patrols.

The largest segment of the SAPS 2012/13 Annual Report is titled 'Performance Information'. It features data ostensibly gathered through roadblocks, patrols, and other operational activities. Because police work is low-visibility work, it is the data that police generate which serves as evidence of work completed. The listing of such evidence informs the police claim to make authoritative pronouncements about the country and, in the words of Loader and Mulcahy: 'have [their] power of naming not just taken seriously but taken for granted' (2003:46). The data adds a layer of formality and common-sense to *public performance deceptions*. Counting and listing suggests there is something of value to be counted and listed. This entrenches the idea that what the SAPS counts represents what the SAPS is accountable for. Using data in this way, police become the manufacturers and gatekeepers of *official wisdom* on crime and policing (Manning 1997:122), while shielding from public view the backstage, where the dirtier work takes place.

Some of the action types and quantities listed in the SAPS 2012/13 Annual Report are: roadblocks (46,079); stop and searches (2,902,917); vehicle searches (7,392,543); and person searches (20,357,564). Notably, the latter is 40 percent of the country's population. The same report claims that in 2012/13 the SAPS arrested 1,682,763 people – more than half of whom were arrested for crimes less serious than shop lifting (SAPS 2013a).

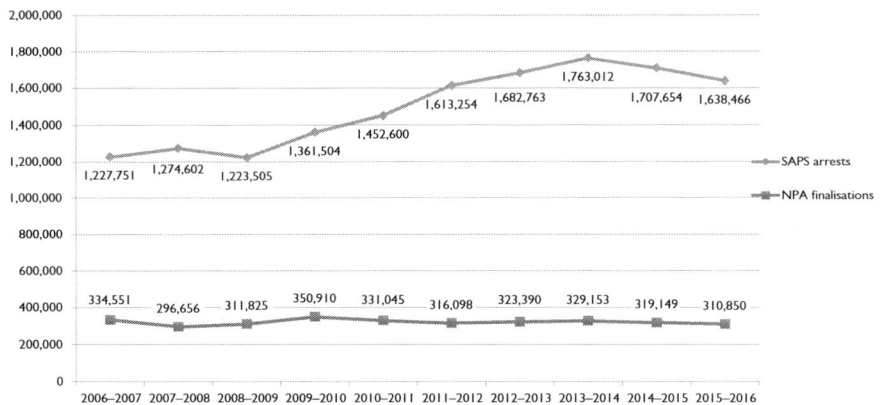

*Figure 3.1* SAPS arrests and National Prosecuting Authority finalisations 2006/07–2015/16

The information is reported with confidence and pride, as if evidence of a police organisation fulfilling its mandate. The figures say to South Africans, 'Of course these are the things you expect of police, and look how many of them we have achieved!' But the figures are almost unbelievable. A critical observer must read them as exposing not only deception, but unnecessarily punitive policing.

Figure 3.1 clearly illustrates that despite the SAPS arresting over 500,000 people more in 2013/14 than in 2006/07, the number of cases which the National Prosecuting Authority finalised did not change. The SAPS work may look good on paper but it does not necessarily make the criminal justice system more efficient or just.

Apart from the invasiveness and coerciveness of acts such as stop and searches, they obscure two important points. The first is that the figures reduce millions of complex social interactions between the state and its citizens to a handful of figures. Second, they hide what are very flawed systems of data generation. I have given an example of the latter by describing the pushing through of student detectives in training. The Annual Report for 2012/13 claims that of 5,068 recruits trained that year, 99 percent were 'found to be competent' (SAPS, 2013a:36). Such claims are common to SAPS reports, but it is very difficult to fail in a system that is rigged to ensure success, if only on paper.

\*

I have illustrated *data performance deception* elsewhere (Faull 2013). That related to Crime Prevention Unit (CPU) officers in Mthonjeni tasked with visiting taverns and shebeens to capture basic information and so map the precincts' alcohol retail landscape. Taverns and shebeens are viewed by city and national governments as generators of crime and vulnerability.

The operation was guided by a pro-forma sheet that officers were required to complete at each venue. But, rather than enter every venue and examine them in person, some officers simply called managers outside and completed the forms from the comfort of their cars. Officers did not check identity documents, as required, nor whether what they were told was true or not. They wanted to fill in the forms and be done with it.

I had the opportunity to shadow Patterson's officers carrying out the same task some months later. Where Mthonjeni's officers spent five minutes, Patterson's spent half an hour to an hour at each venue, not only inspecting the premises but chatting cordially with owners. When the record-taking officer ᵗʰᵉ sheet he did so in a manner that appeared considered, reading each himself, following the words with his pen, before ticking *yes*. Because he appeared so careful, I assumed he was completing But at the fifth tavern I looked over his shoulder as he ticke 'Are any persons under age at the premises?' I pointed out replied, 'I see what you mean; it should be *no*.' The forr filled in, at least for this question, at all premises visited. It made me wonder what other inaccuracies might have been recorded, and how common they might be in the millions of forms SAPS officers complete each year.

*

The examples discussed thus far do not suggest any significant intent to deceive. Rather, they indicate the imprecise manner in which *evidence* of police performance is produced, and how this normalises what the public (and police) expect of the SAPS. The next three examples illustrate more intentional deceit through data.

*

At the end of each shift, Mthonjeni's CPU commanders were required to record and report to the cluster the numbers of actions carried out that day or night. These included Vehicle Check Points (VCP),[1] stop and searches, and tavern visits. But shift commanders were also at times expected to attend management meetings early in the morning following late-night shifts. As such, data would sometimes be captured well before the end of a shift so that the commander could return home to sleep. Lacking confidence with computer work, Mthonjeni's Captain Thangana asked me to assist him with this task on a few occasions. This gave me a front-row seat to the manipulation of data. For instance, only a few hours into an eight- or ten-hour shift, Thangana would ask me to help him capture the required figures. Because the shift had barely begun, the data had to be estimated. Similarly, following an operation in which patrollers, armed with search warrants, raided five homes looking for drugs, Thangana set about capturing the results of the operation, which he had not participated in. He soon realised that officers had failed to record the names of residents at some of the houses raided, as required by the SAPS computer system. To get around this, he made the names up. The spreadsheet also required that he note whether the raided homes were close to churches and schools; whether they were council-built or private. He told me to simply tick the *no* and *council* boxes as others had done for previous operations. He had not been on the raid, but I had, and I was fairly sure that some of his information was incorrect. He also told me to input four VCPs carried out, and 60 people stopped and searched, for the night. One might think this a high number for an eight- or ten-hour shift, but the fact that the captain thought them reasonable illustrates the type of work he believed his superiors expected of his unit. The numbers we entered into the computer are the numbers that make up the SAPS annual reports and their performance claims. They are the acts which police believe signal their dedication to their mandate. But, like the possibility that they may fulfil their crime prevention mandate, they are largely imaginary.

*

The second example relates to VCPs in Yorkton. There, shifts were regularly tasked with conducting five or six VCPs per shift (one per patrol van). This involved setting up a small roadblock, stopping passing cars, checking license details, and searching for illegal substances or weapons. However, most of the VCPs recorded in the station records during my time there never took place.

This is how it worked: The officer would park on the side of the road where the VCP was meant to be carried out. This was so that the car's AVL (Automatic Vehicle Location system) would show it had been in the area. The officer, at times asking for my assistance, would then write down the make and licence information of passing cars before inventing names and licence numbers for their drivers, and recording them on an official form. At the end of the shift, the forms would be handed to the shift commander as evidence of cars stopped when, very often, none had been stopped at all. On those occasions when cars were stopped, when a public performance deception was enacted, no action was ever taken against drivers. Again, this included ignoring un-roadworthy vehicles, expired licences, overloaded taxis, and unfastened seatbelts. Although the officer would threaten people with fines, he did not carry a fine-book, because he had no intention of issuing any. A few times, perhaps emboldened by their wealth and fancy cars, drivers challenged the officer, asking him what the purpose of the stop was. On such occasions he would either ignore the question or mutter something non-committal about it being 'police work' or 'routine stops', suggesting that whatever police are seen to be doing should be accepted as what police should be doing. Of course he could not divulge that it was a *public performance deception* intended to generate misleading data. These interactions illustrate the vagueness of what police work entails. Like stop and searches in Mthonjeni, VCPs normalised invasive police practices in public space, coupling the actions with popular assumptions about police work in the minds of both the public and the police.

Importantly, the Yorkton VCP officer would usually only fill in a one-page form for each claimed VCP. Each VCP was meant to last a full hour. As one officer told me, management must have known the data reported was fake because an hour-long VCP in Yorkton's busy streets would generate many pages of data. My VCP experiences suggested that management knew they were being deceived, and that they were okay with it. Everyone was deceiving, while pretending not to know they were being deceived.

*

The final example relates to Yorkton's ghost squad. The policing area is home to some of Cape Town's most active, moneyed night life. It is also home to a vibrant recreational drug trade. Yorkton's ghost squad was made up of about eight men, all in their 20s and early 30s. Tattooed and pierced, they would walk the streets dressed in casual clothing, in search of drug users.

The Yorkton area's night life is concentrated around a main strip of bars and clubs. One might expect the job of tackling a drug trade in such a concentrated space – and one with an impressive CCTV footprint – to be fairly easy. In 2003/04 the station recorded just over 800 'drug-related' crimes. In 2012/13, this figure stood at almost 2,000 (ISS 2016).

At the station, the ghost squad kept to themselves. While I was not able to shadow them, rumours about their work flowed freely through the station. The most common, confirmed to me by a member of the squad, was that they only arrested drug buyers, never dealers. The reason was simple: drug-related crime fell into the category *crimes dependent on police action*. Higher numbers were viewed as evidence of police at work. If drug dealers were arrested and the trade squashed, there would be fewer buyers to arrest and it would be more difficult to meet targets. So, while the squad knew in which buildings drugs were sold, rather than going inside and arresting the sellers, they waited outside and arrested their clients.

A month before I left Yorkton, an alleged street dealer died in the station's cells. When I arrived for the day shift, hours after the death, the rumour at the station was that he had swallowed the drugs he was carrying, and had died. But I soon realised that many officers did not believe the story. They knew it was common for the ghost squad to strangle people whom they thought had swallowed drugs, to prevent this. In this instance, they suspected the squad had murdered him. Did this mean someone would speak out? It didn't seem likely. Anyone who suspected anything, anyone who was willing to speak to me about it, said they wanted nothing to do with the investigation. They would put their heads down and get on with their work. At the end of the day, this was what was important to them: covering their asses and holding onto their jobs. In the meantime, the ghost squad would continue arresting drug users in order to produce an illusion of police efficacy.

### Internal deception and external deception

The formal, systematic manner in which the SAPS generates misleading data is supported by regular, informal, *internal deception*, lies and, as in the case of the ghost squad, silence. Internal deception refers to the ways in which SAPS officers and groups seek to deceive one another to sustain predictability and to minimise risk to their ontology. Similarly, the public is sometimes deceived to protect an officer's interest; an *external deception*. These practices, such as calling in sick to work, are not unique to the SAPS, but do appear to be endemic in the organisation. An accompanying trend of theft within the organisation results in many officers plainly distrusting their colleagues. This erodes officers' pride in the organisation and their association with it, and so their self-esteem.

Absenteeism in the SAPS has been a concern for a number of years. The SAPS 2013/14 Annual Report states that 80 percent of the workforce took an average of ten sick days in 2013/14, while 19 percent of misconduct cases dealt with that year related to absenteeism without cause (SAPS 2014). In 2012, the Democratic Alliance, the country's main opposition party, made a number of startling claims about absenteeism in the SAPS, including that 85 staff at one station were absent for an average of 77.2 days each in 2011 (Kohler Barnard 2012). The Khayelitsha Commission also identified absenteeism as a serious challenge for the SAPS.

My sense is that many SAPS officers believed sick leave needed to be used, regardless of one's health. Some officers spoke about this openly. For instance, Yorkton's Constable Hendricks told me he always took all his sick leave, often to go partying:

> You only live once and I'm going to make the most of it. I know I have responsibilities to the organisation but the SAPS is not going to shut down just because I don't come to work.

With income and employment secured, he felt free to focus on the social aspects of his identity and to pursue ontological security.

Similarly, Constable Ndungwane in Mthonjeni joked that if he was not granted leave to return to the Eastern Cape in December, he would claim that his child was ill and that he needed to stay home with him. To this his colleague, Constable Deyi, responded with his own story, laughing throughout:

> Last year I did the same. My Christmas leave was denied. Then on the 23rd of December I saw an opportunity. A truck hit a child in Mountain View. It ran over its legs and crushed them. So I went to that White Captain, because she's sympathetic – the Colonel is hard and would have told me to be strong, and she called the social worker and told them I was not okay. They were very happy that I called them and said the police should call them more often. They booked me off as unfit. The next day I went to the Eastern Cape and didn't come back until after my holiday.

While he may well have needed what the SAPS calls *stress leave*, Deyi chose to present his story as if he had cunningly manipulated the system; as if it were normal in the SAPS.

Because abuse of leave is common in the organisation, extreme measures are taken to catch abusers: Following the Yorkton parade one morning, I accompanied Warrant Officer Kriel to visit two officers who had reported being sick because, he said, 'They are often bullshitting.' The measure was extreme. One of the officers lived 70 kilometres out of the city, taking us out of the precinct for three hours. Moreover, having visited the first officer's house, Kriel was unable to locate the second. She lived in Mfuleni, an area on the outskirts of the city in which the many RDP built houses generally look similar. When people on the street denied knowing where the officer lived, Kriel dismissed their statements with derision, saying, 'People always deny knowing who lives in a house if it's the police asking.' Not only did he question his colleague's claims of illness – in his words, 'To them [sick leave and family responsibility leave] is their right; they must take all the leave available to them,' but he mistrusted the public, too.

Driving back to Yorkton, Kriel shared a story which gave context to the visits to sick officers' houses. He began, dramatically and without warning, 'A few years ago I lost it.' He had been working as a detective at the time, and began investigating a group of corrupt SAPS officers. He arrested some of them but they were quickly given bail and began threatening him. He said that one had confronted him while with his family; that he, Kriel, had wanted to 'kill him right there'. A few days later he resolved to murder the man, and had been on his way to do so when police intercepted him. He was sedated and put on long leave. But what Kriel wanted me to understand was that:

> Because of that experience, I will never be friends with a police officer again. I don't trust the police and I tell my family not to trust the police. If the Colonel or Captain visit my house when I'm sick, they know they are not allowed to come inside. They know they are not welcome.

While Kriel's distrust of SAPS officers was extreme, it was not as rare as one might expect of members of the same *team*. Constable Bhele, also at Yorkton, told me he had been robbed by police from another station. He had been off duty, had been very drunk, and was speeding in his car (an offence he, like many officers, admitted freely). Because he was so intoxicated he did not realise he was being chased until he found himself surrounded by police. He recalled dozens of guns pointing at him, being thrown to the ground, and patted down by multiple hands. One of the officers came across his SAPS appointment certificate (ID) and the group let him go. But when he arrived home he realised they had stolen his cell phone and cash. 'Until I experienced this I didn't believe people when they complained that police robbed civilians,' he said. 'Now I do'.

This deep mistrust between colleagues manifested in mundane ways, too. For example, Mthonjeni's detectives almost never left their offices unlocked, no matter how short their absence. This was not because they contained anything of particular monetary value, but rather, detectives feared their colleagues might steal their stationery, coffee, or milk. There was also the vague possibility that someone might steal a docket and sell it to an accused person.

Similarly, officers would openly deceive one another or the public in order to protect their interests or hide inactivity. It was not uncommon for patrol officers to report to radio control that they had attended to a complaint when they had simply not been able to find the complainants. Officers dispatched to complaints at times also pretended to be busy, or asked probing questions before deciding whether or not to respond. While on patrol with Constable Moshoeshoe in Yorkton, for example, he received a call for assistance from the neighbourhood watch. Although we were only patrolling quiet back roads, Moshoeshoe's response was calculated, 'I am busy with a docket, but what is the problem? Maybe I can help.' When the neighbourhood watch said they needed assistance to search someone, Moshoeshoe agreed to help. As we drove he volunteered, 'I lied to them about being busy because I don't want to be called to see a person who has been beaten.' A few days earlier he had told me he did not agree with the violence some of his colleagues and neighbourhood watch members used. I pointed out that, had the call related to an assault, he could have intervened in defence of the victim. But his preference was simply to avoid confrontation, so he told a little lie to buy himself time, and to push back against an occupation that threatened to shape him in ways that made him uncomfortable.

This was another *internal deception*, one communicated over an official radio to a formal SAPS partner. But the manipulation of truth was more common in police–public engagements – *external deceptions*. I often witnessed officers giving false information to members of the public, generally to avoid work, but also to spite people. Examples included sending complainants to other police stations – claiming crime could only be reported in the area in which it occurred (false); telling people they could only pay fines at the court, not the police station (false); patrol officers telling victims to report directly to the police station because the patrollers needed to attend to other business (false); patrol police telling a victim they would only arrest an accused person, whom we could see, on Fridays so that they spend the weekend in jail (true but abusive); and police claiming an inability to open an attempted rape case because the mother of the young victim had been drinking (false and ridiculous).

### A culture of suspicion

Literature on police culture is replete with reference to organisational *cultures of suspicion* (e.g. Reiner 2010; Cockcroft 2013). The suggestion is that police work requires that officers remain suspicious of everything and everyone. However, this generally refers to the detection of illegal activity. The culture of suspicion to which I refer is different. While SAPS officers remain alert and suspicious in accordance with the literature – indeed, while they are particularly suspicious of predominantly poor, Black men – they are also deeply suspicious and mistrusting of many claims of victimisation from the public, and of each other, in ways that are not as common in the literature. This is not to suggest that police suspicion of peers has not been noted in the past; it has (Manning 1974; Reuss-Ianni & Ianni 2005), but rather, that in the same way that any lie affects its teller (Bok 1978), with every lie police tell one another, the bonds within the SAPS suffer. It is as if, while all know they are part of a *team* working together to create a front stage fiction, they are unable fully to abandon their deception in the backstage.

This was most notable at Yorkton, and amongst Mthonjeni's detectives: environments with demographic diversity. Because of South Africa's economic, spatial, and racial divide, many *race* stereotypes prevail. A survey of 25,000 Gauteng residents in 2013 found 73 percent of Africans agreeing that 'Blacks and whites will never trust each other.' Forty-four percent of Whites, 55 percent of Coloureds and 61 percent of Indians felt the same way (SAPA 2014). To live in a racially integrated area, attend a racially integrated school, or work in a racially diverse workplace that is not stratified by race, one needs money. Money and class, to some extent, temper old racial divisions. But most SAPS officials do not have that much money, nor do they work in heterogeneous or power-neutral environments. Instead their occupation makes regular reference to race labels to describe victims and suspects (e.g. referring to 'Three Coloured males', or the euphemistic phonetic alphabet example, 'Three Charlie males', instead, in the interests of political correctness),[2] and guide action, while they engage in daily squabbles over the police radio about which language should be used on air. English is the official language for SAPS radio communication, but is the mother tongue of only a minority of officers. Officers regularly speak to each other in different languages, inevitably excluding some listeners.

*

SAPS officers distrust one another, but they are also suspicious of the public in ways that echo the literature on police organisational culture. This was clearest at Yorkton, where many officers refused to believe the numerous, generally middle-class or international tourist people wanting to report street robbery (almost 3,000 per 100,000 in 2012/13), or pickpocketing and theft (around 17,000 per 100,000 in 2012/13), who daily queued to report their victimisation (ISS 2016). Rather, police felt they were abusing the SAPS to lodge false insurance claims. I believe this doubt was partly born of the fact that many officers did not have sufficient assets or income to be insured themselves. As such, they did not know that cash could not be insured, nor that excess must be paid for general claims. While officers never turned such victims away, they derided them in private. It was as if the claimed value of the items allegedly stolen from the wealthy victims was so incongruent with the worlds the officers inhabited that the only plausible explanation was that victims were lying. Backstage derision (Goffman 1959) of this sort builds morale amongst teammates, patching over some of the mistrust between officers.

Officers' distrust may also have been born of the jealousy and resentment Steinberg (2008b) and Ashforth (2005) have suggested South Africa's precarious majority feel towards the materially comfortable. As long as South Africa remains the socially and economically fractured society that it is, such suspicion and derision will likely remain. Because police work was, for most of those I shadowed, first about income and ontological security – the support of children and social networks – it made sense that they projected the same attitudes onto the public, especially those who were living the life they wished to live themselves, but which for most remained out of reach.

Because so many officers were deceiving their superiors, deceiving the organisation, deceiving each other, and deceiving the public, it seems unsurprising that some assumed everyone in turn was out to deceive them. This is particularly so in a country where, as the surveys cited above suggest, people are generally distrustful of one another and of the SAPS. The irony is that SAPS officers are simultaneously suspicious of their colleagues while conspiring to protect their violations. Because a majority of the SAPS *team* is involved in the manufacture of a façade, not to mention those involved in the dirtier side of backstage corruption, torture, and murder, many are both bound to, and under threat from, their teammates and fellow conspirators. Their personal narratives are entangled in an organisational narrative that vies to shape them.

## Small deceptions and big lies

Others have explored these themes before me. Hornberger has suggested that deploying violence behind an official image of respectful, human rights-based policing is 'actually in itself a form of violence' (2011:152). Similarly, in relation to imprisonment, Super has suggested the prison has become a symbol of government's willingness to *rehabilitate* offenders (2013). Together they suggest the language of *human rights* and *rehabilitation* functions as a screen behind which punitive practices persist. Thus far I have illustrated the very mundane manner in which these deceptive fronts are rendered in the everyday policing of South Africa. They are, of course, part of deeper flaws in the SAPS, including criminality and abuse. In the remainder of this chapter, I outline how these practices relate to the work of the Independent Police Investigative Directorate (IPID), the Marikana Commission of Inquiry, the Selebi corruption saga, and everyday policing as documented by the Khayelitsha Commission.

### The IPID

The IPID is responsible for investigating allegations of specific crimes committed by police officers, and deaths as a result of police action or in police custody. While the IPID appears impressive on paper, a large portion of all cases referred to it are closed as 'unsubstantiated'. According to the IPID, this means 'there is no evidence to support the allegations contained in the case and IPID cannot make a recommendation of wrongdoing' (IPID 2016:1). In 2015/16, of the 3,050 cases IPID accepted, 907 (30 percent) were closed as unsubstantiated. Table 3.1 illustrates the percentage of complaints closed in this way in 2012/13, the year I conducted this fieldwork, and more recently in 2015/16 (IPID 2013, 2016). While the proportion of cases closed as 'unsubstantiated' decreased, it remained high, particularly when one considers that the figures exclude the numerous cases IPID chose not to investigate.

Laying a complaint with the IPID is not particularly easy, nor is the IPID particularly well known among the general public. While the SAPS is compelled to refer any of the abuses listed in Figure 3.1 to the IPID, it is very likely that many aren't reported. And when they are, it should not be surprising that IPID struggles to build its cases when the SAPS is an organisation primed to protect its members. Even where officers may strongly object to the actions of their colleagues – such as with the suspected murder of a drug dealer by Yorkton's ghost squad – they may opt to avoid rather than support investigations, if only to avoid

*Table 3.1* Complaints closed by IPID in 2012/13 and 2015/16, 'unsubstantiated' and total

| Alleged offence | 2012/13 Total | 2012/13 (%) | 2015/16 Total | 2015/16 (%) |
|---|---|---|---|---|
| Deaths as a result of police action | 67 of 72 | 93 | 61 of 145 | 42 |
| Death in police custody | 39 of 44 | 89 | 98 of 194 | 51 |
| Discharge of an official firearm | 49 of 56 | 88 | 327 of 492 | 66 |
| Rape by a police officer | 4 of 5 | 80 | 12 of 28 | 43 |
| Torture | 0 of 0 | N/A | 13 of 31 | 42 |
| Assault | 220 of 301 | 73 | 289 of 848 | 34 |
| **Total** | 379 of 478 | 79 | 800 of 1738 | 46 |

unsettling their already precarious lives. Thus, a more accurate description of the IPID's decision to close so many cases as 'unsubstantiated', would be 'police officers did not want to talk to us'. This has significant repercussions for police accountability and could be instrumental to the multi-faceted deceptions SAPS officers regularly deploy.

### Selebi's corruption conviction

In January 2000 the then Minister of Safety and Security,[3] Steve Tshwete, gave a speech that began like this:

> This is a great moment in the history of the South African Police Service in particular and in the people of our country in general. For the first time ever since its establishment in 1913, the national command of the Service is today handed over to a Black commissioner … We … celebrate the historic gesture and … affirm that our country is indeed on course.

The minister was speaking during the handover of SAPS leadership from George Fivas, the last White officer to lead the SAPS, to Jackie Selebi, who was both the first African to head the organisation, and the first lateral (civilian) entrant to do so. The appointment of Selebi was important, not only for the SAPS, but for the whole country. It reminded South Africans that things were changing.

Born in Johannesburg two years after the formal institution of apartheid, Selebi's was a life shaped by the apartheid state and its racist police force. He spent many years in exile, returning to South Africa only after the ANC was unbanned in 1990. What better justice than for such a man to take the reins of a once-oppressive machine?

But, over many years, astute observers would come to realise that through Selebi, a faction of the ANC aligned to then President, Thabo Mbeki, was using the SAPS to wage battles for power and patronage within the ANC. While Mbeki protected Selebi for many years, both eventually lost favour within the ANC.

This lead to Selebi being charged with corruption in 2007, and Mbeki being ousted from office by an ANC faction aligned with (then Deputy President), Jacob Zuma, in 2008.[4]

In Selebi's 2010 trial, convicted smuggler and Johannesburg underworld king-pin, Glenn Agliotti, admitted to paying Selebi over R1.2 million (£65,600) in bribes, and to buying expensive clothes and shoes for his family. In return, Selebi furnished Agliotti with confidential information. But here's the thing: Selebi did not need Agliotti's money. As National Commissioner of the SAPS, his annual salary probably placed him in the top 1 or 2 percent of salaried South Africans.

The court found Selebi guilty of corruption and sentenced him to 15 years in prison. During the trial, Selebi repeatedly lied under oath. In his judgment, Judge Joffe lamented Selebi's actions and character, saying he had shown:

> Complete contempt for the truth … It is never pleasant to make an adverse credibility finding against a witness. It stigmatises the witness as a liar, a person of low moral fibre. It is a stigma that remains forever. It is so much more unpleasant to make such a finding against the person at the head of SAPS.

Judge Joffe's words were the antithesis of those spoken by Minister Tshwete at Selebi's swearing-in ceremony. Rather than proving to South Africans that the ANC could govern, Selebi had brought the SAPS and the ruling party into disrepute, and significantly damaged the image of both.[5] The narrative of a National Commissioner's fall from grace may not seem relevant to the personal identities or lives of front-line SAPS officers, but it is. Not only did Selebi's crimes tarnish the reputations of all associated with the SAPS, but during my eight months with police in 2012/13, Selebi remained a figure of derision and embarrassment for many.

Of course the guilt of one man does not mean all, or most, SAPS officers are ethically compromised. But the fact that a person in such an important public position felt he could abuse his power for personal gain and then evade sanction by simply denying allegations in court suggests an arrogance born of a belief that his colleagues would not question him, and that his political allies would protect him. Sadly, neither of the two National Commissioners appointed since Selebi's fall, has completed their contract terms. Both were terminated early, following findings against them. The first was Bheki Cele, whom the country's Public Protector found guilty of maladministration in 2010. The second was Riya Phiyega, whom the Marikana Commission found wanting.

### The events at Marikana

The Marikana Commission found that SAPS leadership, headed by Phiyega, submitted a *tailored version* of events leading up to the massacre, and that it was manufactured during a special retreat attended by senior leadership in the weeks following the event (Farlam 2015). Contrary to SAPS claims that the decision to move to its *tactical phase* to disburse and disarm striking miners – the decision that resulted in the deaths of 34 miners – was a response to an escalation of risk on 16 August, the Commission found that the decision had been made the night before at a meeting which the SAPS tried to hide from the Commission. When senior officers who were part of that meeting were sent questions by the Commission's evidence leaders, their answers left the Commission (Farlam 2015:184):

> With a feeling of absolute despair. These are the most senior people in the South African Police Service. They're asked some very important questions … [about] the greatest catastrophe since we achieved democracy, and the answers are evasive and they are non-responsive.

Among the many deceptions noted, the Commission found the testimony of National Commissioner Riya Phiyega 'not only unhelpful [but] distinctly evasive' (Farlam 2015:444). Sworn statements submitted to the Commission by officers involved in the first of two shooting scenes were found to, 'all sing much of a tune and they don't offer you much of a clue . . . they're a frustrating bunch of statements' (Farlam 2015:517).

It seems clear that what the Commission had observed, was the practice of everyday deception which I had seen, carried through to the most serious of deceptions: collusion to avoid culpability in murder (Farlam 2015).

### The Khayelitsha Commission

Like the early shielding of Selebi by President Mbeki and SAPS leadership, efforts to establish the Khayelitsha Commission of Inquiry were hampered by SAPS and political attempts to protect the organisation.

First, the Commission was founded only after the SAPS failed to respond to the Khayelitsha community's many formal complaints about policing in the area. When SAPS Head Office eventually responded with an internal investigation, it was shallow, did not consult communities, and did not result in any change. In fact, the investigation could be called an *internal deceit*. With a paper trail suggesting complaints had been investigated, SAPS top management could tell itself it had held Khayelitsha's police accountable. It had not.

At the beginning of the Commission's work, all requests to SAPS station, cluster, and provincial management were ignored, but for one acknowledgement of receipt. Following a second failed attempt to make contact with these officers, the Commission served subpoenas on SAPS managers to compel their cooperation. It was then that the Minister of Police intervened, challenging the Commission in court, a move that appears to have been a desperate attempt to prevent the SAPS' fictional front from being exposed. Indeed, in some respects the Commission exposed as fiction the SAPS claim that it is an effective, rational, evidence-based organisation made up of well-trained officers carrying out common-sense crime-prevention activities. It highlighted the failure of Khayelitsha SAPS stations to provide even the most basic police services or to treat victims with dignity. It also exposed the fact that the SAPS Performance Chart only measures *outputs* rather than *outcomes*. In the absence of the latter, the Chart serves as another tool through which the SAPS deceives itself and the public.

## The good shift: a perfect lie?

In this chapter, I have illustrated how officers' personal identities are shaped by the social performances prescribed by, and emerging in response to, the SAPS organisational culture, and how this shapes their work. The multiple deceptions I observed are part of a broader culture of mistrust that pervades South African society. Once recruited, officers seek to maintain strategic symbolic fronts to ease organisational pressure and satiate public scrutiny. I have focused on organisational deceptions, and how social performances contribute to officers' own suspicion and mistrust of the public, and of each other. In so doing, I have suggested that the SAPS shapes both officers' personal identities and the way they do their work.

In the absence of the good shift, the SAPS is a team of actors working together to present a fictional front. The SAPS organisational culture rapidly socialises recruits to embrace their prescribed roles as reproducers of this front, so shaping their personal identities. Its purpose is to present the organisation as one that is rational and rule-bound, and to make its presence and practices common-sense in the citizen mind. It is a fiction which the SAPS does not want challenged, so the *team* employs secrets, smoke and mirrors, to deflect interrogation, and leverages its autonomy to define its own criteria for *mistakes*, *truth*, and *police work*. SAPS annual reports are designed and produced with front stage audiences in mind. They appear objective and are certainly valuable to the public, but also strategically present what the police want the public to know. They contribute to common-sense interpretations of who and what the SAPS should be, and how the public should judge it (Loader & Mulcahy 2003; Manning 2009).

SAPS officers' knowledge that organisational performances are misleading, erodes their trust in SAPS processes and logics, and their attachment to, and pride in them. This detachment opens a space in which many officers distance themselves from a personal identity invested in the organisation. Instead they frame themselves as visitors passing through the SAPS on their way to better things. As I explore in Chapter 4, many officers planned to leave the SAPS if opportunities emerged elsewhere. Such attitudes, together with the realisation that a job in the SAPS offered opportunity and security difficult to match elsewhere, resulted in a form of cognitive dissonance: embarrassment of association with a tainted organisation, and the desire to make it something better through which long-term ontological security might be secured.

That the SAPS deceives is not surprising. Lies and deception are built into the generic public policing model. Pressure to produce evidence of work done, when so little of what police do is measurable, encourages deceit. The more officers think of themselves as involved in a *war on crime*, as SAPS officers often do, the more easily the *ends justify the means*, and lies are defended (Alpert & Noble 2009). Casual lies are diametrically opposed to the interests of the public, who rely on police for honesty and transparency. Where an officer is publically exposed as a liar, the whole team is discredited (Goffman 1990). But officers are internally castigated if they do not achieve *successes* at work. This leads to shame, which, as I discuss in Chapter 5, can lead to violence. One way of protecting against shame, is to employ strategies that preserve positive self and organisational images (Tyler & Feldman 2005). Where the means to sustain team pride and individual self-esteem is a choice between brutality and deceit, perhaps deceit is the lesser evil.

I have suggested that the SAPS symbolic front is informed by four categories of deception: (1) public performance deceptions; (2) data performance deceptions; (3) internal and external deceptions; all of which build on and feed into (4) a culture of suspicion. If the test of an acceptable deception in a democratic state is that it is openly debated and consented to in advance, then a great deal of what SAPS officers do in their daily work is unacceptable. Where deceptions hide torture, abuse of force, and even murder – as alleged at Yorkton and Marikana, a police organisation's legitimacy is in great peril.

The impact of SAPS organisational deception is clear in a retrospective examination of the Marikana, Khayelitsha, and Selebi scandals, and in the number of criminal cases the Independent Police Investigative Directorate (IPID) closes each year, unresolved, due to lack of evidence. From the ill-referenced, contradictory, and out-of-date training material to the pushing through of recruits; from the staged operations on the street to the forged data fed up the organisational hierarchy; and the lies told by SAPS leaders on the most public of stages, the SAPS is an organisation hiding behind a multi-layered mask, and a vast, intricate performance, working to justify its place and practice in contemporary South Africa. In the midst of this, and in the overlap of organisational deceit, societal deceit, and officers' personal identities, officers do what they must to forge a secure sense of self and, with it, colonise their futures.

## Notes

1 Usually smaller than standard roadblocks, at times staffed by as few as two police officers.
2 Other examples include: 'Alpha' instead of 'African', 'Whiskey' instead of 'White', 'Bravo' instead of 'Black', and 'Indigo' instead of 'Indian'.
3 Today known as the 'Minister of Police'.
4 Zuma, too, had only managed to come to power through political interference with the criminal justice system. He had been removed as Deputy President following the corruption conviction of his financial adviser. Subsequently, 573 charges against Zuma were dropped. By 2016 the phrase *state capture* had become common parlance in South Africa. It inferred that President Zuma – who was once head of intelligence in the ANC underground – had captured the criminal justice system, as well as key parastatals, in an effort to plunder the state coughers.

5  Some saw the conviction of such a senior and politically connected figure as a sign that the country's justice system was rigorous and independent. But, as Gareth Newham pointed out soon afterwards, Selebi had been investigated by the prosecuting authority's own investigative branch, the Scorpions. Under Selebi's watch, the first steps to dismantle the unit had begun, and soon after his conviction the Scorpions were merged with the SAPS, effectively diluting their expertise, resources, and independence, and shielding the politically connected from police reach. Selebi appealed his conviction, but it was upheld and in December 2011 he began his prison sentence. In June 2012 he was released on medical parole – much to the chagrin of many South Africans who saw it as a sign of political meddling. In January 2015 Selebi died, aged 67. At his funeral, friends and comrades tried to smooth over his muddied past, claiming he had in fact been a crime intelligence agent spying on Glen Agliotti. But the claims were weak, making them appear like the desperate cries of a government and liberation party scrambling to salvage its crumbling legitimacy. Selebi's successor, Bheki Cele, was another career politician appointed by the President. But, unlike Selebi, Cele was widely popular in the SAPS and with the public at large, mostly for his aggressive anti-crime and pro-police stance. But, in a fashion reminiscent of Selebi's downfall, in 2012 the Public Protector found that Cele had mismanaged costly building purchases for the SAPS, so that he too was relieved of his post. Cele's successor, Riya Phiyega, another lateral entry, has failed the SAPS and country dismally in leading what the Farlam Commission found to be a concerted attempt to hide and cover police actions at Marikana.

# References

@CityPress, 2013. Dying for a Job. *City Press*. Available at: www.citypress.co.za/news/dying-for-a-job/.

Africa Check, 2015. AfricaCheck: Are Foreigners 'Stealing Jobs' in South Africa? *Daily Maverick*. Available at: www.dailymaverick.co.za/article/2015-04-20-africacheck-are-foreigners-stealing-jobs-in-south-africa/#.WBUMltV97IV.

Afrobarometer, 2013. *Summary of Results: Afrobarometer Round 5 Survey in South Africa*, Cape Town, South Africa. Available at: http://afrobarometer.org/sites/default/files/publications/Summary of results/saf_r5_sor.pdf.

Afrobarometer, 2016. *Summary of Results: Afrobarometer Round 6 Survey in South Africa, 2015*, Johannesburg, South Africa. Available at: http://afrobarometer.org/sites/default/files/publications/Summary of results/saf-r6-sor.pdf.

Alesina, A. & La Ferrara, E., 2002. Who Trusts Others? *Journal of Public Economics*, 8(2), pp. 207–234.

Alpert, G.P. & Noble, J.J., 2009. Lies, True Lies, and Conscious Deception Police Officers and the Truth. *Police Quarterly*. Available at: http://pqx.sagepub.com/content/12/2/237.short.

Altbeker, A., 2005. *The Dirty Work of Democracy: A Year on the Streets with the SAPS*, Johannesburg and Cape Town: Jonathan Ball.

Anderson, B., 1991. *Imagined Communities: Reflections on the Origin and Spread of Nationalism*, London: Verso.

Ashforth, A., 2005. *Witchcraft, Violence, and Democracy in South Africa*, Chicago, IL, and London: University of Chicago Press.

Ashraf, N., Bohnet, I., & Piankov, N., 2003. *Is Trust a Bad Investment?* Working Paper No. 2004–07, Basel: Centre for Research in Economics, Management and the Arts.

Bok, S., 1978. *Lying: Moral Choice in Public and Private Life*, New York: Vintage Books.

Bray, R., Gooskins, I., Kahn, L., Moses, S., & Seekings, J., 2010. *Growing Up in the New South Africa: Childhood and Adolescence in Post-Apartheid Cape Town*, Cape Town: HSRC.

Brodeur, J.P., 2010. *The Policing Web*, Oxford: Oxford University Press

Brogden, M. & Shearing, C.D., 1993. *Policing for a New South Africa*, London: Routledge.

Bruce, D., 2012. *Marikana and the Doctrine of Maximum Force*, Johannesburg: Parktown Publishers.

Burger, F.J., 2006. Crime Combating in Perspective: A Strategic Approach to Policing and the Prevention of Crime in South Africa. *Acta Criminologica*, 19(2), pp. 105–118.

Burns, J., 2004. *Race and Trust in Post-Apartheid South Africa*, Cape Town. Available at: http://opensaldru.uct.ac.za/bitstream/handle/11090/644/csssr-saldru-wp78.pdf?sequence=1.

Cawthra, G., 1993. *Policing South Africa*, London: Zed Books.

Cockcroft, T., 2013. *Police Culture: Themes and Concepts*, New York and London: Routledge.

Comaroff, J. & Comaroff, J., 2004. Policing Culture, Cultural Policing: Law and Social Order in Postcolonial South Africa. *Law & Social Inquiry*, 29(3), pp. 513–545.

Comaroff, J. & Comaroff, J., 2006. *Law and Disorder in the Postcolony*, Chicago, IL: University of Chicago Press.

Curtis, S., 2003. Lies, Damned Lies and Organisational Politics. *Industrial and Commercial Training*, 35(7), pp. 293–297.

Davis, R.C., 2012. *Selected International Best Practices in Police Performance Measurement*, Cambridge: RAND Corporation. Available at: www.rand.org/content/dam/rand/pubs/technical_reports/2012/RAND_TR1153.pdf.

Demombynes, G. & Özler, B., 2005. Crime and Local Inequality in South Africa. *Journal of Development Economics*, 76(2), pp. 265–292.

Elgar, F.J. & Aitken, N., 2011. Income Inequality, Trust and Homicide in 33 Countries. *The European Journal of Public Health*. Available at: http://eurpub.oxfordjournals.org/content/21/2/241.short.

Eterno, J.A. & Silverman, E.B., 2010. Understanding Police Management: A Typology of the Underside of Compstat. *Professional Issues in Criminal Justice*, 5(2&3), pp. 11–28.

Farlam, I.G., 2015. Marikana Commission of Inquiry: Report on Matters of Public, National and International Concern Arising Out of the Tragic Incidents at the Lonmin Mine in Marikana, in the North West province. Available at: www.sahrc.org.za/home/21/files/marikana-report-1.pdf.

Faull, A., 2010. *Behind the Badge: The Untold Stories of South Africa's Police Service Members*, Cape Town: Zebra Press.

Faull, A., 2013. Policing Taverns and Shebeens: Observation, Experience and Discourse. *South African Crime Quarterly*, 46, pp. 35–48.

Faull, A., 2014. Performance Measurement in Police Agencies: A Report Written for the Commission of Inquiry into Allegations of Police Inefficiency in Khayelitsha and a Breakdown in Relations Between the Community and the Police in Khayelitsha. Available at: www.khayelitshacommission.org.za/bundles/bundle-twelve/category/266-1-expert-reports.html.

Faull, A., 2016. Measured Governance? Policing and Performance Management in South Africa. *Public Administration and Development*, 36(2), pp. 157–168.

Fleming, P. & Zyglidopoulos, S.C., 2008. The Escalation of Deception in Organizations. *Journal of Business Ethics*. Available at: http://link.springer.com/article/10.1007/s10551-007-9551-9.

Frydl, K. & Skogan, W., 2004. *Fairness and Effectiveness in Policing: The Evidence*, Washington, DC: National Academies Press.

Gibbs, A., Govender, K., & Jewkes, R., 2016. An Exploratory Analysis of Factors Associated With Depression in a Vulnerable Group of Young People Living in Informal Settlements in South Africa. *Global Public Health*, pp. 1–16. DOI: 10.1080/17441692.2016.1214281.

Gilligan, J., 2000. *Violence: Reflections on our Deadliest Epidemic*, London: Jessica Kingsley.

Goffman, E., 1959. *The Presentation of Self in Everyday Life*, New York: Doubleday.

Goffman, E., 1990. Stigma: Notes on the Management of Spoiled Identity, London: Penguin.

Grover, S.L., 1993. Lying, Deceit, and Subterfuge: A Model of Dishonesty in the Workplace. *Organization Science*, 4(3), pp. 478–495.

Herman, A.A. et al., 2009. The South African Stress and Health (SASH) study: 12-month and Lifetime Prevalence of Common Mental Disorders. *South African Medical Journal*, 99(5 Pt 2), pp. 339–344.

Hornberger, J., 2011. *Policing and Human Rights: The Meaning of Violence and Justice in the Everyday Policing of Johannesburg*, Abingdon: Routledge.

IPID, 2013. *Annual report 2012/13*, Pretoria: IPID.

IPID, 2016. *Annual Report 2015/16*, Pretoria: IPID.

ISS, 2016. ISS Crimehub. *Institute for Security Studies*. Available at: www.issafrica.org/crimehub/.

Keita, 2014. Occult Crime Unit: Enforcing Christianity Through a Net Widely Cast. *News 24*. Available at: www.news24.com/MyNews24/Occult-crime-unit-enforcing-christianity-through-a-net-widely-cast-20140304.

Keyes, R., 2004. *The Post-Truth Era: Dishonesty and Deception in Contemporary Life*, New York: St. Martin's Press.

Klockars, C.B., Kutnjak Ivkovich, S., & Haberfeld, M.R., 2003. *The Contours of Police Integrity*, London: Sage Publications.

Kohler Barnard, D., 2012. Sick Leave Abuse Rife in SAPS – Dianne Kohler Barnard. *Politics Web*. Available at: www.politicsweb.co.za/party/sick-leave-abuse-rife-in-saps-dianne-kohler-barna.

Kriegler, A. & Shaw, M., 2016. *A Citizen's Guide to Crime Statistics in South Africa*, Johannesburg and Cape Town: Jonathan Ball.

Kutnjak Ivkovich, S. & Sauerman, A., 2012. The Code of Silence: Revisiting South African Police Integrity. *South African Crime Quarterly*, 40, pp. 15–24.

Kutnjak Ivkovich, S. & Sauerman, A., 2013. Curtailing the Code of Silence among the South African Police. *Policing: An International Journal of Police Strategies & Management*, 36(1), pp. 175–198.

Lancaster, L. & Kamman, E., 2016. Risky localities: Exploring a Methodology for Measuring Socio-Economic Characteristics of High Murder Areas. *South African Crime Quarterly*, (56), pp. 27–35.

Lawrence W., Sherman, D.C., Gottfredson, D.L., MacKenzie, J.E., Reuter, P., & Bushway, S.D., 1998. *Preventing Crime: What Works, What Doesn't, What's Promising*. US Department of Justice, Office of Justice Programs, National Institute of Justice. Available at: www.ncjrs.gov/pdffiles/171676.pdf.

Lee, R., 2012. Death in Slow Motion: Funerals, Ritual Practice and Road Danger in South Africa. *African Studies*, 71(2), pp. 195–211. Available at: www.tandfonline.com/doi/abs/10.1080/00020184.2012.702965.

Lipsky, M., 2010. *Street-Level Bureaucracy: Dilemmas of the Individual in Public Services*, New York: Russell Sage Foundation.

Loader, I. & Mulcahy, A., 2003. *Policing and the Condition of England: Memory, Politics and Culture*, Oxford: Oxford University Press.

Manning, P.K., 1974. Police Lying. *Journal of Contemporary Ethnography*, 3, pp. 283–307.

Manning, P.K., 1997. *Police Work: The Social Organization of Policing*, Prospect Heights, IL: Waveland Press.

Manning, P.K., 2009. Policing as Self-Audited Practice. *Police Practice and Research: An International Journal*, 10(5–6), pp. 451–464.

Manning, P.K., 2010. *Democratic Policing in a Changing World*, Boulder, CO: Paradigm Publishers.

May, J. & Norton, A., 1997. 'A Difficult Life': The Perceptions and Experience of Poverty in South Africa. *Social Indicators Research*, 41(1/3 [Quality of Life in South Africa]), pp. 95–118. Available at: www.jstor.org/stable/27522258.

Mmotlane, R., Struwig, J., & Roberts, B., 2010. The Glue That Binds or Divides: Social Trust in South Africa. *HSRC Review*, 8(3), pp. 4–5.

Moore, D.S., 2006. *The Basic Practice of Statistics*, 4th edn, New York: W.H. Freeman.

Muir, W.K., 1977. *Street Corner Politicians*. Chicago, IL: University of Chicago Press.

Myhill, A. & Bradford, B., 2013. Overcoming Cop Culture? Organizational Justice and Police Officers' Attitudes Toward the Public. *Policing: An International Journal of Police Strategies & Management*, 36(2), pp. 338–356. Available at: www.emeraldinsight.com/doi/10.1108/13639511311329732.

O'Regan, J.C. & Pikoli, A.V., 2014. *Towards a Safer Khayelithsa: Report of the Commission of Inquiry into Allegations of Police Inefficiency and a Breakdown in Relations Between SAPS and the Community of Khayelitsha*, Cape Town: Khayelitsha Commission of Inquiry.

Pinker, S., 2011. *The Better Angels of Our Nature*, New York: Penguin Books.

Posel, D. & Hinks, T., 2013. Trusting Neighbours or Strangers in a Racially Divided Society: Insights from Survey Data in South Africa. *Journal of African Economies*. Available at: http://jae.oxfordjournals.org/content/22/1/136.short.

Reiner, R., 2010. *The Politics of the Police*, 4th edn, Oxford: Oxford University Press.

Republic of South Africa, 1996. Constitution of the Republic of South Africa. Available at: www.thehda.co.za/uploads/images/unpan005172.pdf.

Reuss-Ianni, E. & Ianni, F., 2005. Street Cops and Management Cops: The Two Cultures of Policing. In T. Newburn, ed. *Policing: Key readings*. Cullompton: Willan Publishing, pp. 297–314.

Roberts, B.J. & Gordon, S.L., 2016. Pulling Us Apart? The Association Between Fear of Crime and Social Cohesion in South Africa. *South African Crime Quarterly*, April(55), pp. 49–60.

Roeder, O., Eisen, L., & Bowling, J., 2004. *What Caused the Crime Decline?*, New York: Brennan Center for Justice at New York University School of Law.

Samara, T.R., 2011. *Cape Town After Apartheid: Crime and Governance in the Divided City*, Minneapolis, MN: University of Minnesota Press.

SAPA, 2014. Blacks, Whites Don't Trust Each Other – Survey. *News 24*. Available at: www.news24.com/SouthAfrica/News/Blacks-whites-dont-trust-each-other-survey-20140814.

SAPS, 2010. *Basic Development Learning Programme: Module 1 – Professional Conduct Learner's Guide*. Pretoria: SAPS.

SAPS, 2013a. *Annual Report 2012/13*, Pretoria. Available at: www.saps.gov.za/about/stratframework/annual_report/2012_2013/ar2013_00_front_content.pdf.

SAPS, 2013b. *Performance Chart Learning Programme*, Pretoria: SAPS.

SAPS, 2014. *Annual Report 2013/14*, Pretoria. Available at: www.gov.za/sites/www.gov.za/files/SAPS%257B_%257DAnnual%257B_%257DReport%257B_%257D20132014.pdf.

SAPS, 2015. *Sector Policing Operational Guidelines*, pp. 1–48. Available at: www.saps.gov.za/resource_centre/publications/sectorpolicing.php.

SAPS, n.d. *Code of Conduct*, South African Police Service. Available at: www.saps.gov.za/about/conduct.php.

Shearing, C.D. & Ericson, R.V., 1991. Culture as Figurative Action. *The British Journal of Sociology*, 42(4), pp. 481–506.

Sherman, L.W., 2009. Evidence and Liberty: The Promise of Experimental Criminology. *Criminology and Criminal Justice*, 9(1), pp. 5–28. Available at: http://crj.sagepub.com/cgi/doi/10.1177/1748895808099178.

Skolnick, J.H., 1966. A Sketch of the Police Officer's 'Working Personality'. In J.H. Skolnick, *Justice Without Trial: Law Enforcement in a Democratic Society*, New York: John Wiley, p. 279.

Skolnick, J.H., 2008. Enduring Issues of Police Culture and Demographics. *Policing and Society*, 18(1), pp. 35–45. Available at: www.tandfonline.com/doi/abs/10.1080/10439460701718542.

Stanko, B., Jackson, J., Bradford, B., & Hohl, K., 2012. A Golden Thread, a Presence Amongst Uniforms, and a Good Deal of Data: Studying Public Confidence in the London Metropolitan Police. *Policing and Society*, 22(3), pp. 317–331.

StatsSA, 2014. *General Household Survey, 2013*, Pretoria. Available at: http://beta2.statssa.gov.za/publications/P0318/P03182013.pdf.

StatsSA, 2015. *Exploration of Selected Contact Crimes in South Africa: In-depth Analysis of the Victims of Crime Survey Data*, Pretoria. Available at: www.statssa.gov.za/publications/Report-03-40-03/Report-03-40-032014.pdf.

StatsSA, 2016. *Quarterly Labour Force Survey Quarter 4: 2015*, Pretoria. Available at: www.statssa.gov.za/publications/P0211/P02114thQuarter2015.pdf.

Steinberg, J., 2008a. *Thin Blue: The Unwritten Rules of Policing South Africa*, Cape Town: Jonathan Ball.

Steinberg, J., 2008b. *Three Letter Plague: A Young Man's Journey Through a Great Epidemic*, London: Vintage Books.

Steyn, J., 2015. 'Darker Shades of Blue': A Ten Year Gender Comparison of Police Culture Attitudes in the South African Police Service. *African Journal of Public Affairs*, 8(2), pp. 166–189.

Steyn, J. & Mkhize, S., 2016. 'Darker Shades of Blue': A Comparison of Three Decades of South African Police Service Culture. *South African Crime Quarterly*, (57), pp. 15–26.

Super, G., 2013. *Governing Through Crime in South Africa: The Politics of Race and Class in Neoliberalizing Regimes*, Oxford: Routledge.

The Planning Commission, 2012. *National Development Plan* (November). Pretoria: The Planning Commission.

Tyler, J.M. & Feldman, R.S., 2005. Deflecting Threat to One's Image: Dissembling Personal Information as a Self-Presentation Strategy. *Basic and Applied Social Psychology*, 27(4), pp. 371–378.

Vigneswaran, D.V. & Hornberger, J., 2009. *Beyong 'Good Cop'/'Bad Cop': Understanding Informality and Police Corruption in South Africa*, Johannesburg: Forced Migration Studies Programme, University of the Witwatersrand.

von Holdt, K., 2010. Nationalism, Bureaucracy and the Developmental State: The South African Case. *South African Review of Sociology*, 41(1), pp. 4–27. Available at: www.tandfonline.com/doi/abs/10.1080/21528581003676010.

WHO, 2010. *Estimated Road Traffic Death Rate (per 100,000 population), 2010*, Geneva. Available at: www.who.int/gho/road_safety/mortality/rate_text/en/index.html.

Wicks, J., 2016. 'It's Just the Facts' – Penny Sparrow Breaks Her Silence. *News 24*. Available at: www.news24.com/SouthAfrica/News/its-just-the-facts-penny-sparrow-breaks-her-silence-20160104.

Wilkinson, K., 2014. Why the Matric Pass Rate Is Not a Reliable Benchmark of Education Quality. *Africa Check*. Available at: http://africacheck.org/reports/why-the-matric-pass-rate-is-not-a-reliable-benchmark-of-quality-education/.

World Bank, 2016. *Poverty and Shared Prosperity 2016: Taking on Inequality*. Available at: https://openknowledge.worldbank.org/bitstream/handle/10986/25078/9781464 809583.pdf.

# Chapter 4

# More than police work

Precarity, policing, and personal identity

## The world behind the uniform

Deception is integral to the daily functions of the SAPS. SAPS officers are both producers and recipients of these deceptions. By toeing the institutional line officers reproduce the myths central to public policing while easing the organisational strain placed on them as individuals. By not questioning incompetence, by turning away from illegality, and by enacting deceptive performances, police succeed in the ways the organisation wants them to and avoid life-complicating attention from superiors.

Of course, these deceptions do not go completely unquestioned. Individuals, civil society groups, an independent media, and formal oversight bodies, are just some of the parties questioning the narrative of South Africa and its police, authored by the SAPS. The conviction of former National Commissioner Selebi, the killing of miners at Marikana, and the findings of incompetent policing in Khayelitsha were all scandals that shook the SAPS' official front and revealed elements of its back stage.

But there is another deception central to the lives of SAPS officers with which many struggle. This is the notion that the SAPS should secure their material ambitions and ontological needs, hopes that are central to the narrative of a successful South African in the early twenty-first century.

To live in modernity is to live with risk. Individuals' desires and ambitions inform actions that are calculated and considered against an unprecedented awareness of alternative actions and outcomes, in a world that is increasingly transparent (Giddens 1991). In South Africa, the possibility of working for the SAPS must be considered and contrasted with the alternatives. What does a job in the SAPS offer that others don't? How does it relate to officers' self-narratives about the past, present, and future?

In this chapter, I illustrate how most officers are recruited from contexts of precarity. The job serves primarily an instrumental purpose: it opens a road to upward mobility. As such, it reduces risk, feeds ambition, and improves officers' prospects of securing ontological security. It is against this exploration that the deceptive and violent police practices discussed thus far, and the violence and contributions to disorder discussed in subsequent chapters, are best understood.

*

In a society characterised by poor educational outcomes and mass unemployment, the SAPS is a portal to an easier world, offering life-long job security and a starting salary nearly twice that of the average African male-headed household. As such, policing is an occupation rich in life-changing potential. But, while the job certainly changes officers' lives, the change is not always as hoped. Most police belong to intimate networks of people whose potential has been systematically stunted for generations. Within these networks sharing is common; what belongs to one must be shared with all (Ashforth 2005). Self-pride is frowned upon. It ignites jealousy and invites attack, spiritual or physical (Ashforth 2005). So, while on the one hand even the most junior officers earn a decent income, it seldom belongs to them alone. It must be shared, and shared with humility. As a result, it is far more common to hear police lament that they do not earn enough to survive than to hear them celebrate their privilege like Skrikker in Chapter 1. Goffman calls such performances *negative idealization* (1959:49). While people aspiring to climb the socio-economic ladder may idealise those of higher standing, he suggests they may play up their lower status where it benefits them. To feel confident in one's membership of a stable political community is to feel secure (Walker 2007). This is presumably true even when that community is materially poor. So, where a job in the SAPS may change an officer's life – securing their material needs and improving their prospects beyond those of their neighbours – it can simultaneously open new fault lines that fracture ontological security. By advertising their financial struggles, SAPS officers create buffers against intimate networks that desire a share of their fortune. Their complaints of being underpaid also provide them with a defence against a security-obsessed public demanding the impossible: a crime free South Africa.

The dismantling of apartheid and lifting of race-based discrimination in the early nineties produced hope and expectation in most South Africans. The first two decades of democracy saw attempts to embrace free-market neo-liberal economic and social policies, and to support citizens just enough to help them help themselves. This paradigm suggests that if government provides a baseline of services and a market-friendly foundation for investors, individuals and businesses will carve out their own successful futures. But in the face of widespread deprivation, a culture of conspicuous consumption consistently and crassly reminds the poor majority what they lack.

Police work is symbolic work; it shapes communities and nations. Similarly, a job in the SAPS shapes officers' lives, symbolically and instrumentally, as their personal narratives become entangled in those of the organisation. To appreciate this, one must consider the job in the context of officers' personal narratives. Though varied, these are often united by the themes of original poverty, a struggle for upward mobility, and a vision of a better future for one's children. Almost no officers I met wanted their children to join the SAPS. Rather, they saw their employment in the organisation as a stepping stone from which they could propel them, and so a piece of themselves, into a brighter future. To me it seemed that I was glimpsing a generation in transition. Those born into the families of police officers will benefit from the rewards their parents' jobs offer. At the same time, the South African public will receive a service delivered by officers understandably preoccupied with their own aspirations in a country where life for most remains incredibly precarious.

## Gompo: a job that changes the world

I want to return to the four students writing in their pocket books in Gompo's early autumn light. They were the organisation's future. Where had they come from? What paths had they walked before arriving at that table? During my days with them, they allowed me insight into the stories through which they made sense of their lives.

When I introduced Student Constable Mmaya in Chapter 3, I described him as 'an artist turned police recruit'. I learned about his artistic past while chatting to residents of the village in which I had rented a house, 15 kilometres from Gompo. The village had attracted the attention of wealthy, skilled South Africans and the international donor community, and so was home to various experiments in rural health provision and income generation under *The Arago Fund*. The fund's website describes it as offering support to the most vulnerable of people affected by poverty and disease. Before joining the SAPS, Arago had been Mmaya's life blood. Like so many officers, he had been recruited from the country's most vulnerable.

When I asked Mmaya how he had come to join the SAPS, he responded like this:

> I matriculated from high school in 2000. Then I sat at home because there was no money for further study. I started working at the Arago Art Project. It was my first time to do art. I was very fortunate to be selected as one of four people from the project to be sent to PE[1] to study fine art, so I have a three-year diploma. I then returned to Arago where I applied my skills as an artist. But then I decided to join the SAPS. You can't support yourself with community projects. You can have money for food and clothes but that's all. It's not enough.

Mmaya had joined the SAPS in the hope that it would offer the *enough* he sought; a path towards ontological security in a context of precarity.

Mmaya told me that when he had completed his police training he would be posted in a small town police station, 65 kilometres from his Gompo home. He was grateful that it was not too far. He didn't own a car so would have to rent accommodation in the town, but was happy that he would be close enough to return home on his rest days.

Almost every African police officer I had met during my six months in Cape Town spoke of the Eastern Cape as *home*. It was where they had been born, where they knew their ancestors to have lived, and where they imagined themselves growing old and being buried. But while they pegged the narrative of their own beginning and end to the rolling hills in the country's south-east, they knew the bulk of their working lives would be spent in Cape Town. So Mmaya was lucky. For his part he had only visited Cape Town once: 'to visit a friend, but I wouldn't want to stay there. It's a rough place. The way people live there is not right.' It was a view of cities shared by most of Gompo's officers. They were places of jobs and opportunity, but also of violence and risk. Cape Town was viewed as particularly violent; a place where police were hunted and killed. A posting in a small town close to his village excited Mmaya.

If Mmaya's story was different from those of many other officers I met, it was not because he had come from harsher conditions, but because he had been luckier than many. While it had taken him 11 years between leaving high school and securing permanent employment in the SAPS, he had been fortunate enough to complete a sponsored tertiary qualification and to have some work during that time.

The phrases 'there was no money' and 'the money ran out' were common to the self-narratives officers shared with me. They were almost always used to explain why tertiary study could not be pursued; to indicate the loss of a dream and explain the accident of their occupation. For these officers they hoped the SAPS might fill the space left by the dreams they had deferred to their children.

*

Gompo's Student Constable Cethe was luckier than Mmaya. He had joined the SAPS directly out of high school, but this had not been his plan. As he told me:

> I live 10 kilometres from Gompo, in Bruce village. I went to school near the police station here. I walked to school every day; it took me 40 minutes each way. Every day when I got home I washed my shirt, then went to soccer practice at five. When I came home, I ironed my shirt, watched TV, and went to sleep. In the morning I left home at seven again.

As an afterthought he added, 'I wasted my time doing pure maths and pure science for matric because now I have ended up in the police.'

The single school shirt and long walk to school were indicative of the poverty in which he was raised, while the school subjects were reminders of opportunities lost. Maths and science are considered the most important school subjects for those hoping to enter industry- or business-oriented tertiary degree programmes, which in turn represent the potential for significant financial reward. Cethe was signalling to me that he had once had very different dreams for himself.

Mornings and afternoons in Gompo's policing area still saw dirt roads lined with children walking to and from school. Not every village had its own school, and most residents could not afford transport, so that the daily on foot migration was a feature of the arid landscape. But Cethe was not unhappy that his daily walks had led him to the SAPS. When I queried what sounded like a tone of res-ignation in the telling of his story, he responded, 'When you are inside the SAPS you see that it is nice. There are lots of opportunities. But to the person outside they just see a uniform chasing a suspect.' It seemed that he saw his future in the SAPS as one that might meet his needs, even his ambitions, but that he feared being reduced to something inferior in the eyes of the public: an agent of the state who did its begrimed bidding.

Sitting around the table with the four students I asked them what they thought of SAPS salaries. 'Right now it's not a salary,' responded Mmaya. 'It's a stipend. But as long as you are not a baby factory, then the police salary is a good one.' I asked what he meant. Cethe laughed, 'It's very common for a policeman to have six babies with different women.' Mmaya finished the thought, 'As long as you don't do that, the money will go far.'

It was a reference to notions of sex, reproduction, and family in the country, in which masculinity can be emboldened through proven fertility, but weakened where fathers cannot or do not financially support their children (Hunter 2006). In 2013, 39 percent of South African children lived with only their mothers, while just 4 percent lived with only their fathers. Just 33 percent lived with both parents (SAPA 2013).

The SAPS is a male-dominated organisation. While I explore aspects of South African masculinity in more detail in Chapter 5, at this point it is helpful to touch on fatherhood. In the introduction to their edited volume on the subject, Richter and Morrell provide the following overview: historically – though per-haps especially since the country's industrialisation – many South African men have not fully participated in their children's lives. Half of 22,000 children born at a Soweto hospital in the early 1990s had no male support, while 26 percent of 11 year olds in the early 2000s reported almost no contact with fathers since birth (Richter & Morrell 2006). Some of these trends likely have roots in the migrant labour system established in the early colonies and formalised under apartheid. African fathers working on mines spent the bulk of their time living far from their families. On the one hand this meant many assumed a responsibility to sup-port a distant homestead financially – a part of them and their narrative located far away. But it also meant an assumption that women would parent, leading to paternal neglect and abandonment (Richter & Ramphele 2006). There is evidence that these trends are slowly reversing, but their inertia remains. Of 67,000 court orders (mostly to men) to pay child maintenance in 2002, Richter and Morrell write, only 7,000 were paid. Most young people in Cape Town live in homes forged around maternal kin networks (Bray et al. 2010). Absent and unsupportive fathers increase the burden on women, already bearing the brunt of the social strains wrought by the country's HIV/AIDS pandemic.

Results of the 2011 census confirm the extension of a four-decade trend, which has seen fewer couples choosing to marry. Hunter suggests this is in part because men cannot afford the bride price expected for a traditional marriage (2006). To restore the value of fatherhood, Richter and Morrell write, South Africa must tackle both the unemployment disproportionately affecting the African population, and the historical emasculation forged over centuries of White exploitation (2006). In some respects, a job in the SAPS promises to address both these factors for male officers. Still, I met many with children not living with them, often born to different women. The resulting pressure to support them threatened their upward mobility, masculinity, and prospects of ontological security.

*

Following Cethe and Mmaya's joke about babies, Student Constable Debeza asked me if I had children. She was surprised when I said I did not. 'I have one,' she volunteered. 'She's four years old.' Debeza was in her early 20s. I asked if she would like her child to join the SAPS someday. She exploded in exaggerated gasps, 'Yoh! No, no, no, no!' If so, I asked, why had she joined? 'Job scarcity,' she replied. 'Most of those in our intake joined because of job scarcity. They didn't want to be police but once you are in there you start to like it and develop a passion.' She continued, reflecting on this change in herself:

> It's strange when you go from shouting at police to liking the police. I was shouting at the police before I joined; when they closed the tavern when we were still having a good time. Now I won't. It was wrong. And I will tell my sister not to shout at the police either.

Giddens calls moments of great change, such as deciding to get married or switch careers, *fateful moments* (1991). They are points in life, such as joining a once despised police service, where the appeal of fortune is strong, but where ontological security is challenged. After all, how does one reconcile becoming that which one previously despised? Only by significantly revising one's self-narrative (Giddens 1991). For many, joining the SAPS required re-interrogating and re-writing the stories they told themselves about themselves and their relation to the SAPS. A large part of this included resigning themselves to any stigma attached to the job, in return for a reduction in other risks and progress towards a more ontologically secure state of being.

A person who suddenly develops a stigma quickly experiences a change in personality (Goffman 1990). They know how they are perceived by others because they were once part of those who judged the similarly afflicted. Offered a job in the SAPS, South Africans who once judged the police from the outside easily join the SAPS team and play the part expected of them. For some this includes deceiving and deploying violence against those who would challenge their claim to a secure occupational identity.

The similarity in Debeza and Cethe's revised narratives made me wonder if it had been strategically deployed by trainers when they welcomed the students to the SAPS. If so, one might imagine trainers pre-emptively seeking to strike down the resentment they knew many new recruits might bring with them to the SAPS, and to shape it into something positive. Yet however much Debeza told herself she enjoyed her work, she did not wish the job on her family or child. She was grateful for the work, but they deserved better.

\*

At some point during my time at Gompo I told the students that they were lucky to be training in rural areas where rent was cheap. I had been struck by how little those officers without homes in the area were paying, usually less than R100 (£5.50) a month. The highest rent was paid by Lieutenant Nkomo, who lived in the nearby SAPS barracks; he paid R1,000 (£55) a month. The police station and barracks were by far the newest and sturdiest buildings in the area, and among few with indoor plumbing. Despite this, officers preferred paying token rent to look after the dilapidated rural homes of those who had migrated to cities. Because so many officers had grown up in poverty, they were happy to forego the luxury of indoor plumbing for the money they saved and the promise of the better life it represented.

Mmaya told me that when he moved to take up his permanent post in the small town 65 kilometres away, he would rent a shack in the township outside town: 'I don't need to be one of those city coconuts,' he told me. 'I have lived in the city before; I don't need to now.' He said the shack would cost him R300–R500 (£16.50–£27.50) a month and that it would be only a 20-minute walk from town. Saving money for the future was more important than living in a brick house.

On a sunny afternoon a month later I asked Mmaya and Cethe what they would do with their first salaries as fully fledged constables. Despite his prior song and dance about eating and drinking through his back pay, Cethe's response was serious. 'I have family responsibility,' he said. 'I must support them: my mother, father, sisters, and brother. They are not working.' A week later I passed Cethe's family home while on patrol. It was a small rectangular structure on an overgrown plot, possibly big enough for two small bedrooms. Its outer walls were dirt-covered white and one of its barred windows was broken. Cethe would later describe the *rondavel* he hoped to build for his parents, with a second for himself, over the property's wild grasses. His answer to my salary question was emblematic of a theme that ran through the lives of most of the officers I shadowed: they felt pressure to support others financially.

Mmaya's answer to my salary question was different, but equally representative of those I had shadowed, 'I must be honest with you, Andrew; I need wheels.' He was grinning from ear to ear.

## Instrumentality and police work

For many, perhaps most, of the student constables and constables I met during my fieldwork, a job in the SAPS meant two things: a responsibility to support immediate and extended family, and access to new goods. Considering that South African society is intentionally structured to grow a black middle class on a foundation of historical race-based inequality and deprivation, this is unsurprising. After all, government is South Africa's biggest employer and the SAPS is one of government's biggest departments.

The idea that police officers have personalities predisposed to upholding the law and promoting justice is central to state-promoted policing narratives in liberal democracies. But in most societies, what is as true today as it was at the birth of modern policing, is that the men and women who make up the ranks of police agencies are often recruited from a society's poor. They take the jobs because they need work. They are given a foot up over their peers, encouraged to believe and promote the state's ideologies, and used to control the communities that raised them. The same has been true in South Africa, and remains true today.

To illustrate these trends in the South African context, and to locate them in relation to violence, shame, and respect in the daily work and lives of SAPS officers, the remainder of this chapter describes the paths some officers walked before their employment in the SAPS, and touches on the work that they pursue on the side to help realise their dreams and ambitions.

\*

Gompo's Constable Mbelani was born and raised in a village an hour's drive from the station. He told me about it a few hours before the end of an eventless shift:

> I am from a village in the Patterson area. I grew up with my mother, brothers, and sisters, and attended my local village school. Halfway through high school I moved to a school closer to Patterson: it had a better matric pass rate. It's a common trend in the area, everyone moving to attend better schools. There are schools that have closed down because everyone leaves. My first school used to have about one thousand students; now it only has something like one hundred and ninety.

While he didn't frame it as such, Mbelani's observation was one of class migration, underpinned by the same fluctuations in social structure that saw African residents moving into Skrikker's Cape Town suburb, as noted in Chapter 1.

Mbelani continued:

> After school I moved to Woodside to study financial management at an FET college.[2] It was a two-year course but after one and a half years I decided to drop out. I lived in Extension 6[3] and the college was on the other side of town. I didn't have money for transport so had to walk there and back every day. It took over an hour. Class only ended at 8.30 in the evening. I would only get home an hour later and would be too tired to study for my tests, so I dropped out and applied to the SAPS. I kept my phone on all month, waiting for them to call, but they didn't.

The phrase 'I dropped out' was about as common as 'the money ran out' in the stories SAPS officers told of their lives. They were the signposts marking the forks in their biographical roads, after which the SAPS became their destination. 'The other thing is that Woodside is a crazy place,' he continued:

> While living there I was shot at, chased with *pangas*, chased with an Okapi [knife] … This scar on my arm, I was coming home from the club and saw these people fighting over a lady. I tried to break them up and one of them stabbed me on the arm. Then they laughed, stopped fighting, and left. I was just trying to help that lady.

Mbelani's arm carried a scar 15 centimetres long, running from the elbow to the wrist. Over my weeks at the station he would recount in detail his many encounters with violence and death in Woodside, including how he had almost stabbed someone in a premeditated revenge attack a few days after being robbed. When I asked him if he had reported any of the incidents to the police he said that he had not. Even in retrospect, as a police officer, the idea did not seem obvious to him. But those stories came later. On that uneventful afternoon, Mbelani had more to say about his journey to the SAPS.

> The people in Woodside like to slaughter things. They are from the rural areas and are used to it. The youth are dying there; they are dying. Every weekend blood is spilled. I was living in an RDP house there with a friend. He had his room; I had mine. Then one morning I woke up and just told him I was leaving. I couldn't take it anymore: there was too much crime. The next day he left, too. I returned to my home village. About a month later the SAPS called.
>
> I didn't enjoy my course in Woodside but I hadn't ever imagined joining the police either. When you are growing up you think of being a nurse or

a teacher or a lawyer, never a cop. But now that I am in the SAPS I have grown to like this job, I enjoy it. Now that I am here, there are so many options. You can be a cook or a sports trainer or a teacher. I got lucky getting this job, *yoh!* I got lucky.

Working in the rural areas like this I can save lots of money. The first thing I must do is buy a car, before the end of this year. I need something which matches my level, constable, something like a VW Polo. Most constables are buying cars like that. It will be about R2,400 (£132) or R2,800 (£154) a month, then insurance. So it's affordable with what I earn. My rent is only R100 (£5.50) a month. I stay up the road here. I have an outside tap and boil water with the kettle if I want to have a bath. But if I was living in town my rent would be R1,000 (£55) or R1,500 (£82), so I am lucky. Once I have a car I must save for a cow. You know with Xhosa people, if you have cows but no money, you are still rich! If you need money you sell one. Many people send their children to study by selling cows. Then when they graduate the children get a job and buy the cows back.

I don't yet have a wife or children, but I do have to pay for my family. The more money you have the more problems you have.

There it was again, the future car embodying the life the young officer hoped to live, but the family pulling him back; bringing him 'problems'. Steinberg found the same among the police he shadowed almost a decade before me (2008). They were men and women whose parents had toiled to provide them with the education and language skills required to enter the SAPS. In return, the officers were obliged to share their relative wealth, not only with their parents, but with their siblings, whose own futures had been sacrificed to provide for the officer-to-be. Young constables' money is seldom theirs alone, and while constable salaries are fairly good by South African standards, at approximately R14,500 (£765) a month in 2016, 'the money runs out' fairly quickly.

\*

Intra-familial remittances have a long history in South Africa, closely tied to inequality and exploitation. All share roots in migration, and continue to ripple through South Africa's social fabric.

For most of the nineteenth and twentieth centuries, rural–urban migration in South Africa was driven by economic and tax systems designed to control and leverage cheap African labour. When diamonds and gold were discovered in the late nineteenth century, White miners were treated better than Black. Confined to single-sex compounds, African miners could not return to their rural homes at will, nor could they co-habit with their families. Mine life introduced them to European criminal and civil codes that shaped gender, sexuality, marriage, property, land tenure, succession, and inheritance (Marks 2009). When they returned home, usually once a year, it was with experience, wages, and ideas about identity, class, and Christianity, which shook up rural life (Etherington et al. 2009). The introduction of cash to the countryside led to new patterns of consumption and class consciousness (Etherington et al. 2009). When migrants returned to mines and cities, they held onto their rural ties, remitting money to those they left behind. This insured them against unemployment and reserved them a place for retirement (Posel 2004) and burial (Lee 2011).

While plenty has changed since these early migrations, their impact remains. In 1993, over 70 percent of the money received by the country's poorest residents came in the form of private cash transfers (Seekings & Nattrass 2005). Most of the miners killed at Marikana in 2012 were originally from, and supported, families in rural villages. Similarly, the Khayelitsha Commission described the township as a 'threshold to the City', with 69 percent of its adult residents having been born in the Eastern Cape (O'Regan & Pikoli 2014). This figure rises to 93 percent in the poorest parts of Khayelitsha. It is likely that many of these people grew up in the rural Eastern Cape, and that they moved to Cape Town in search of work, intending to support those left behind and to provide opportunities to their city-born children.

While government grants have replaced remittances as the most important source of income for poor South Africans, the perceived obligation to support kin remains powerful. This was true for many of the officers I shadowed. When they spoke of money it was often couched in language suggesting investment in, and identity shaped against, rural communities and vulnerable relatives whom they felt obliged to support. As such, their personal identities – the stories they told themselves about themselves and their networks – were steeped in precarity.

Post-apartheid state welfare has significantly altered labour market remittance patterns in the country. In 2002, between a quarter and a third less money was remitted to rural households that received pension grants than to those that did not (Jensen 2004). In 2008, nearly half the country's unemployed lived in households supported by an employed person, while 13 percent received only remittances (Leibbrandt et al. 2012). The number of unemployed people with no links to labour market (remittance) networks rose from 30 percent in 1997 to 42 percent in 2008, probably because income from grants replaced some remittances (Leibbrandt et al. 2012). By 2015, 46 percent of households received at least one grant from the state, making grants the second most common household income (StatsSA 2014a; StatsSA 2014b). But remittances remain important, as do the social expectations tied to them, especially for African South Africans.

Findings from the Cape Area Panel Study published in 2010 revealed that 40 percent of young African adults felt obligated to support two or more kin, compared to only 2 to 3 percent of White and Coloured respondents (Seekings & Harper 2010). This weight of obligation is surely in part born of the vulnerability of the social networks in which they are embedded: 51 percent of African respondents considered at least one kin member to be poor, compared to only 3 percent of Coloured and 1 percent of White respondents (Bray et al. 2010). In this context it is not surprising that so many police officers spoke of the burden to support kin. Like Cethe and Mbelani, they felt obliged to help those close to them whose lives were significantly more precarious than their own. While the state's grant-providing machinery may have shifted the burden of the poorest from remittances to welfare, the expectation of familial support continues to weigh on the minds of those lucky enough to escape original poverty.

\*

As if to avoid the weight of the story he had just told me, Constable Mbelani moved the conversation from his life to his day. He and Constable Mashile had been called to a village where two teenagers had assaulted an elderly man. With great drama he explained how he and his partner had chased the teens up and down hillsides while the villagers stood and laughed. 'They will never help,' he said:

> Only for something serious like a rape or murder. But they must *feel* the police. At least now they've seen us and will *feel* us. They will know what happens when they throw stones, and they won't do it again.

He was inferring that he and his partner had adequately performed the roles expected of them, in front of a sufficiently large audience, and that the result would be a community respect for police authority. He laughed, recounting how he had been drenched in sweat by the time they apprehended the younger teen, and how the older had got away, 'But we know where he lives. We will get him.' These were the privileges of rural policing – today's escape was tomorrow's arrest. As long as a suspect was known, they had nowhere to go.

Mbelani had removed his pepper spray from its belt pouch and had started flicking its safety cover as he talked. I asked if he had had to use it with the teenagers. 'No,' he responded:

> You can't use this stuff on a child, they might go blind. But if you spray a mentally disturbed person with this it doesn't do anything. They will stand there with their eyes open, tears coming down their face, but they will just keep talking.

He told me he had done just this with a man accused by a village community of being a rapist:

> That guy was lucky because those villagers can be vicious. When those people come together they are dangerous. They are used to slaughtering animals and things. That's why those places like Woodside and the cities are so dangerous. It's those people who come from the farms; they move to the cities and the towns and then they kill each other. Even the people in the locations in the cities will say that these people have their origins in the rural areas, but when they come together they fight. Then in December they all move back to the rural areas and they fight here.

He chuckled as he told the story. I found his take on migration fascinating after the way officers in Cape Town had talked about the Eastern Cape. The two narratives overlapped, but contradicted one another in important ways. A dominant view among Mthonjeni's police was that it was the young men born in Cape Town, the *Cape Borners*, who were behind the township's crime, specifically because they had not grown up in rural areas where they would have learned respect. They said that Mthonjeni's crime declined over December when people travelled back to the Eastern Cape, but framed this not as the result of rural marauders taking their crime home, but as Cape Borners taking the city's crime to the countryside.

Constable Mbelani had described both Woodside and the rural villages as hotbeds of violence. I asked him whether he would prefer to live in a city or the countryside. He responded with muddled confidence:

> Even the people who move to the cities retire in the rural areas. They come back here and do nothing. I like it here. When I go to PE to visit I get bored. Even here I am bored; there is not much to do. At least in the cities you can go out if you have money. But the cars are all going *whoop-whoop*, and there are crazy people up all night. Here everyone is asleep at night because there is nothing else to do. But I am from here, so I'm fine with it.

It was a confusing response. It seemed he believed life in the city was good if one had money, but that his salary did not go far enough there. If he was going to be bored at home, he preferred to avoid the aggravating presence of those who had money to spend; those who reminded him of what he did not have. I asked how he had entertained himself as a child in his village:

> When I was growing up in the rural areas we would play games; pretend we were action heroes from TV; or we would shoot birds in the trees and eat them. Sometimes we stole peaches from the trees in people's yards. If we were caught doing something wrong, we were badly beaten and wouldn't do it again. We did other bad things, but not what we had been beaten for. Even at school they would hit us on our hands with a stick. It still happens today: children are being hit in school. They know it is their right not to be hit; they know it is abuse, but when the school tells parents they will kick children out for smoking *dagga* or pills, the parents say, 'Don't kick them out, just give them a beating.' They support it.

It was a reference to the everyday violence of his youth, and the violence to which many children are still subjected in South Africa (Artz et al. 2016). Mbelani's stories were full of violence. He laughed about the notion of 'grounding' children as punishment, which he knew of through American TV. He had learned his childhood lessons through force; he had *felt* the presence of authority and the judgement of his actions; and he believed it had made him better. This was the story he told himself about himself, and about how to bring about order.

How had we gone from stories of hardship and aspiration, to ones of police work, violence, and coercion? While I doubt he intended it, I think the themes are intimately related. To strive in a context of precarity is to be vulnerable. To find oneself unintentionally working for the SAPS requires the rewriting of one's self-narrative, convincing oneself and others that the new narrative is true, and that police should be respected. One of the easiest ways to do this is by describing the narratives of others as illegitimate. The *skollie* and the *criminal*, are among the simplest at hand. They were the nodes to which Mbelani and other SAPS officers could return when they felt their sense of self beginning to unravel. Through them they pushed past the idea that they were accidental police officers, and positioned themselves instead as important, contributing members of society.

*

Again, Jock Young's work on identity in late modernity provides a useful framework for understanding the anxieties of South African life, including the lives of its police (1999, 2007, 2011). Although South Africa is not a *late-modern* state, there is plenty of overlap between the late-modern project and the country.

In the second decade of the twenty-first century, South Africa, like late-modern societies, is characterised by diversity and stratification. Since the emergence of global capitalism in the nineteenth century, market forces have upturned material certainty and uncontested values, and replaced them with risk and uncertainty. This has led to economic and ontological precarity, tied to increased, but unmet, expectations of living lives like a minority elite rendered ever more visible by technology and (social) media. The result is that people constantly strive to be and have more. Energies are focused on self-realisation, while the neo-liberal state champions the notion that individuals are responsible for their own fortunes (Young 2007).

As occurred through South Africa's early mine migrations, changing proximities (urban and virtual) have introduced South Africans to a plethora of new ideas, information, and material goods over the last two centuries. These have been felt most powerfully in the democratic era. Uncensored media have spread new narratives about the groups to which people think they belong, and those they have never met. South Africans have learned that their cultures, beliefs, and practices are not necessarily best or correct, and that some are rendered illegitimate by the country's constitution. Pluralism and doubt have replaced certainty.

Of course, such changes are inevitable, but in South Africa they gained momentum in the late eighties and early nineties as influx control broke down. Africans previously restricted to homelands moved to cities in great numbers. In Young's late modernity it is the foreign *other* against whom citizens strengthen their sense of self, but in South Africa the *other* was internally manufactured. South Africans were increasingly exposed to people, products, and ideas from which they had previously been kept. In this context, old stereotypes of rural- and urban-born youth morphed. In the *new* South Africa, precarity became personal, as millions of people left long-established communities. Such moves allow individuals the space to re-author personal narratives, but can also challenge ontological security as they encounter new choices and risks.

Waged work is central to personal identity, a source of reward and mobility that both promises and withholds happiness. But the wage-earning system is unequal, making the development of positive self-narratives difficult for those it does not favour. At the same time, family and work no longer offer the security of trajectory or biography they once did. Failure to thrive in the market economy can cause humiliation, which some may respond to with consumption and, as I suggest in Chapter 5, violence. Constable Mbelani talked of his being hired by the SAPS as *lucky*; it was not something he had planned or been able to exert much control over. He couched this luck in a narrative of precarity. But, secure in the SAPS, his next big goal was to buy himself a new car, to own something he could touch and feel that had been denied to those who came before him, and in the process, to create an ontological reference point that reminded him that his was a life getting better.

To pursue ontological security in a context of precarity, one must erect barriers against those who threaten one's sense of self. Where the state manufactures the category *criminal*, the exercise is simplified. *Criminals* become the *others* against whom self-narratives take form. The officers I shadowed were both part of this state labelling apparatus, and benefited from it when forging their own self-narratives. This is exemplified in how Mbelani, Cethe, and Deyani described the fateful moments when they *realised* they liked working for the SAPS. Suddenly an organisation which they once despised had become a container in which they could re-write the story of their lives. This re-write was aided by their exposure to the precarious *criminal*, against whom a positive self-narrative was likely simpler to forge.

A job in the SAPS provides officers a vantage point from which they can look both up the class hierarchy at those whose lives they envy, and down at the poor. The poor remind them from where they have come, but also to where they might fall should they not make a success of the police occupation. In response they carry out the dirty work required of an exclusionary social and economic system, labelling some *criminal* or *skollie* along the way. The resultant *entanglement* can produce a state of *liminality*, of never quite arriving, which shapes officers' identities and work. This is what Mthonjeni's officers did with their incessant stops and searches, and what Yorkton's detectives communicated with their violence while tracing. These exercises in othering, together with the uniforms, insignia, cars and firearms of the SAPS, provide officers with anchors through which to steady their sense of self when they find themselves adrift on an ocean of precarity.

## Mthonjeni: of home, township, village, and violence

Rewind four months to my time in Mthonjeni. Arriving for a 6.00 a.m.-to-2.00 p.m. shift with a CPU I found the officers gathered around a table. They cracked jokes while they prepared their pocket books. Captain Jacobs passed around a Crime Intelligence report containing information on gang members wanted by the SAPS. I asked whether the names of the gangs had any relevance. Warrant Officer Jiyana responded with a smirk, 'You are the one who is from Cape Town, Andrew. You must tell us what they mean.' Then, after a short pause, 'Take us back to the Eastern Cape. We don't know this place.'

He glanced in Constable Deyi's direction, 'Deyi, are there gangs in your home village?' Deyi replied, 'No.' Despite Jiyana and the three constables having spent half their lives in Cape Town, they did not think of it as *home*. Home was in the rural Eastern Cape.

The conversation shifted to crime in Umtata, the former capital of the Transkei. Jiyana shared a story about the town:

> It is a dangerous place. The people from the villages are committing the crimes there. The ones born in Cape Town are raised on cornflakes and oatmeal; they are slow like chickens eating all day; sitting under that light; getting fat and growing quickly. But in the Eastern Cape they grow up chasing cows and goats on the hillside. When they come to Cape Town they can still run and jump, only here they jump over walls as if they were goats, while they run from police.

Jiyana grinned at his wit. It was the same narrative I would later hear in Gompo, but not the narrative most common at Mthonjeni, not even within this CPU. It was much more common for these men to blame the 'chickens eating all day' for a violence they believed sprang from the young men's city-born greed.

The group broke for patrol. I was posted with Deyi and Ndungwane. We collected Constable Yoyo – the shift's only woman – at her shack which she rented near the station.

A few hours into the shift I asked the constables what they thought they would be doing if they didn't work for the SAPS. Ndungwane had fallen asleep, so only Deyi and Yoyo answered. Deyi began:

> Before I joined the SAPS I was a taxi driver. I started driving when I was in high school. The taxis used to pick me up outside school and then I would work. I didn't have a licence at the time.

I asked if he had ever been stopped by police:

> I was once almost arrested. I was driving people from Cape Town to the Eastern Cape in December. I was pulled over in Leeu-Gamka and didn't have a licence. But we negotiated with the police and offered to buy them some cool drinks.

In South Africa buying a police officer a cool drink is a euphemism for paying a bribe. When I asked how much the cool drinks had cost him he said it had been

R250 (£13). Asking if the SAPS had not looked into his past during recruitment he replied that he had not even had an interview. Yoyo said that when she had applied to the SAPS she had been interviewed but could not remember anything about it. 'They didn't ask anything important,' she said, 'Just the usual, "why do you want to join the police?" and so on.'

I heard the same from others over the months. It seemed that interviews for trainee posts in the SAPS achieved little more than the ticking of a box, much like those I had been instructed to tick as part of my fraudulent firearm test, described in Chapter 3.

'When I joined the SAPS in 2008 I didn't really like the job,' continued Deyi. Then after a short pause, 'Actually, I still don't like it. You have to get angry with people. I wasn't raised like that.' It seemed he did not like the role the SAPS had scripted for him, and continued to struggle to assimilate aspects of the work into his self-narrative. But it was a secure job that paid far better than driving a taxi. Not liking the work was not going to make him walk away from it.

Returning to my question about work outside the SAPS, Yoyo said that if she had the means she would start her own business, but when I asked what kind of business it might be, she said she had not thought that far, 'I just know that it must be in town, not the location. Here in the location they rob the shops all the time.' For Yoyo a *business in town* symbolised freedom and money, and an escape from the violence that surrounded her at work and home. It was as simple as it was obvious that almost any South African struggling to make ends meet would leap at the opportunity for permanent employment in a tainted organisation that promised them a more comfortable, predictable life.

*

That morning's patrol was quiet; the 6.00 a.m.-to-2.00 p.m. shifts generally were. The most entertaining part of the day was giving a lift to a drunk SAPS officer whom we found standing in the middle of an intersection trying to hail a taxi. He belonged to the railway police unit stationed nearby and was relieved when Ndungwane offered him a lift. 'Thank you,' he gasped. 'These *cockroaches* don't trust you when you are in uniform. Nobody wants to stop for me!'

After dropping him at work, the CPU constables burst out laughing, having found his intoxication hilarious. I asked if his drunkenness (possibly while carrying a firearm) was not something they should intervene in. 'No,' came the answer, 'He was reporting for duty. That is for the station commander to sort out.' They were turning a blind eye, making sure their own performance was sufficient, while judging but ignoring, the dangerous behaviour of their colleague.

An hour before shift-end, Deyi said it was time to pick up the relief officers and head home. The first stop was Yoyo's. Her shack was only 300 meters from the station, wedged between the cramped dirt embankment that surrounds Mthonjeni's brick and mortar houses. She lived with the township's poorest residents, metres from where one of Mthonjeni's detectives had been stabbed in the face during a tracing operation the previous month. Like many others, she lived there in order to save and send money to the Eastern Cape, where her mother was raising her child.

In subsequent weeks Yoyo told me how difficult it was to live in the community she policed: 'It's not easy. The *skollies* talk to me in the street; make comments like "We need to do something about this constable." I just tell them to do what they must do.' But it seemed clear that living there scared her. This is why her colleagues had collected and dropped her at home. The short walk to the station, in uniform, wasn't worth the taunting, stress, and danger that would threaten the narrative through which she made sense of her life in the SAPS. She was in Cape Town, doing dirty work to support her mother who came before her, and the children she would leave behind.

*

Occasionally I joined Mthonjeni's officers, together with the city's Law Enforcement and Metro Police officers, on operations targeting the illegal sale of alcohol in unlicensed taverns (e.g. Herrick & Charman 2013; Faull 2013). I spent one of these with Constable Qoboza who had tasked a *trap boy* with purchasing beer at a neighbourhood shop. It was entrapment targeting a small trader, but seizure of alcohol and the shutting down of illegal taverns are key to SAPS' public performance and data performance deceptions, and Constable Qoboza thought the effort worth it. Three cars full of uniformed bodies parked around the corner from the target and waited. To pass the time, Qoboza told me about his life.

'I'm from the rural areas,' he said, 'I started school at the age of ten. I'm now 37. I have children. My daughter is brilliant!' His face lit up when he talked about her:

> She is ten years old now and is already in grade three. So if you think that I started school when I was ten and she is already two years into school at the same age … it's amazing!
>
> My children live with their mothers. You know it's our culture to have children with different women, one with that woman, another with that woman, and a third with another woman. But it's changing because it's expensive to have children these days.
>
> I got my first job in 2001. I was 26. I worked in a factory that made fake leaves, the kind used to decorate walls. I worked from 5.30 in the afternoon until 6.30 in the morning and was paid R50 (£2.70). I couldn't believe how little it was, but we had to take it or leave it.
>
> My next job was as a garden boy. I earned R80 (£4.30) a day, so R400 (£22) a week. That's when I applied to the police. In college I was being paid R2,800 (£154) per month after deductions.
>
> I've been in the police for eight years now. I'm due for promotion soon. I earn R11,500 (£631) per month and receive about R8,900 (£488) after

tax and deductions. It isn't bad. When I become a sergeant I will earn 15 or 16 thousand. The SAPS pays well considering you only need matric. I try to have a positive attitude about everything. This is why I appreciate my salary.

I was studying for my diploma in policing before, but I stopped after two years. I realised people were being promoted without any additional education, so it doesn't make a difference.

It was fairly common to meet constables pursuing diplomas and degrees in policing through the country's biggest distance-learning university, the University of South Africa (UNISA), or the Tshwane University of Technology (TUT). Few studied anything else. But it was also common for those who had completed the degrees to lament that they did not lead to promotion. This was often what they were really after: a piece of paper that would lift them into a new pay grade. Not once has a police officer told me they learned anything valuable or interesting while pursuing this degree. To them it seemed to be another performance; a *data performance deception* (discussed in detail in Chapter 3), bridging their private and occupational worlds to please an audience that could advance their career. It's unlikely to be what the SAPS intended, but it is perfectly understandable.

My appreciation for the place of education in officers' lives would develop in subsequent months, but to clarify I asked Qoboza, 'You were studying only to secure a promotion?'

Yes, but now I want to study commercial forensic investigation because there are lots of posts at the forensics laboratory and they all start there at warrant officer. Warrant officers start at about R19,000 (£1,043) a month; good money!

So Qoboza had not lost all interest in studying, though it was linked to advancing in rank and salary as rapidly as possible. I certainly do not mean to demean him by this. The same current runs through most occupations and is relevant to most people, myself and academia included. But if one is to understand who SAPS officers think they are and how it shapes their work then this is key.

The trap operation was being held near a football stadium, a developed area. We were parked in a side road lined with houses. The trap was due to take place around the corner – a different world, made up of corrugated iron sheet-shacks so tightly packed together that only small footpaths allowed navigation between them. Qoboza pointed to a sturdy house across the road; it was larger than most in the area bordering the informal settlement. 'This probably costs about R350,000 (£20,210) in Cape Town,' he said:

But in East London[4] it would only be R120,000 (£6,586). I used to own a house in Eersterivier [in Cape Town] but I sold it to buy a house in East London. I was able to pay that new house off immediately because it was so much cheaper.

My brother is now staying there but I don't charge him rent because he looks after it for me. I currently stay in my mother's two-room flat in Mthonjeni, very close to the police station. She's now living in East London.

I asked if he planned to move to East London too, 'No, I don't see myself moving there until I'm finished with the police; until I retire.' It was an imaginary journey that occupied the minds of many of Mthonjeni's police. They only pictured themselves returning *home* to the Eastern Cape upon retirement.

At first I was surprised that Qoboza was not renting out his house in East London. His had been a life of struggle, securing stable employment only at the age of 29. With children to support and only eight years of steady income behind him, I assumed he would have leapt at the opportunity for additional income. But over time it became clear that for almost all SAPS officers, family came first, and family often meant hardship. Of course my ignorance was the product of privilege. Within most South African families, it is expected that kin support and share with one another. As such, it is not the wealthy and liberal, but rather the working poor bound to networks of precarity who share with others the greatest portion of the little they have.

*

In Chapter 2 I mentioned that when I first met Yorkton's Constable Moshoeshoe he had recently moved house. Having come to Cape Town from the Free State – a province in the centre of the country – he had spent his first years in Cape Town, living in a shack in Harare, a township on the city's sand-covered south-eastern edge. He had since bought a house in Mitchell's Plain, a far more developed, formerly Coloured part of the Cape Flats. 'The area was too dangerous for me to stay,' he had said of Harare. 'It was full of *skollies* who would rob people on their way to and from work.' As he spoke he held his right hand over his stomach with his index finger and thumb extended, 'This is how I would carry my firearm under my jacket while walking from my shack to the bus stop and back when I was going to work.' He said he was always *one up* – a bullet in the chamber, ready to shoot.

Moshoeshoe had feared the *skollies* would take his life because they wanted his firearm, and he carried the firearm to protect his life. It was a dilemma of which many SAPS officers spoke. When I asked why they did not leave the firearms at the police stations when booking off duty, some like Moshoeshoe replied that the *skollies* wouldn't know that they didn't have a gun with them; would just see the uniform and attack. This sense of danger bound officers together, justifying the extra-legal force they sometimes used, and the deceptive performances behind which they hid it.

Knowing he could afford to rent a room almost anywhere in the city on a constable's salary, I had asked Moshoeshoe why he had chosen to live in a shack in Harare. 'I own the shack,' he replied. 'The problem with renting is that I have children and my mother is also sick. Sometimes they come and stay with me. If I have a landlord, then I must negotiate every time and they will say no.'

I asked if he had sold his shack when he moved. 'No,' came the response, 'I gave it to my brother-in-law. You can't sell when there are others in the family who are suffering.'

*

It was the same for Mthonjeni's Constable Qoboza. Although his had not been an easy life, and owning a house was an important accomplishment for him, he could not rent it out to others when he had relatives who needed accommodation. Later in the day Qoboza told me of his hope to buy a second house. He was planning for his future and believed it would be bright.

As we waited for the *trap boy*, Qoboza pointed to the stadium, 'I have some friends who play there,' he said. 'They are professional soccer players. They earn R27,000 (£1,482) a month with bonuses for wins and goals. These youngsters are making money!'

Not surprisingly, money, salaries, and comparative income were among the topics most commonly raised by the officers I shadowed. How much were others earning? How rich was I that I could study in my 30s? Where did they feature on this continuum? They were constantly measuring themselves against those around them, and against those of whom they read in newspapers or saw on television. Often, comparisons left them grateful for the opportunities and income which the SAPS provided them. But at other times they felt trapped on a trajectory which, while upward bound, saw their lives improving at a pace incongruent with their aspirations.

I asked Qoboza if he thought his life had improved as a result of his job in the SAPS, 'Yes, definitely,' he replied. 'It's good to have a job and money, and to learn every day.' But he complained that the community did not understand the law or like the police. He said he had been on a date with a woman who, on learning of his occupation, told him her family members didn't like the police. When he asked her why, she had said that her brother had robbed a shop; then shot at police while he fled the scene. Police had responded by shooting and killing him. 'And she put it just like that,' he said, pointing out that her brother committed the crime and fired at police first, 'But she still blames the police.' He said lots women in Mthonjeni liked male police officers because of their stable salaries, but that if police needed information relating to crime, no one would share it. In this way, officers were attractive for the comforts they could purchase their lovers and partners, but were given the cold shoulder when carrying out the work that earned them the salaries others envied. It struck me that something similar was true for many officers: the job offered them a wealth of opportunities, but it required that they do things many would rather not do.

While the public expects the SAPS to prevent crime, in many of the country's most dangerous areas, witnesses and informers fear speaking to police for fear of retribution by an accused's family (O'Regan & Pikoli 2014; Faull 2016). Qoboza's date story hinted at the breakdown in relationship between communities and police detailed by the Khayelitsha Commission. While the woman knew her brother had committed a serious crime, her family took priority, not dissimilarly from the ways police worked for their own families.

Changing the topic, I told Qoboza that I would soon be heading to the Eastern Cape to carry on my work with police there. 'In the Eastern Cape you will find police playing cards all day,' he responded:

> Some of them have no work to do. They can visit a house party while on duty, sit down and relax, and be given meat to take away and eat on their shift. There, the people won't complain, but if a policeman is seen at a party in Cape Town they will film him with a cell phone.

Here was another *other* against whom Qoboza could compare and legitimise his self-narrative. Rural police were people with whom he shared a job, uniform, and employer. But where he felt township-based officers were treated with suspicion and contempt by the public, he believed rural police were respected by the communities they served. Qoboza steered the conversation to his youth:

> When I was a child I belonged to gangs. We would steal things from neighbours. There was no electricity then and people would cook their meat on fires outside. We would throw stones at the house and when the people left the fire to investigate, we would steal the pot. We had our own food at home but we were just doing it for fun. In those days we didn't know about violence; we didn't use weapons and didn't confront people. These days when people steal cattle they knock on the door and demand the cattle at gunpoint. They use *muti* so that they can sense if the police are approaching while they commit their crimes.

It was another contradiction in Qoboza's depiction of the rural Eastern Cape. While he tried to present his youth as peaceful and idyllic, he recounted memories of his own crimes. Then, while trying to present rural life as peaceful, he found himself describing armed robbery. As with so many such narratives, the boundaries were blurred. Qoboza wanted to present the rural Eastern Cape as a place of peace in contrast to the violent city, but also wanted to present it as a place that was no longer the paradise in which he had been raised. Perhaps, like Young's late modernity, South Africa has become a land of inordinate and competing truths within which it is difficult to secure a truth about oneself, for oneself.

An elderly man walked past the van and nodded a greeting our way. It was the beer seller Qoboza had hoped to trap. He'd seen through the plot. This part of the operation was over.

## Yorkton: police work is (not) enough

At least three of the officers I worked with at Yorkton were involved in significant money-generating initiatives in addition to their police work. Sergeant Louw introduced me to his over coffee.

It was shortly after 6.30 a.m. in Yorkton; the morning parade and briefing had just been concluded. I had been assigned to work with Sergeant Louw for the first time. 'Do you want some *good* coffee?' he asked as I approached him amidst the scattering uniformed bodies. Of course I did. He led me out of the station to a trendy, upmarket coffee shop. I fumbled with my wallet, happy to pay for the coffee as a token of appreciation for the time he would spend with me that day, despite my thinking it unreasonably expensive. I often bought coffee, cool drinks and chips for the SAPS officers. It was an easy way to express gratitude, and officers almost never objected. So it was to my surprise that Sergeant Louw told me to put my money away, 'There are two things I don't compromise on,' he said, 'Good food and good coffee. I spend R200 a day on coffee.' He claimed it with pride. Then, as if to explain it definitively, 'I have another job. I'm a fitter and turner.' He said that his brothers were also in the trade, and that they split the work between them so that they could cover for him when he had police duties.

Over a number of shifts together, Louw would tell me how he had grown up moving from town to town as his father had chased employment. He said he was incredibly naughty as a child always getting into trouble. He reminisced about being shot at while stealing fruit from a farmer's orchard, and about shooting a bull's testicles with his BB gun. He was always punished, he said, but always went back for more.

In the adult world he claimed to have shot and killed over 300 people while on duty for the SAP and SAPS. It's a difficult claim to believe, even if one imagines the most unregulated extremes of apartheid policing. While he claimed these lives with pride, he also blamed them and what he alluded to as various assault charges against him, for his being the oldest member of the shift while still relatively junior in rank. Despite these setbacks, Louw held himself with confidence. On the surface at least, he seemed ontologically secure.

Patrolling the Yorkton area, he would point out the large houses he had worked on as part of his side job, describing their interiors and the characters of their owners. He was proud of both his occupations and the money they brought him. They offered him a lifestyle that overlapped in some small way with the wealthier residents of the streets he policed. In this, Louw was luckier than many of his colleagues. As a White South African, his parents and siblings – though not wealthy – had access to opportunities denied most of his colleagues' familial networks. As a result, his money was his to spend and so shaped his self-narrative in celebratory, rather than lamentable, ways.

*

Yorkton's Warrant Officer Kriel was also White and also had a business on the side. Like Louw he insisted on paying for my food and drink on alternate occasions. His primary side business involved home renovations and repairs for which he employed a number of full-time staff. He was also involved in buying, selling, and letting property. While he patrolled the city, he coordinated the activity of his employees by cell phone.

Kriel lived with his wife, and one of his two sons, in one of the city's more affluent suburbs. His house, which I visited, was not particularly lavish, but compared to the RDP houses and backyard shacks in which many of his colleagues lived, it was a palace. Kriel told me he joined the SAPS in order to avoid going to prison. From the age of 15 he had begun racing motorcycles. Other bikers thought he had promise and, with them, he began committing petty crimes. To break away from this group, he told me, he had joined the SAP.

When I told Kriel I had previously thought he was a captain, he responded with a sardonic laugh, 'I'm White! No chance of that.' He was cynical about South Africa's affirmative action-based (employment) redress policies. He probably invested so much in his other businesses because he believed he had reached a promotion ceiling in the SAPS. He lamented having to send his son to an expensive private college after he had failed to secure a place at a public university, believing that both he and his son were the victims of anti-White discrimination.

Another of Kriel's theories was that government was not interested in reducing crime, because its prevalence justified the hiring of more police officers, so creating jobs and pandering to the vulnerable majority. He cited as proof of this the Yorkton ghost squad's strategy of only arresting drug buyers. When I pointed out that safe cities would likely attract investment and encourage economic and job growth, he shut me down, saying the government had no long-term vision.

But he had long-term vision. 'I don't do this work for the money,' he told me. 'I have my companies for that. I do this because I enjoy it.' He said he might retire from policing once his children were out of university. While he inferred that his SAPS salary was not needed, he complained about what he believed were the exorbitant costs of the private educations he was providing to his sons. While he seemed cynical about the country, Kriel's rough exterior masked a hidden optimism. It bubbled to the surface each time he talked about his children; their potential and promise, despite the challenges he thought their whiteness brought them. He saw hope in all the country's youth. 'The younger generation is going to change things,' he told me. 'The current generation is too tribal; they just follow their elders.'

Kriel referred to Constable Moshoeshoe as an example of tribalism. He said he was in his mid-30s but 'only a constable' and did not value education. While I did not say anything to Kriel, days earlier Moshoeshoe had told me that education was 'the key to success', and that he blamed his father for failing to provide it to him and his siblings. As a result, theirs had been a life of struggle. Moshoeshoe had told me with pride that his fiancé was studying to be a nurse while he supported her financially. He knew the value of education; he just came from a far more precarious background than did Kriel. But this was not for me to share. Instead, I asked Kriel why he thought so many constables, like Moshoeshoe, were recruited in their late 20s and early 30s, rather than out of high school. 'Because the youngsters are educating themselves and aiming for better things,' came his reply. 'More than the SAPS can offer.' It seemed Kriel was a proponent of the mantra: 'Unlike my generation, new SAPS recruits are only here because it was the best job they could find.' While he saw young people in general as aspirant, he seemed unaware that his colleagues were dreaming of, and working towards, bigger and better things, much like himself.

\*

It should by now be clear that apartheid's race categories played a significant role in determining the material and ontological security of the officers I shadowed, and thus influenced the way they worked. Black officers were most vulnerable, White officers least. Coloured officers, like Yorkton's Constable Hendricks, fell somewhere in between.

During my first shift with Hendricks I learned that he was pursuing an undergraduate degree in psychology. As we patrolled Yorkton's suburban streets I asked him what had drawn him to the subject. He answered with a story:

> It started when my father died, when I was in standard four.[5] So I grew up without a father which means I grew up without a role model. That's how I started drugs when I was 17, in my final year of school. I want to be a child psychologist because the children are the future.

He stopped the car to search three teenage boys. When he was done he told me he had not arrested them because 'they were under eighteen so I would have had to call a social worker and the parents, and they were first time offenders'. He would make similar comments during future shifts, presenting himself as empathetic to young people. But in this instance the young men had done nothing wrong. It seemed an obvious example of a self-narrative, in this instance Hendricks' desire to see himself as an ally to the youth, shaping his social performance and police work.

Hendricks was in his late 20s and had been in the SAPS for seven years. Unlike most constables he was not worried about when he might be promoted because he did not plan to stay a police officer for very long; he had other plans. As the hours past he shared the rest of his story, and his plans, with me.

> When I was eighteen I decided to study oceanography at a technical college. I had always loved nature. I still do. I had been interested in psychology but was too late to apply in time. At college I met a Chinese woman. She was 18 and was driving a Mini Cooper. Her brother was also driving a smart car.

I was attracted to the money and wanted to know how they were making it. I started dating the woman and discovered that her father was a drug lord. She and her brother were selling his drugs on campus, cocaine and *tik*.[6] I moved in with her and started to help them sell. It all started going bad when we started testing the product ourselves. We became addicted. Her father found out and made his children leave South Africa. I remained addicted and found myself stealing globes from my mother's car's headlights so that I could smoke.

My mother was unemployed and I decided I needed to earn money for the house. I went door to door asking people if I could clean their yards. When people asked how much I charged I told them they could decide how much I deserved once I was finished. Some people gave me R10; some people gave me food. If I said I didn't want food they called me ungrateful and chased me away. Some people deducted R3 from my pay if I asked for water.

After that I started hanging out on street corners in places where people picked up day labourers for jobs. But I was the skinny Coloured guy behind all the big Black guys so nobody chose me.

I went to a job agency, the kind where you go at 6 a.m. and if somebody calls needing a worker then they send you off. I got some casual work through them; then I got a month's contract at a dairy. They paid R900 (£50) per week but the agency kept R450 (£25) of it.

From there I got a job as a driver for an engineering company. They offered me R3,000 (£165) per month. *Yoh*, it was a lot for me! It was like having R15,000 (£825).

It was while working as a driver that Hendricks had applied to the SAPS. He believed that the path he had walked from fatherless child to drug seller and addict, from desperate job seeker to police constable, would make him a good child psychologist. He had completed one year of his studies and needed another three or four before he could practice. He was not in a hurry though. 'I know I want to be a psychologist,' he told me. 'That is my goal. That will be the last thing I overcome. But I'm not in a rush. I have a job and I enjoy it. I want to qualify by the time I'm 35.'

Working as a constable was Hendricks's primary job, but it was not his only source of income. In another long story, he told me that he was also an occasional sex worker. He said he earned between R350 (£19) and R1,200 (£66) for sex work, depending on the service he provided. His girlfriend did not know about this side occupation. From what he said of her, she was also young and aspirational. She had already secured a university degree for herself, and was enrolled for a second. Together, the pair were a couple from humble beginnings, taking the opportunities that came their way and chasing what they saw as a glittering future.

\*

The SAPS is akin to a container jammed full of personal narratives, each informed by, and informing, the organisational narrative. Together the narratives shape the manner in which police practise their craft, which in turn shapes South African communities. While officers' personal narratives are contrasting and varied, dominant themes include coming from a life of hardship and using the SAPS as a vehicle through which to improve one's lot, as well as those of one's familial networks. But, as illustrated through Kriel and Louw, the narrative is not the same for everyone, with White police the most obvious exceptions.[7]

## Of life, lottery, and longing

In the 2014/15 financial year the South African Police Service advertised 3,977 jobs, for which it received almost 200,000 applications (SAPS 2015). From these it employed only 2,827 people. To secure a job in the SAPS requires perseverance, patience, and an inordinate amount of luck. As long as there remains mass unemployment and widespread poverty in South Africa, a job in the SAPS will be something to be coveted, even if applying to or working for the organisation forces applicants to re-visit the stories they tell themselves about themselves in ways they may never have expected.

It is against the precarity from which most officers are drawn, and in the instrumentality of the job to their lives, that the police practices and deceptions discussed thus far, and the police violence and order-shaping work discussed in remaining chapters, are best understood. Through attention to the ways officers' personal narratives are entangled in societal and SAPS contextual forces, one begins to understand how entanglement – and for some, the *liminality* – shapes police practice.

Almost none of the police I met had planned to be police officers. On the contrary, many had grown up actively deriding and looking down on police, some admitting to having broken the law as children and adults. They had turned to the SAPS when earlier dreams had slipped out of reach. Often, they told themselves, these dreams had been lost because they had lacked money for tertiary education. As such, they framed themselves as victims of an unfair society, and the SAPS as a repository for high school-only graduates. But once employed by the SAPS, they told themselves that their views had changed. They became hopeful of promotion – even if they believed it unlikely – and were appreciative of the avenues to personal development which the job offered. As they assimilated into the SAPS team they felt stung by the judgements of the public they served, and feared the guns of the brazen *skollies* who they imagined themselves pitted against.

But even those who celebrated the job, like Warrant Officer Skrikker and Constable Qoboza, remained on the lookout for opportunities in other sectors. Meanwhile, they deferred their dreams to their children, cocooned in visions of a more prosperous, safe, and predictable future. Until they could return to the rural Eastern Cape – their *home* – to retire or be buried, they sought to invest in cars and houses but also in education, symbols of success in the bling and hustle of the young democracy. In so doing they sought to consume their way out of the cycle of poverty into which they were born. This was hampered by the weight of the familial networks which called on them for financial support. Most officers presented themselves as respectful of these responsibilities and as willing to share what they could.

Many women officers seemed to be single parents, while some men and women had grown up in single parent homes, or had been raised by grandparents. Some male officers had children with different mothers, spread across the city or across provinces. While officers generally wished the best for their children, they struggled to balance their personal ambitions with the reach of their salary. Where they held tenuous ties with former lovers, relationships were at times considered burdensome. With rural–urban migration, a movement of youth away from elders, and men away from women, family responsibility has shifted from fathers to mothers.

That officers invested in both the city and countryside – most clearly in the expansion of their houses – is an important indicator of South Africa's trajectory, should it manage to generate comparably remunerated employment on a broad scale. Unlike the police Steinberg met in Johannesburg who overextended themselves to move to expensive suburbs, the officers I met lived in either very modest settings – including in shacks, so that they could save or share money (including with children and relatives in the Eastern Cape) – or were expanding the RDP and township houses in which they lived. In this way they were investing in the spaces in which, and people with whom, they felt they belonged. They were channelling resources into parts of Cape Town and the Eastern Cape that had historically been neglected or only modestly developed. They were (re) distributing their relatively meagre privilege in ways that will likely make South Africa more secure. If the idea that police can significantly reduce crime is a fiction then this point is particularly ironic. Where SAPS officers succeed in making South Africa safer, it may not be through their patrols or investigations. Rather, it may be through improving the lives of family and friends as a result of the stability and income which their work provides them.

When I write of this police majority I do not include most White officers. For their part they entered the SAPS on very different terms from most of their colleagues. They are part of networks of individuals who are both self-sufficient and at times able to provide them with new income and opportunity streams. Kriel and Louw both framed their police work as a choice, saying they did not do it for money. In this way they claimed an agency which distanced them from their colleagues, many of whom they saw as having joined the SAPS because it was the only job they could find. The non-policing income-generating activities that Kriel and Louw were engaged in were part of the formal economy, with the potential for substantial reward. In contrast, where African officers imagined starting businesses on the side, they usually involved informal taxis, *spaza* shops, and the sale of alcohol. These are the activities that drove township commerce in the shadow of apartheid's anti-competition laws, and so the activities that appeared within reach to those from disempowered networks. In this way, it is the relative agency and privilege of White officers that exposes the comparable lack of their African colleagues.[8] Similarly, none of the white officers I met spoke of having to support anyone other than their immediate (nuclear) family. The money they earned was theirs alone.

In Chapter 2 I recounted a narrative which many officers I met used to explain the country's violent crime. At its core was the idea that young men were being born in cities where they were poorly socialised and drawn to crime. It is a narrative which is almost a century old. But the views of rural officers in Gompo and Patterson, like Constable Mbelani, were different. Mbelani believed it was the countryside that made rural men violent, and that they took their violence to the towns and cities. The narrative previously sketched, though dominant in Cape Town, was not sufficient for rural officers, so they turned it on its head and blamed the rural youth for the country's crime. Perhaps this was in part because they did not necessarily imagine themselves staying in the countryside. Outside the job, life was relatively dull. Cities offered the fertile soil in which dreams could grow. They were where specialised police units were based, where new challenges could be faced and new skills learned, not to mention where most non-state jobs were located. While they saw cities as places where police were in peril, they also saw them as places where their careers might flourish, so did not dismiss them entirely. Like Young's late modern societies, South Africa is not a place where anyone is very secure for very long, and so rural officers let their minds flirt with visions of urban futures.

But, I believe, there is another presence behind the ways police spoke of young men – whether countryside or city born – in such menacing tones: they were reminders that officers' place in the world was precarious and under threat, often by young men whose lives at times closely resemble their own. In this way, the idea of a rural home served two purposes. First, it was a place to which officers attached their identity, but, more importantly, it was one in which at least some material and ontological security could be imagined in a country seemingly awash with insecurity. In this way they acknowledged that risk was everywhere, and security guaranteed nowhere.

Imagining a future with new, positive self-images requires a constant search for paths that lead away from pervasive risk. It was these paths that had drawn most officers to the SAPS, and similar paths that may lead them away from it. Whether in the city or countryside, most officers were on the lookout for the next step up to a better, easier life. This aspiration, and the responsibility to support precarious networks, shaped the way they policed South Africa.

## Notes

1 Port Elizabeth, a city nearly 250 kilometres away, also in the Eastern Cape Province.
2 Further Education and Training College.

3 Amongst the poorer parts of the town, on the outskirts, consisting of many government built (RDP) houses.
4 The second biggest city in the Eastern Cape Province.
5 The sixth year of primary school.
6 Crystal Methamphetamine.
7 This is not to say that white SAPS officers generally come from wealthy backgrounds, they do not. But compared to the levels of deprivation experienced by most South Africans since the late nineteenth century, theirs' are privileged backgrounds.
8 It has been empirically shown that self-perceptions of (subjective) well-being are significantly higher among Whites than Africans (Posel & Casale 2011).

## References

Artz, L., Burton, P., Ward, C., Leoschut, L., Phyfer, J., Loyd, S., & Kassanjee, R., 2016. *Research Bulletin: The Optimus Study on Child Abuse, Violence and Neglect in South Africa*, Cape Town: Centre for Justice and Crime Prevention. Available at: www.cjcp.org.za/uploads/2/7/8/4/27845461/cjcp_ubs_proof_18.pdf.

Ashforth, A., 2005. *Witchcraft, Violence, and Democracy in South Africa*, Chicago, IL, and London: University of Chicago Press.

Bray, R., Gooskins, I., Kahn, L., Moses, S., & Seekings, J., 2010. *Growing Up in the New South Africa: Childhood and Adolescence in Post-Apartheid Cape Town*, Cape Town: HSRC.

Etherington, N., Harries, P. & Mbenga, B., 2009. From Colonial Hegemonies to Imperial Conquest, 1840–1880. In R.R. Carolyn Hamilton & Bernard K. Mbenga, eds. *The Cambridge History of South Africa*. Cambridge: Cambridge University Press, pp. 319–391.

Faull, A., 2013. Policing Taverns and Shebeens: Observation, Experience and Discourse. *South African Crime Quarterly*, 46, pp. 35–48.

Faull, A., 2016. Measured Governance? Policing and Performance Management in South Africa. *Public Administration and Development*, 36(2), pp. 157–168.

Giddens, A., 1991. *Modernity and Self-Identity: Self and Society in the Late Modern Age*, Cambridge: Polity Press.

Goffman, E., 1959. *The Presentation of Self in Everyday Life*, New York: Doubleday.

Goffman, E., 1990. *Stigma: Notes on the Management of Spoiled Identity*, London: Penguin.

Herrick, C. & Charman, A., 2013. Shebeens: Conduits or Victims of Crime? The Multiple Criminalities of South African Liquor and its Regulation. *South African Crime Quarterly*, (45), pp. 25–32.

Hunter, M., 2006. Fathers Without Amandla: Zulu-Speaking Men and Fatherhood. In L. Richter & R. Morrell, eds. *Baba: Men and Fatherhood in South Africa*, Cape Town: HSRC Press.

Jensen, R.T., 2004. Do Private Transfers 'Displace' the Benefits of Public Transfers? Evidence from South Africa. *Journal of Public Economics*, 88(1–2), pp. 89–112.

Lee, R., 2011. Death 'On the Move': Funerals, Entrepreneurs and the Rural–Urban Nexus in South Africa. *Africa: The Journal of the International African Institute*, 81(2), pp. 226–247.

Leibbrandt, M., Finn, A., & Woolard, I., 2012. Describing and Decomposing Post-Apartheid Income Inequality in South Africa. *Development Southern Africa*, 29(1), pp. 19–34. Available at: http://dx.doi.org/10.1080/0376835X.2012.645639.

Marks, S., 2009. Class, Culture, and Consciousness in South Africa, 1880–1899. In R. Ross, A.K. Mager & B. Nasson, eds. *The Cambridge History of South Africa Vol 2*. Cambridge: Cambridge University Press, pp. 102–156.

O'Regan, J.C. & Pikoli, A.V., 2014. *Towards a Safer Khayelithsa: Report of the Commission of Inquiry into Allegations of Police Inefficiency and a Breakdown in Relations Between SAPS and the Community of Khayelitsha*, Cape Town: Khayelitsha Commission of Inquiry.

Posel, D., 2004. Have Migration Patterns in Post-Apartheid South Africa Changed? In *Conference on African Migration in Comparative Perspective*. Johannesburg, pp. 1–21. Available at: http://s3.amazonaws.com/zanran_storage/time.dufe.edu.cn/ContentPages/222055987.pdf.

Posel, D. & Casale, D., 2011. *Relative Standing and Subjective Well-Being in South Africa: The Role of Perceptions, Expectations and Income Mobility*, Durban. Available at: www.econrsa.org/system/files/publications/working_papers/wp210.pdf.

Richter, L. & Morrell, R. eds., 2006. *Baba: Men and Fatherhood in South Africa*, Cape Town: HSRC Press.

Richter, L. & Ramphele, M., 2006. Migrancy, Family Dissolution and Fatherhood. In L. Richter & R. Morrell, eds. *Baba: Men and Fatherhood in South Africa*, Cape Town: HSRC Press.

SAPA, 2013. Only 33% of SA Kids Live with Both Parents. *News 24*. Available at: www.news24.com/SouthAfrica/News/Only-33-of-SA-kids-live-with-both-parents-20130311.

SAPS, 2015. *Annual Report 2014/15*, Pretoria. Available at: www.saps.gov.za/about/stratframework/annual%7B_%7Dreport/2014%7B_%7D2015/SAPS%7B_%7DAR%7B_%7D2014-15%7B_%7Dfor%7B_%7Dviewing.pdf.

Seekings, J. & Harper, S., 2010. *Claims on and Obligations to Kin in Cape Town, South Africa*, Working Paper 272, Cape Town: Centre for Social Science Research. Available at: www.cssr.uct.ac.za/publications/working-paper/2010/claims-and-obligations-kin-cape-town-south.

Seekings, J. & Nattrass, N., 2005. *Class, Race and Inequality in South Africa*, New Haven, CT: Yale University Press.

StatsSA, 2014a. *General Household Survey, 2013.*, Pretoria. Available at: http://beta2.statssa.gov.za/publications/P0318/P03182013.pdf.

StatsSA, 2014b. *Transforming the Distributional Regime: Poverty Trends in South Africa: An Examination of Absolute Poverty Between 2006 and 2011*, Pretoria. Available at: http://beta2.statssa.gov.za/publications/Report-03-10-06/Report-03-10-06March2014.pdf.

Steinberg, J., 2008. *Thin Blue: The Unwritten Rules of Policing South Africa*, Jeppestown: Jonathan Ball.

Walker, N., 2007. The Necessary Virtue of the State. In I. Loader & N. Walker, eds. *Civilsing Security*, Cambridge: Cambridge University Press, pp. 170–194.

Young, J., 1999. *The Exclusive Society*, London: Sage.

Young, J., 2007. *The vertigo of late modernity*, London: Sage.

Young, J., 2011. *The Criminological Imagination*, Cambridge: Polity Press.

# Chapter 5

# Ambition, shame, violence, and respect[1]

## Overlap and entanglement

So far I have described and unpacked the key practices, worldviews, and lived experiences that appeared central to the occupational lives of the officers I shadowed. My aim has been to sketch the overlap and entanglement of individual trajectories; national and local context(s); the functioning of the police bureaucracy; and the resultant impact on police practice. I have suggested that in contexts characterised by unemployment, crime, and general precarity, a job in the SAPS changes one's life. At the same time, police work is symbolic, cultural work. It shapes communities and nations. Through their employment as police officers, a select few of the country's precarious majority are given a foot up the income ladder. In return, they are expected to do the dirty work of the state. They buy into the fantasy that coercive policing reduces crime, and enact deceptive performances and fabricate data to save face when it doesn't. I have illustrated this using the idea of the 'good shift', and the deceptive performances enacted in the absence of such shifts. I have shown that deception is employed to keep the SAPS public façade intact. In many instances, those whom the police marked through their stops and raids were people raised in communities much like their own. Many police returned home to relatively poor, violent neighbourhoods after work, so that their private lives were shaped by the violence they believed they were expected to prevent in their occupational lives. Violence followed them everywhere.

Finally, I have framed police as people who turned to the SAPS for employment after other dreams and imagined futures had drifted beyond reach. One might describe them as *accidental police officers*. Some recalled disliking the police before joining, while others admitted to crimes committed as teenagers. Upon joining the SAPS, however, many found themselves re-writing their self-narratives. They told themselves that they enjoyed the work, and distanced themselves from their prior views of police. Earning more money as police than they might have imagined, and more than most family members, they were weighed down by the expectation that their fortune must be shared with kin, often scattered across the country. Sharing constrained their aspirations of upward mobility and material consumption. Some of those who could supplemented their income by moonlighting or starting small businesses on the side. Ultimately though, it seemed officers invested most in their children. They did not want them to be accidental police officers, so they invested in their education in ways their own parents had not been able to do for them. In so doing they presented the SAPS as a repository for those determined enough to finish high school, but unable to have studied further. Some officers resented the fact that they still lived in RDP homes or backyard shacks, but did so in pursuit of other material, familial and ontological aspirations. They were excited about where their police salaries might lead them but sceptical about their chances of promotion. Theirs were often dreams perpetually out of reach, so that many felt trapped in states of liminality. This shaped the lens through which they viewed themselves and their jobs, and so how they went about their work.

In this chapter, I re-visit and unpack the theme of police and societal violence touched on in previous chapters. Building on the contextual foundations provided thus far, I discuss police violence in relation to violence in South Africa more broadly, socially and historically; the ways in which police officers talk about, experience, and deploy violence in their work; violence as it relates to South African masculinities; violence in relation to feelings of shame and respect; and violence as a means of communication. I conclude by exploring how violence delivered by the state shapes South African society, and how violence seeps into and spills out of both the SAPS as an organisation, and the private lives of its officers.

## Marikana: August 16, 2012

At this point it is helpful to re-visit Marikana and the events that took place just one week into my fieldwork.

On August 16, 2012, following two weeks of labour protests during which two police officers, two mine security staff, and four miners were killed (allegedly by miners), police opened fire on hundreds of striking miners, killing 34 and wounding 78.

More than the daily complaints about the SAPS' failure to prevent crime; more than police leaderships' infamous calls to 'shoot to kill' criminal offenders between 2008 and 2011;[2] more than the conviction of the SAPS National Commissioner, Jackie Selebi, for corruption in 2010; more than police beating to death Andries Tatane as he marched for access to water in 2011; and more than the Khayelitsha Commission of Inquiry into a breakdown in the relationship between the community and the SAPS; what is often called *The Marikana Massacre* has become the most visible scar on the face of the SAPS.

It was against this background that I collected the data for this book. The subject of Marikana, or 'that thing in Marikana' as some officers referred to it, regularly came up in conversation with those I shadowed. Although some expressed sadness at the killing of the workers, almost without exception, they tried to convince me that the officers who had pulled their triggers that day had done so lawfully and professionally; that they had done nothing wrong.

Considering that peer solidarity is a long-established characteristic of police organisational culture (Reiner 2010; Cockcroft 2013), perhaps this should not be surprising. But I believe there was more to why SAPS officers so quickly defended the slaughter of 34 men at the hands of their colleagues; something closely tied to the culture of deceit described in Chapter 3. Put simply, it was that officers abhorred being disrespected. On accepting their jobs in the SAPS they had agreed to re-write their self-narratives, and to buy into the state's narrative that hard work pays; that one reaps what one sows. That day in Marikana, like every day on the streets of the country's cities and towns, their colleagues had stood their ground in the face of workers and, so they told me, *criminals*, who sought to enrich themselves by demanding hand-outs, cutting corners or committing crime. Their colleagues had done the work they believed they had been employed and deployed to do, the work they believed the system required them to do. And yet, they were being punished for it – not just the officers in Marikana, but by association, every member of the SAPS. That's why the officers I shadowed so quickly sided with their colleagues 1,500 kilometres away.

## Policing, symbolic power, violence, and respect

That most police in Mthonjeni felt the public did not respect them was evident within my first days at the station. Station mythology abounded with stories of officers attending complaints and returning to their vehicles to find the tyres slashed or wheels stolen; having stones thrown at their cars; and being unable to conduct foot patrols because the community would attack them. This, despite plenty of evidence to the contrary, including the weekly outreach patrols by predominantly unarmed administrative staff wearing police vests. Almost identical claims were made by police at the three stations being probed by the Khayelitsha Commission.

In Chapter 4 I mentioned Constable Yoyo's fear of walking the 300 metres from her shack to the police station. Another constable who lived 500 metres away paid to take a taxi to work each day for the same reason, even though he was a detective, so did not wear a uniform. Many officers refused to walk the 50 metres to a shop that shared a wall with the station for fear of being attacked for their firearms, while others told me that when they were off duty they would not tell people that they were police officers because this would put them in danger. They saw these (potentially) violent attacks as signs of disrespect – of a public that did not view them as human.

How did these ideas about danger and disrespect manifest in officers' daily work? While many talked of the need to treat the public with respect in order to earn their trust, this sentiment was seldom extended to groups thought to be regular offenders, like the imagined *skollie*. The word was used to describe young men, usually African or Coloured and poor, perceived to be criminals. But this demographic represents almost half the country's population. It also mirrors the communities from which most police are drawn. Many officers seemed to believe that the best way to teach a *skollie* respect was through force.

## Mthonjeni: violence in the township

Conversations with two Mthonjeni CPU constables, Nzo and Mqhayi, while on patrol in the early hours of a Saturday morning, illustrate some of the undercurrents informing officers' thoughts on respect and force. I asked the constables if they thought the community respected them. Nzo was the chattier of the two and replied immediately, 'No, they don't respect us anywhere in South Africa. You try and arrest someone and they will throw stones at you.'

Nzo was from the Eastern Cape but had moved to Cape Town in the mid-nineties to finish high school. He lived in Khayelitsha's Site C, one of the poorer sections of Cape Town's largest township. He said he enjoyed the area but lamented that many of his school peers had become *skollies*. Some had even been arrested for murder, or 'killed [by] each other,' he said. Although he still lived in Khayelitsha, he avoided his old friends.

After finishing high school, he studied engineering for two years before 'the money ran out'. He was first hired as a typist for the SAPS before being accepted for training as a police officer. His plans for the future were to finish building his second house (his first being at *home* in the Eastern Cape) before enrolling in a correspondence course to complete his engineering diploma. With that in hand, he hoped to leave the SAPS. I asked him why he wanted to leave the organisation:

> Because they have taken [away] all the powers of the police. Even if they point a gun at you, you can't shoot them. You must wait for them to shoot you first and then you can only shoot. The community just stand and insult you. It's not right anymore. You explain to [a victim] the processes they will go through if you open a case for them; you try to help them and tell them you can take them to a certain point, but when the case doesn't go any further, they accuse you of corruption. If we are called to a domestic violence scene and we beat the man, then the woman will complain. They call the police for everything, for a birth, for a death, for sickness, but when you get there they fight with you.

I asked Nzo what his ideal job in the SAPS would be, were he to remain in the organisation:

> It would be fine if I was a captain. At least then I would be respected by the other members. I would like to work at a senior level at the forensics lab, but I also enjoy the action in police work. When I arrest people I have to

struggle with them, but once I have them in the cells, I give them advice; tell them to take short courses [to improve their chances of employment]. In the morning they thank me, or when they see me in the streets at a later stage, they salute me.

It was a short tale of a police officer who felt unappreciated, of force used to restrain, and of advice offered. Most importantly, it was about earning the respect of men who had previously shown none.

Nzo started complaining about 'the senior police', how they were just out to punish their juniors:

If I receive information that there is something in a house, like a gun, I might not have time to get a warrant. But if I search that house and the occupants complain, I will immediately be arrested.

He recounted a house raid in which he had taken part. The 'elderly woman' occupant had accused him of stealing R300 (£16.50) from under her bed. He claimed that station management had wanted him and his colleagues to be arrested immediately but that they had gone back to the house and found the R300 under the woman's mattress, absolving them of the accusation – at least in his version of the event. The story's theme was that both the public and police management were out to get junior officers, that everyone was against them.

Having patrolled for a few hours we were flagged down by a man and woman in their early 20s, lone figures on the deserted street. It was after 1.00 a.m. and, in my sleepiness, I did not immediately register the shock on their faces or the tears in the woman's eyes, but the constables did. In a matter of seconds, they had stopped and leapt from the car, drawn their firearms, and were running towards a cluster of shacks. 'They were robbed of a cell phone at gunpoint,' Nzo muttered to me as he disappeared out of sight. Alone with the victims, the woman repeated words of distress over and over. The man remained silent, shocked. Two minutes later the constables returned and holstered their firearms. Without even stopping to face them, Nzo said something to the two victims and they began walking away. As quickly as we had stopped, we were back on patrol.

If the constables' initial response – the drawing of guns and hurrying into the darkness – was symbolically meaningful, its power was contradicted by what came after. Whereas the initial search and threat of deadly force by officers appeared in service of the victims, the remainder communicated disinterest and resignation. There had been no request for a description of the attackers; no report over the radio; no asking the victims if they wanted to open a case, if they needed counselling, an escort home, or anything else. The one thing the constables had done was draw their firearms – the extensions of their occupational identities that communicated a willingness to use lethal force. It seemed they believed that by demonstrating, through performance, their willingness to run towards danger and to shoot in defence of the victims, they were fulfilling their mandate. It was a powerful act, but where it should have been followed by compassion – even a simple bureaucratic note – there was only silence and the dark of the night.

Minutes later, the ordeal was repeated. This time we were waved down by a number of women complaining of footsteps on the roofs of their shacks. The SAPS Tactical Response Team (TRT), also patrolling the area, rounded the corner as we alighted our vehicle, and joined the search for the few minutes for which it lasted, but nothing and no one was found. Soon we were on the road again, minimal communication having taken place between officers and complainants, and with no information shared over the radio.

The heavily armed TRT had been established two years earlier to tackle high-risk crimes like cash-in-transit heists, but were regularly deployed to the Mthonjeni policing area as a 'force multiplier' conducting 'crime prevention' alongside the station's CPU. Pulling away from the TRT I asked the constables what they thought of the unit. At the time the media had been painting them as violent and abusive. Nzo responded:

> They are good but we don't have a backbone in the police. The [SAPS management] don't appreciate what the TRT are doing and so they are demotivated. Since they have been deployed here there has been a big decrease in crime. People respect them.

I asked why he thought people respected them. 'Because they beat people,' he replied. 'If they have suspects, they torture them and the person gives up everything. It's good.' I asked whether he knew what kind of techniques they used. 'They use that one with a bag over the head of the old days,' he said referring to the waterboarding used by apartheid's SAP.

*

The sentiment expressed by Constable Nzo and the tacit agreement of his mostly silent colleague bring together a number of themes in this book. Nzo, like so many others, had come to the police after lack of money had meant earlier dreams were deferred. The injustice of South Africa's past had delivered him into adulthood without the means to enjoy the consumption that signals success in the *new* country. In its place he had turned to the SAPS but found himself frustrated by managers and members of the public who seemed not to recognise the ambitious, hard-working person he thought himself to be.

Where he was not shown respect, Nzo suggested he sought it through force: literal force, such as his claim of beating abusive husbands; performative force, such as the pulling of his firearm; and rhetorical force, through his support of torture. But, it seemed, he also sought respect in softer ways, by, for instance, providing what guidance he could to those who found themselves in his custody. And when they saluted him, he filed the memory away with others that supported the story he told himself about himself, even if others didn't believe it to be true.

While Nzo may not have actually assaulted a wife-batterer or seen TRT officers using torture, that he suggested as much was notable. Stories told by police generate meaning, both for police and the policed. The selection of some themes – such as assault, torture, and disrespect – over others lends them credence and power to shape organisational culture (Holdaway 1983) and thus personal identities. The themes covered that night included: (1) that many South Africans are poor; (2) that without money one's education, opportunities, and dreams are limited; (3) that the SAPS offers opportunities to those who have lacked; (4) that members of the public do not respect police officers and often complain about, or falsely accuse them of, abuse and criminality; (5) that SAPS managers do not trust their subordinates and are quick to punish them; (6) that force and torture reduce crime; and (7) that the state has disempowered police officers by introducing strict limitations on their use of force, which further diminishes the public's respect for them.

What I have shown in this book thus far is that these themes pervade every aspect of SAPS daily rituals, and so the lives of its officers. To the themes touched on by Nzo, we might add officers' general mistrust and lack of respect for colleagues, the organisation, and the public. While these themes manifested differently across stations and individuals, I found them everywhere. Their conjuring and repetition aided officers in their efforts to interpret and make sense of their worlds, themselves, and their actions. Ultimately, through both talk and action, police communicate symbolic meaning (Loader 2006), serving as both minders and reminders of community (Walker 2002), of the way things are, and the way those in power think they should be.

*

A growing body of research suggests that procedurally fair, respectful treatment by police promotes compliance with both police and the law, including in the absence of police (Sunshine & Tyler 2003; Tyler 2004; Hough et al. 2010; Bottoms & Tankebe 2012; Stanko et al. 2012; Bradford et al. 2014). Even without knowledge of such evidence, a reasonable person might expect that fair treatment by police would more likely earn them respect and promote compliance than would use of force. This reasoning is accepted by many in the SAPS, but it is accompanied by the equally common view that violence earns respect. The following examples, I believe, illustrate this most clearly.

I have elsewhere described an experience of closing down a tavern with Mthonjeni's Warrant Officer Jiyana (Faull 2013). It was a weekend night and the street outside the tavern where Jiyana had stopped our patrol van was crowded with patrons illegally drinking in public. Jiyana used the car's loudspeaker to gently and respectfully ask people to stop drinking, but our presence and his words were ignored. He immediately summoned the tavern owner and asked her to shut the tavern down. It seemed he wanted to punish the crowd for ignoring him.

We drove around the block and returned. This time Jiyana directed his loudspeaker address at an individual, telling him to empty his drink on the ground. This the man did, and walked away, but everyone else carried on as before. As we pulled away, a deep thud echoed through the car – someone had hit it with a large rock. 'They think I will run,' muttered Jiyana, 'but I won't. I will close it down.'

Jiyana's anger was quiet. He parked the van around the corner and called for backup. In the wing mirror I noticed a violent assault taking place 100 metres behind us, but when I alerted Jiyana he said they deserved to be assaulted, 'If you spend time attending to these petty beatings then you can lose time' (Faull 2013:44). Because the young people were drinking in public, because they were out late at night, and because they had ignored his requests to disperse, they deserved to be punished, he thought. They had offended him.

Setting the car in motion once again, we rounded another corner, continuing a circuit of the block. Jiyana shouted through the window at two teenage girls, telling them they would be raped if they walked and drank in public. Like the other drinkers, they ignored him.

Rounding the block's last corner, we were met by two backup vehicles outside the tavern. Tavern staff had already closed its gate and were sweeping the street outside. Patrons ambled into the darkness. I commented to Warrant Jiyana that he had succeeded in closing the tavern. His response was one of pride:

> I was successful because I was gentle with them. Because of this, when I come to close them down in December, I will be safe. If you assault them they will throw stones at your vehicle.

His statement was deeply ironic. First, we had had a large rock thrown at us despite his gentle approach. Second, he had purposefully not intervened in what appeared to be a violent assault, precisely because he wanted the patrons to suffer, apparently because they had ignored him. And, third, while the tavern complied with Jiyana's request that it close its doors, its patrons had entirely ignored our presence, choosing instead to disperse because the tavern had closed, rather than because police had instructed them to do so. It seemed the authority lay with the tavern, not the police.

Of course, the fact that the tavern owner closed the premises indicated that Jiyana and his colleagues had some authority. It was just that the intended authoritative power of the police presence had been neutralised by the patrons, and probably only recognised by the tavern owner because she could lose her licence to trade.

## Yorkton: violence in the affluent city

When I described Yorkton's police precinct in Chapter 2, I emphasised the difference between its demographics and those of the other stations. I also noted that many Yorkton residents had more social and economic capital than the police officers working there. I suggested that wealthy White residents were treated with more deference than the Black and poor. While I inferred that patrol police were less likely than Mthnojeni's to use violence in public space, I noted that they still used it. I described Constable Hendricks' choking various people, predominantly because they questioned his authority; Constable Moshoeshoe's hesitation in attending complaints for fear of being exposed to his colleagues' violence; and the ferocity and contempt displayed by detectives tracing suspects on the Cape Flats. Despite all of this, Yorkton's police were infinitely more tolerant of people on the streets late at night, less suspicious of young men in general, and believed that most of the local community respected them.

Even so, it was at Yorkton that it became most clear that one should not challenge a SAPS officer unless one is willing to be arrested or assaulted. This was apparent because (1) officers at the station used the charge of *riotous behaviour* to detain anyone they wanted to punish, including anyone who questioned their authority; and (2) detainees who challenged officers in the holding cells had a good chance of being slapped into silence, despite their being monitored by CCTV.

Contempt for a disrespecting public is not unique to the SAPS. Loftus, for example, reports watching English police put people through an 'attitude test'. People stopped for casual questioning passed the attitude test by 'being polite, apologising or admitting guilt, essentially by feigning respect for the police' (Loftus 2010:10). The act served as a reminder of police authority, and officers' thirst for respect.

In Mthonjeni and Patterson, a version of the attitude test played itself out in frenzies of stop and search. But, it was in the holding cells of Yorkton, where detainees are 'processed' before being allocated a cell, that I witnessed a more violent version of the test. People were slapped and punched, sworn at, laughed at, or ignored, often only because they dared to ask a man in uniform why they had been taken into custody. Despite it being a legal requirement, I had never known a SAPS office to formally state the reason for arrest when forcing someone into the back of a van, and this remained true throughout my 2012/13 fieldwork. In addition to CCTV cameras recording holding-cell activities, these abuses took place in front of other police, including commissioned officers, none of whom ever intervened in their colleagues' violence. Indeed, removed from the public gaze, the violence was a performance by (male) police officers for (male) police officers, an intra-group enactment of how violence earns respect. The performance of, and silence around, violence in this private police space served to remind officers of their occupation's powerful recourse to force. And while this informal violence went against all SAPS policy, the silence around it meant, at some level, the organisation accepted it. It is this silence, part of the deception described in Chapter 3, which allows for routine abuse of force and other violations. Considered through von Holdt's lens of South African bureaucracies (von Holdt 2010), the silence is a form of organisational and state face-saving.

SAPS officers know that abuse scandals dirty the organisation's image and that the dirt may rub off on them. By not reporting, or by actively turning away from colleagues' transgressions, they protect themselves. After all, the less popular the SAPS is, the harder it is for officers to feel ontologically secure.

On a number of occasions officers told me, in celebratory tones, of the silencing effect of a slap to the face of a disrespectful individual. Apartheid's SAP officers jokingly referred to it as 'the charge office slap' (Faull 2010:202). Violence and police occupational space have a long history in South Africa. In 2012/13 these slaps were referred to as if they were a cunning trick of the trade; a slight movement of the hand that brought about compliance and respect.

\*

One Friday night I was in the processing room of the Yorkton cells with Constable Hendricks. He was writing up the paperwork for a drunken naval cadet who had driven his car into a row of stationary vehicles. Already in the holding area were a man in his late 20s and his partner. The man was shouting over and over, 'Beat me! Beat me! Tomorrow I will come with my lawyer and we will win! Why have you arrested me? What did I do?' But the officers were more interested in his partner, a dreadlocked man who sat in silence. He refused to give up his belt and personal items, which must be handed to officers before detainees are locked in the cells, but which some are reluctant to do for fear that officers will steal them. Officers grabbed the man by his hair and pulled him to the ground so that his head hit the concrete. Colonel Cruz, the shift commander, stood at the gate to the cells, watching. His eyes followed his officers as they dragged the man out of sight, and in a tone of subdued concern he said, 'Don't beat him. Don't beat him.'

A minute later another detainee was brought in. He too shouted questions, asking why he had been arrested, pleading. The arresting officer needed the man's name in order to complete a form, but he refused to give it. Constable Hendricks looked up from his work and, with a grin, said, 'Take him to the back'. The arresting constable took the cue, 'Do you want me to take you to the back where we can talk man to man?' Again, the detainee remained silent. The constable led him out of sight and I heard a slap. The cell sergeant, a woman, looked up at me, 'I always get afraid when they go back there.' She did not like what had happened, but she was not going to intervene.

The constable and his victim returned immediately, the latter following in wide-eyed silence, on the verge of tears. Over the next hour his mouth bled and swelled. 'I have a wife and child at home,' he told the officers, 'What am I supposed to tell them when they ask what happened here? And you are the South African Police Service?' He turned to the colonel who stood in the doorway and stuttered, 'They beat me! Why did they beat me? Why must I go to prison? You kill people! You kill people!' The statement connected the *charge office slap* to the slaughter of miners at Marikana. The colonel ignored him, but Constable

Hendricks looked up. Shifting his accent and language, as if to signal to the man that they both came from the same, hard, Cape Flats, he silenced him with an expletive 'Hou jou bek, jou poes!'[3]

Eventually Hendricks and I headed back to the streets. We spent the rest of the night driving up and down Yorkton's main strip, often lingering on the side of the road ostensibly looking for pickpockets, but really just looking at women. At one point a man walked up to Hendricks' window and dropped a bundle of notes into his lap, 'Money talks, eh?' Hendricks' response wasn't what the man expected, 'No man, you're disrespecting me. That's a slap in the face. Don't think that you can do with me what you do with the other police you meet here.' He handed the money back to the man who sheepishly walked away. I asked Hendricks who he was. 'A friend of a friend who worked in a club,' he replied.

There was an irony in Hendricks's 'slap to the face' analogy, considering the literal slaps we'd earlier heard in the Yorkton cells. Importantly, he compared the analogous slap to disrespect. While he did not infer any disrespect for his colleagues who slapped detainees, in this encounter he signalled a disrespect for colleagues who accepted bribes. It was evidence both of his disrespect for some of his colleagues, and an acknowledgement that a slap, whether physical or symbolic, was an act rich with disrespect. Yorkton's officers sought respect through slaps, and took offence to words and gestures – metaphorical slaps – which, in conveying disrespect for officers, challenged the stories they told themselves about themselves which they believed to be true.

## Gompo: violence in the village

In Gompo and Patterson in the rural Eastern Cape, police used force differently from their city and township colleagues. In Chapter 2 I recounted the beating of a young knife-carrying Patterson teen and how officers had laughed and released him once they realised his flight from them had 'only' been motivated by his possession of the weapon. For their part, the beating had nothing to do with the knife but rather with the fact that the teen had run from and so disrespected them.

More interesting, particularly in the Gompo area, was the use of symbolic violence. The station area and the tasks officers carried out there were very different from those of the urban stations. Due to the precinct's size and the number of villages within it, urban-like patrol was not feasible and police–public interaction was rare. It was also apparent that police working in the area felt, far more than their city counterparts, that the communities in which they worked respected them. There might be a number of explanations for this, including that police work was one of the only professional occupations in the area, other than teaching. It may also relate to the comparably light criminal case burden which rural police faced (10 or 20 cases per month rather than 3,000 in the city). And yet, rural officers still, in part, saw themselves as disciplinarians.

\*

One quiet afternoon in Gompo, a village resident called the station to report that her son had stolen money from her, and to request that the police 'teach him a lesson'. I accompanied Constable Botile and Student Constable Cethe to the village.

Arriving at the house, Botile disembarked the van alone, an improvised wooden baton in hand. Cethe, who remained with me in the car, joked that the baton was to keep dogs at bay. Within minutes Botile emerged from the house holding a teen boy by the scruff of his neck. Cethe and I climbed out of the car, and the student helped Botile bundle the teen into the back of the van. Then, without any communication from Botile, so that he must have known what was coming, Cethe told me to stand up-wind. Within seconds, Botile had removed his pepper spray and fired a jet of the silvery liquid into the boy's face. Botile then swung at him with the wooden baton, most of the blows missing the teen, before he locked the van.

Cethe laughed uncomfortably. 'Andrew,' he said, 'You know there are things that happen on the shift which stay on the shift. You were not supposed to see that!'[4] It was a reference to a conversation we had had in previous weeks, and an acknowledgement that such backstage performances were not intended for anyone but police. Within his first year of SAPS training, Student Constable Cethe had already learned that this was how the organisation worked, and he seemed comfortable with it. The violence posed no threat to his sense of self.

With the boy locked in the van, we entered the house where the mother, in angry exasperation, said she believed her son had stolen R1,500 (£82) from her bedside drawer. The boy had been seen drinking over the weekend and she believed he had used her money. Cethe whispered to me, 'She just wants her change back; then it will be fine. We need to make him talk.'

We returned to the car and drove around the village in search of the boy's drinking companion to ask whether he might have paid for the drinks. This would exonerate the boy, and yet the officers had already assaulted him. If nothing else, they had communicated to him and to his mother that the SAPS would unleash its violence upon young men who disobeyed their parents, that violence is legitimate and corrective. We didn't find his companion.

There were a number of other occasions on which parents asked Gompo's police to discipline their children. Twice, teenage girls were accused of having slept at their boyfriends' houses without parental consent. In response, Gompo officers collected them from their boyfriends' homes and brought them to the station where the station commander, Captain Dlamini, shouted at them and made them sweep and mop the station floor. This they did with tears in their eyes while police officers and civilian staff taunted them. Although no force was deployed, it was a violent form of state punishment nonetheless, and one for which the SAPS has no mandate. The castigation reminded the girls that elders must be respected and that police will punish disrespecting youth. That the community called on police to carry out such tasks, I believe, helped officers feel valued and respected.

The liberty with which Gompo's officers felt entitled to deploy force was most clearly illustrated in a claim by the station's Community Liaison Officer,

Constable Bungu. Bungu had put significant effort into arranging a sports day for youth living in the precinct. This included arranging accommodation for the hundred-odd teens due to take part. On the day they were due to arrive, Bungu told me Captain Dlamini was going to address them, adding that this made her happy. 'They are very scared of Dlamini,' she said, 'So it's good that he will speak to them. When he catches them doing something wrong, he doesn't like to lock them up, so he hurts them and takes them home.' I asked if he beat them, to which she replied with loud laughter, 'Yes, he beats them! He beats them!' I asked what parents thought of this, 'Hayi,[5] they like it! They like it a lot. And it works; it really works.' It was just like the 'charge office slap', force and violence conjuring submission and respect.

Bungu told me that before Captain Dlamini had transferred to the station, crime had been much worse, 'There has been a big improvement,' she said. It was clear that she believed Dlamini's informal beatings were the reason things had improved. While on the surface (and in reports to seniors) it appeared that Gompo was carrying out impressive community outreach initiatives such as the sports day, on the backstage a darker police–community relationship played out, a reminder that many South Africans believe violence a legitimate way to solve problems.

## Violence and respect in South Africa

In the remainder of this chapter, I unpack the intersections between SAPS officers' personal narratives, South African masculinities, and general attitudes towards violence. I suggest that, where these overlap and become entangled with one another, officers believe violence earns respect.

The ways in which police officers work is influenced by the occupational culture of their police organisation, and by their personal notions of order (Manning 1978). The latter can be formed during an officer's upbringing, shaped through early socialisation at home and school. Drawing on a breadth of data, Anthony Collins has suggested that many forms of violence are considered by most South Africans to be legitimate; that '[violence is] socially accepted . . . commonly understood as benign, necessary, [and] justifiable' (2013:30).

In 2006, the then Department of Safety and Security (renamed 'Department of Police' in 2010 in an effort to re-imagine and re-militarise the SAPS) commissioned an independent research organisation, the Centre for the Study of Violence and Reconciliation (CSVR), to explore the drivers behind the violent nature of South Africa's crime. One of the findings was that South Africans' 'perceptions and values related to violence and crime' were central to the high levels of violence:

> [The tolerance of violence] reflects widely held norms and beliefs which see violence as a necessary and justified means of resolving conflict or other difficulties ... [including] the perception by young men that they need to be able to use violence to protect themselves and to obtain the respect of others.
> (CSVR 2010:4)

That violence in South Africa is most commonly accepted and practised by young men is important. It has been convincingly argued that the manner in which South African masculinities are constructed contributes to young men suffering grossly disproportionate levels of violence and victimisation (Seedat et al. 2009). This is in part a result of their inability to live up to society's expectations that men should earn good money, be virile, show leadership, and be physically and mentally tough (Ratele 2008). Through analysis of mortuary data, Ratele and Letsela suggested in 2009 that 12 percent of premature male deaths in South Africa were the result of 'masculine beliefs' characterised by sexual dominance and risk taking, and that such traits were amplified in male-centric environments (Letsela & Ratele 2009). A 2010 survey of 1,696 men aged 18–49 found that 28 percent had raped once or more, with most having first done so before the age of 20, having felt entitled, as men, to force themselves upon women (Jewkes et al. 2010). Like many other forms of violence in South Africa, many rapes are perpetrated by people known to their victim (Vetten 2014). Similarly, more than half of women murdered in South Africa are killed by intimate partners (Abrahams et al. 2009).

Police agencies have historically been staffed by men, and characterised by machismo (e.g. Reiner 2010). Although the SAPS has made great strides in gender parity, with women accounting for 36 percent of employees in 2016 (SAPS 2016c), they are less likely to be deployed outside police stations than are men. This, I believe, is because SAPS culture frames women as risks to themselves and their police partner when in public. Conversely, police *men* are expected to be brave and advance toward danger.

In previous chapters I have conveyed a sense of the violence that SAPS officers are exposed to both at work and at home. Against this background it is helpful to consider them, particularly male officers, as members of communities and families where violence, especially that perpetrated by men against men – but also against women and children – has been normalised as a common problem-solving tool. As such, it is unsurprising that many SAPS officers embrace violence as a means to solves problems or earn respect on the job.

I was made aware of the pervasiveness of such views, and of their reach in officers' personal lives, on a number of occasions. Some of these have already been described, such as the murder of Captain Jacobs' friend in Chapter 2, and Constable Mbelani being stabbed in the arm in Chapter 4. In the next section, I offer three more examples that illustrate the ways violence pervades officers' lives.

## A violence brought from home

One Monday morning, Mthonjeni's Sergeant Tambo, Warrant Officer Skrikker's partner, arrived at work with a swollen lip. When I enquired about it he told me had intervened in a fight outside his house between a friend and a stranger, during which he was punched in the face. When I asked whether he had opened an assault case against his aggressor, he laughed, 'No, five other neighbours joined in and we put that guy in hospital.' Despite being a police officer, Tambo had chosen immediate and violent retribution, rather than criminal justice. He had also chosen to assault a man in front of his neighbours, who knew he was a police officer, and was happy to recount the story to me as though it were humorous.

Something similar occurred with Constable November, another Mthonjeni detective. He arrived at a morning meeting wearing sunglasses, and continued to wear them indoors throughout the day. When I asked him about them he removed them to reveal a swollen black eye. He told me he had been drinking with family the previous afternoon, a Sunday, when one of his relatives had grabbed a child by the hair and pulled him violently. November had reprimanded the relative who responded by punching him in the face. When I asked whether he had opened a case against his aggressor, he smiled, 'No, I'm going to wait until he's forgotten about it all and then I'm going to get him.' The inference was that revenge would be violent.

For the last example, we return to Mthonjeni's Warrant Officer Jiyana. While I was on patrol with him one morning, he announced out of nowhere, 'I executed somebody last night.' His words shocked me, but he quickly corrected himself, 'I executed my duty last night.' He told me his teen daughter had been robbed of her cell phone in Khayelitsha a few days earlier and that in response:

> I worked like I always work. I talked to people in the community. I got information where I could, until I found who the boy was and where he lived. Then last night at 3:30 a.m. – because I knew if he was out robbing people he would have to listen to the call of his ancestors and go to sleep around then, because everyone must listen to the ancestors' call – I went to the house where the boy lived with his parents.

It occurred to me that this took place right after Jiyana would have finished his shift, so he would still have been in his police uniform and driving a marked police car.

> I did not wake up his parents but went straight to the boy's room and stood over him. As soon as he woke up he said, 'I didn't do anything! I didn't do anything!' This was a sign of his guilt because why else would he have said these things without talking to me? I gave him a few *klaps*,[6] then took him with me to fetch my daughter to identify him. The boy told me he had sold the phone to a Somali so I made him take me to him. We went inside the Somali's house and I searched it because he didn't want to give us the phone; he tried to hide it. But we found it.

Jiyana was very happy with himself. I asked if he had opened a case against the boy but he had not. For him, the point was that he had been dedicated, clever, cunning, and a little violent (including, perhaps in front of his daughter), and had recovered a stolen phone. The fact that he was acting in his private capacity while wearing a police uniform, that he unlawfully entered two private residences, and that he assaulted at least one minor was immaterial. To him, his actions were not just common-sense, they were praiseworthy.

I've chosen these examples because they illustrate once more that violence is a common feature of the private lives of many police officers. South African police deploy and are the victims of violence, in both their personal and occupational lives. Accounts of extra-legal violence were openly shared with colleagues and me alike, as though there were nothing untoward about them. They help explain how violence is normalised within the SAPS. For many it had shaped their lives long before they became police officers, and continued to do so while they were working for the SAPS.

\*

The normalisation of violence in South Africa is at times bolstered by statements made by public figures and political leaders who seem to think the threat of state violence will reduce crime and build respect. It is a view illustrated by a litany of aggressive rhetoric beginning in the mid-2000s (cf. Faull & Rose 2012: 8–11).

In March 2013, South Africa's then president, Jacob Zuma, stated against all other evidence, that South Africa was not a violent country (SAPA 2013b). His comments were made in the weeks after Olympian Oscar Pistorius shot dead his girlfriend, Reeva Steenkamp, and in response to a litany of international media coverage of the country's relationship with violence. The president's statements contradicted a significant body of evidence that not only suggests South Africa records the highest levels of intimate-partner violence in the world (Mathews et al. 2004; Abrahams et al. 2012) but that it has among the world's highest reported murder rates too (UNODC 2014; Kriegler & Shaw 2016).

President Zuma's claim also contradicted his own assertions. In 2006 he told a large gathering that 'same sex marriage is a disgrace to the nation and to God. When I was growing up, 'ungqingili[7] could not stand in front of me, I would knock him out' (SAPA 2006). The inference was not just that Zuma was homophobic, but that he supported violence as a means to express his homophobia, despite sexual orientation being a constitutionally protected right. The statement was made on Heritage Day, a holiday celebrating the country's history and culture. While Zuma did not intend it thus, violence is a firmly established part of the country's heritage. Zuma himself was in 2006 tried for the rape of Fezeka Ntsukela Kuzwayo, the daughter of his close friend. He told the court she had led him on with her attire, and was acquitted.

In 2011 the trusted *Mail & Guardian* cited a source claiming that Zuma had appointed Bheki Cele as national police commissioner to build a 'mature, visible police force that brought back its fear factor . . . [and portrayed an image] that says the police must be feared and respected' (Tabane 2011).

Other leaders have publicly romanticised violence. In March 2013 the MEC for Education in the Eastern Cape, Mandla Makupula, told school learners that they did not have any rights. Referring to a learner who had taken his father to court because he did not want to go to initiation school (preparation for circumcision and 'manhood'), he told learners, 'I wish he could have been my child, I would have hit him on the head with a *knobkerrie* and he would have gone to that initiation school crying' (John 2013). The department defended his comments, saying:

> The MEC recognised that this was an engagement with young people with a limited attention span, it was important that his remarks were interspersed with a high level of humour and reference to day-to-day experiences.
>
> (Carlisle 2013)

But this defence is equally emblematic of the problem. It unintentionally acknowledges that violence is a common part of young South Africans' lives, and presents it as humorous. A 2013 victim survey of almost 6,000 school learners found that half had been caned or spanked at school by an educator in the previous year, and 12 percent had been threatened with violence by someone at school (Burton & Leoschut 2013).

A 2015 victim survey of 5,000 15 to 17 year olds found that 33 percent had been hit, beaten, or kicked by an adult; 20 percent had been sexually abused; 23 percent had witnessed violence perpetrated by an adult caregiver against a sibling or another adult in the household; 19 percent had been attacked without a weapon and 16 percent attacked with a weapon. Twenty-six percent had been robbed, and 45 percent had been victims of theft (Artz et al. 2016). An unrelated social audit of 244 schools in 2015 found that learners were beaten at 83 percent of the schools, and that beatings were daily occurrences at 37 percent of these (Equal Education 2016). Life history interviews with South African repeat violent offenders suggest that the violence of their crimes has roots in these early childhood experiences (Gould 2015).

In the run-up to the country's 2016 municipal elections at least 20 people were killed in what appeared to be politically motivated assassinations (de Haas 2016). In the same year, a review of 711 cases of child death found that murder was the second most common cause, and accounted for 53 percent of deaths among 15 to 17 year olds. Abuse and neglect accounted for 11 percent of child deaths (Mathews et al. 2004, 2016). Considering that South Africa's recorded murder rate (as a proxy for other violence) was close to a four-decade low, these figures hint at an astoundingly violent society. Child abuse in the country is predicted by the precarious states in which millions of people live, marked by poverty, AIDS-related stigma, bullying, school non-attendance and achievement, sexual abuse, caregiver disability, inconsistent discipline, family conflict, and living with a step-parent (Meinck et al. 2015).

Many SAPS officers are the products of such childhoods, as are the offenders against whom they define themselves. In such contexts, police work involves the perpetual bandaging of a wound that never stops bleeding. While the SAPS and broader government regularly emphasise efforts to protect women and children, the president and MEC's utterances, together with the above data, contradict these claims.

Similar contradictions are evident in South Africa's post-1994 criminal justice policies. While the death penalty was abolished with apartheid, it was replaced with a slew of harsh minimum sentences and steep increases in incarceration, alongside progressive child and restorative justice legislation (Muntingh 2009; Super 2013). Based on 2015 data, the World Prison Brief estimated that South Africa had the 35th highest imprisonment rate in the world (World Prison Brief 2016).

These policies have emerged in a context in which government has struggled to balance its commitments to human and constitutional rights with South Africans' fear-driven lust for punishment. Seventy-five percent of 18 to 34 year olds surveyed in 2013 supported the reinstatement of the death penalty (SAPA 2013a), while vigilante and xenophobia-related violence and murder are common.

In 2015, 37 percent of South Africans avoided public spaces for fear of victimisation, and 69 percent felt unsafe walking in their area of residence after dark (StatsSA 2015). Seventy-seven percent believed government was doing badly at reducing crime and 53 percent feared being a victim of crime in their own home. South Africans see crime as the second most important priority government should address, after unemployment (Afrobarometer 2016). As illustrated in Chapter 3, this fear erodes trust between South Africans (Afrobarometer 2013, 2016; Mmotlane et al. 2010).

In a context of fear and pervasive violence, it is perhaps unsurprising that South African men who find themselves working for the SAPS tolerate or encourage the use of violence to beat respect into others. Julia Hornberger offers further insight on the matter. Exploring attempts to introduce human rights policing to the SAPS at the turn of the century, and having observed the normalisation of violence in daily policing, she suggests that SAPS officers resort to violence because they lack the personal reference points required to position themselves in the middle-class, human rights-oriented front stage proposed in SAPS policies. Instead, she writes:

> Most police officers [invest] in the backstage [which allows] them to get respect from colleagues ... The image of potency allowed by the backstage has helped police officers to remain motivated and avoid feelings of humiliation and inadequacy ... [which arise] where formal education standards are missing, where promotions have come to a halt, where challenges to masculine identity are seen as threatening, where the difference between middle-class values and police officers' bias towards lower and working-class values becomes insurmountable.
>
> (Hornberger 2011:126)

As already suggested, many officers did not agree with their colleagues' abuse of force. Many told themselves that respect was earned by treating people empathetically and respectfully. Focus groups and social attitude surveys suggest that this procedural justice-like approach is what most South Africans want (Bradford et al. 2013; Faull 2011). But the organisational script which says *violence earns respect* appears stronger than its alternatives. Many of those I shadowed seemed to believe it their role to punish.

In the next section I offer three narratives through which SAPS officers justify the violence they deploy. I suggest that amidst the precarity of life, violence is a tool through which officers validate their place in the world as they strive to become ontologically secure.

## Explaining violence: masculinity, the 'good old days', and 'peanuts'

In Chapter 2 I suggested that the gaze of most SAPS officers is trained on the bodies of poor, young, Black men. They stop them, search them, and mark them incessantly. They ritually enact the archetypal roles of hero versus villain, cop versus crook, and *man versus man*. Whitehead suggests that in contexts where a man's sense of being a man comes into conflict with another man *as a man*:

> Violence by [either man] may be regarded as functional in maintaining an idealised and internalised sense of manhood in the face of external realities that point to his inability to do so.
>
> (2005:415)

I am not suggesting that all male officers are inherently violent, nor that those who are represent a hegemonic masculinity (Connell & Messerschmidt 2005) against which all other male officers measure themselves – although they might. Morrell et al. note that violence in South Africa is commonly used by men, but that this does not mean it is part of a national hegemonic masculinity (2013). Rather, it is the context in which violence is practised – in this case the police organisational context – that can establish violence as a legitimate part of hegemonic masculinity, while outside the organisational realm the violence might be considered illegitimate. In many respects, joining a police organisation compels officers to accept, and prepare for the likelihood that they may have to use force in their work, even if they have no history of violence. It is not difficult, particularly in contexts of precarity, to imagine occupational violence seeping into officers' private and social lives.

Another explanation for the acceptance of violence in the SAPS is found in a common organisational narrative that suggests that because apartheid's police could shoot at will, and at times used whips and batons in their work, crime was controlled and police were respected. While emerging evidence suggests that violent crime was no less common during apartheid (outside White space) than it is in 2017 (Kriegler & Shaw 2016; Super 2013), the belief that it was, and that police were obeyed out of fear, is common. These sentiments, shared by many of the officers I shadowed, are captured in the following excerpt from a 2009 interview, which I conducted with a warrant officer in Pretoria:

> Crime is out of control. If they manage to change Section 49 [so that police can shoot more easily], we will be back where we were before. The reason we are where we are is that the criminals have no respect for us. They have far too much leeway; they have far too many rights in this country. Our hands are literally tied behind our backs. I'm not saying we should go out and shoot and kill everyone running around, but they need to give us back our respect. When they give us back our respect, the crime rate will come down.
>
> (Faull 2010:117–118)

It is easy to idealise the past. Despite most officers acknowledging the abuses of apartheid's police, both Black and White, they still imagine the old South African Police *force* as one characterised by meritocracy, justice, and respect. In contrast, some current police have only negative things to say about their colleagues, managers, and the SAPS. Many disrespect and distrust the people they share offices with, as well as the public they serve.

In Chapter 4, I suggested that SAPS recruits revise their self-narratives when they take up their posts. Before joining the SAPS, they looked down on police, but once inside they re-wrote their self-narratives in efforts to silence the voices of contradiction in their heads. 'Once you're inside, you find you like it,' they told me, and I believed them. But this did not mean their employment significantly altered the precarity from which they were recruited. They may have changed their views of the SAPS, but it was unlikely that their friends and family had.

Consider once more that none of the officers I asked wanted their children to join the SAPS. Instead they stressed the importance of education as the key to 'better' employment. Steinberg found the same idealisation of education in the Johannesburg police he shadowed (2008). In that and subsequent work (Steinberg 2012) he suggested that some South Africans, in some contexts, do not consent to being policed by the SAPS. We know that identity is constituted through interaction with others (Jenkins 2008), so for SAPS officers to have their occupational identities challenged (i.e. their claim to represent the state and their deserving respect) is to challenge their sense of self. A challenge to their authority must, no matter how fleetingly, compel them to re-examine their self-narratives, and those they use to understand the world around them. A common product of such re-examination is that the South African public does not respect its police.

I have mentioned that some officers told me that when off duty they would not tell people that they worked for the SAPS. They suggested the information would put them in danger. The same justification was given by officers who chose not to travel to work wearing their police uniform, despite it allowing them free travel on buses and trains, and despite complaints that they did not have the money to live the lives they wanted to live. While there is some substance to their fears, it is also possible that some did not wear uniforms because they felt ashamed. For instance, in 2009 I interviewed a colonel who told me:

> It's becoming embarrassing for me when I am at a private place, for instance at church, and they ask me, 'What do you do?' and I say, 'I am a police officer.' You can immediately see for yourself – these people, if you don't know them well, they will immediately withdraw a bit and think you are corrupt, or illiterate, or a poor performer. It's sad that that's the association with the police.
>
> (Faull 2010:177–178)

I have repeatedly emphasised the precarity from which many SAPS officers are recruited, and the dreams they abandon or defer to their children once employed in the organisation. And yet, despite their apparent sacrifices, securing a comparable job in the SAPS was more than would have been possible to most under apartheid. Of course, to expect officers to be grateful for this is to ignore their humanity. In the *new* South Africa, high school students are told they live in a meritocracy; that they are the authors of their own lives and can accomplish whatever they set their minds to. Beginning basic training in the SAPS, however, signalled to many that this was a lie. For them, accepting the job meant accepting they had been misled. They took the job because it offered the best security and income they could find. Ironically, working for the SAPS requires that officers contain the frustrations, anger, and rage of tens of thousands of other South Africans who have not been as lucky. These are people who, each year, take to the streets in protest; shut down mines and factories, bring city transport and garbage collection to a standstill, block major freeways and force universities to close, all to demand the good life promised by democracy. Given a different roll of the dice, those in uniform would have been those in the crowds of protestors.

Despite officers' awareness of their fortune, it is common for them to complain that they earn 'peanuts'. In 2009 I interviewed a young constable who, in justifying his corruption, told me:

> The SAPS must give members decent salaries to survive. More importantly, though, we need a shelter. I can't provide for my family; that is a problem. I live with my wife and my child. My wife does not work. I have three children. The sad part of it all is that I live in a shack. It is hard for me. I've lived in the shack for three years – my whole police career. I spend my money just paying the rent.
>
> (Faull 2010:208)

At the time, I did not think the constable was being honest with me. I knew what constables earned and knew it was far more than most South Africans. And yet,

I was very familiar with both the organisational and public mantra: 'We can't expect much from our police because they are paid so little.' It has long struck me as one of the few subjects on which South Africans and police officers seem to agree.

In 2006, I compared the salaries of teachers, nurses, fire fighters and police officers to test the claim that police were underpaid. Contrary to popular belief, I found that police consistently earned more money than these allied professions (Faull 2007), yet there was little comparable public sympathy for the others, with the possible exception of teachers. Since then, SAPS salaries have continued to increase at a rate above inflation, while officers continue to complain that they earn 'peanuts'. I heard this many times in 2012/13.

What frustrated me when officers lectured me about how little they were paid was that, compared to most South Africans, they earned very good money. This does not mean they do not deserve better remuneration or conditions of employment, and I know that many would take issue with a well-remunerated White academic suggesting that SAPS officers should be content with their pay. And yet, one cannot ignore that compared to most South Africans, police are well paid. Their incomes and benefits are particularly good if one considers that recruits need only a high-school completion certificate and driver's licence to qualify for the job.

One attempt to define the middle class, though perhaps a more accurate term would be 'middle income' in South Africa, pointed to an 'actual [household] median' of R3,036 (£167) per month and an 'actual middle', accounting for 31 percent of the population, as R1,520–R4,560 (£83–£250) per month based on 2008 data (Visagie & Posel 2013). Visagie describes the 'relatively affluent middle', accounting for another 31 percent of the population, as those earning between R5,600–R40,000 (£307–£2,195) a month (Visagie 2013).

By comparison, in 2006, SAPS constables received a starting salary of R5,916 (£325) per month (Faull 2007), with an additional 17 percent cash equivalent in housing, clothing, medical and pension contributions, and a thirteenth cheque. By June 2010, this figure stood at R8,461 (£464) per month with the same benefits (SSSBC 2011) and, by 2013, officers told me it was approximately R12,000 (£659). These incomes place entry-level SAPS officers firmly in the 'relatively affluent middle' income group.

In contrast, the 2011 national census showed that the average annual income for a female-headed household was R67,330 (£3,695), and R128,329 (£7,043) for male-headed households. Combined, the average household earned R103,204 (£5,664) per year (StatsSA 2014). However, these figures are misleading. South Africa's wealth is not evenly distributed. In 2013, 50 percent of SAPS employees were classified as *Male African* and 29.4 percent as *Female African* (SAPS 2013:175). Census data shows that amongst these groups, average income was significantly lower at R60,000 (£3,293) per year (StatsSA 2014). Similarly, 10.6 percent of the SAPS workforce was classified *Coloured* (SAPS 2013:175). The census shows that, in 2011, Coloured female-headed households earned an average of R51,440 (£2,823) and Coloured male-headed households R112,172 (£6,157). This data show that 90 percent of the SAPS workforce, on average, earns significantly more than the national median, based only on starting salaries.

In 2016, a government advisory panel assembled to consider the feasibility of a national minimum wage, recommended an amount of just R3,500 (£193) a month. It noted that 51 percent of all residents lived on less than R1,036 (£57) per month in 2016, and that a minimum wage of R3,500 would exceed the income of 47 percent of the country's workforce (National Minimum Wage Panel 2016).

A constable's starting salary is twice the average income of an African male-headed household and four times as much as the poorest 50 percent of South Africans earn. And yet, as Visagie points out, 'the middle group in South Africa, comprising 4.2 million households, is quite poor,' and 'The relatively affluent middle class still includes, in its lower ranges, households with a very moderate level of income, i.e. R5 600 total income per household per month' in 2008 (Visagie 2013). While even the lowest ranking SAPS officers sit above this 'very moderate' pay range, it may be fair to describe theirs as a modest income.

Despite having thought plenty about SAPS salaries over the previous decade, it was only during my 2012/13 fieldwork that I appreciated them in context. As I accompanied officers to and from their homes before and after shifts, it became clear that many continued to live in relative poverty. While police salaries are very good compared to national averages, they are hardly sufficient when an officer is the sole breadwinner responsible for the support of unemployed parents, siblings, and children, often split between two provinces (as sketched in Chapter 4). This is particularly true if a constable is city-based and aspires, like Young's vulnerable late-modern subjects (Young 2007), to consume his or her way out of what can be the humiliation of poverty and precarity.

*

SAPS officers walk precarious paths marked by financial aspiration and struggle, together with frequent misrecognition from the public. These factors inform police violence.

David Bruce has suggested that many South Africans suffer low self-esteem and insecurity about their social status, and that this feeds the country's high levels of inter-personal violence, particularly that perpetrated by men. Citing research that correlates low self-esteem and an inflated sense of self-worth as drivers of aggression, he suggests that the most disadvantaged will not necessarily be the most violent (Bruce 2006). Similarly, Gilligan has convincingly suggested that any form of violence is motivated by feelings of shame and a desire to replace it with pride (1996, 2000). Echoing Young (1999, 2007), Gilligan notes that violence is almost always enacted by those who have been socially shamed by the structure and condition of the society in which they live. In other words, where the unemployed, an ethnic group, or the disabled are marginalised within a stratified society, they may be primed for violence to regain self-esteem. This is particularly true among men in social systems that prescribe clear gender roles, and in unequal societies. South Africa is a quintessential example of an unequal society in which men are celebrated for being brave, aggressive, virile providers, and where women have historically been expected to serve them. When these men fail to live up to societal expectations, such as when failing to secure gainful employment, and if they have not been taught alternative coping mechanisms, they may resort to violence to reclaim self-esteem.

Giddens writes that shame is the manifestation of anxiety emerging from attempts to sustain a cohesive sense of self. As such, shame bears directly on personal identity (Giddens 1991). Giddens contrasts shame with guilt, suggesting that the former is about integrity of the self, while the latter is derived only from feelings of wrongdoing. While SAPS officers might know their abuse of force is wrong, guilt may be less threatening to their sense of self than shame, and shame could manifest in the absence of respect-generating violence.

Giddens cites Lewis, suggesting *bypassed shame* is born of unconscious anxieties of self and feelings of ontological insecurity, consisting of repressed fears that one's self-narrative cannot withstand the pressures on its coherence or social acceptability. In short, he argues, pride comes from a self-narrative that can be sustained, while shame manifests where narratives crack under social interrogation. The latter includes lack of coherence of ideals, the inability to find anything worthy of pursuit, as well as instances in which goals are too demanding to be attained (Giddens 1991). One might imagine that these manifest in the lives of South Africans younger than 40 who find themselves working in the SAPS, having previously never imagined themselves doing such work. Such anxieties are likely amplified by what Sarah Henkeman has called the *invisible violence* of Black South African life. By this she means the symbolic, structural, psychological, and physical harm caused to Black South Africans living in a society still structured around Whiteness (Henkeman 2016). Most SAPS officers will have experienced invisible violence for much of their lives, though few will have named it thus. Nevertheless, it is the product of the precarity with which they are so familiar.

Invisible violence primes young men for physical violence, which may be triggered by environments such as those in the SAPS. In addition to the attitudes towards police violence and the acts of police violence already described, the fact that, in 2014/15, 10 percent of SAPS employees were treated for depression and post-traumatic stress (SAPS 2016a), and that 26 percent of officer deaths between March 2012 and December 2015 were suicides (SAPS 2016b), hints at this anxiety, shame, and invisible violence.

It is plausible that some SAPS officers experience emasculation and shame amidst the tensions between their personal and occupational lives. This is likely most pronounced among African officers, many of whom are drawn from the margins of the working poor and are most likely to be sole breadwinners responsible for the sustenance of extended social networks. African men comprise most of the SAPS workforce, followed by African women.

Of course, masculinities in South Africa are not neatly delineated by race. Reflecting on, and generalising, the violence of White male SAPS officers, Schiff suggests that:

The need to conform to strong cultural standards of masculinity within the context of the police can lead to a severely restricted coping repertoire that is unable to conceive of solutions to problems other than within a narrow range of behaviours that are mostly rooted in violence.

(2010: 370)

Male SAPS officers who, in general, have been raised with the expectation that they must provide for their families (and extended families) find they are unable to do so. They have failed in the most intimate of spheres, because they cannot realise the successful life they and society expects of them, and they feel disrespected in the most public of spheres, because they wear the blue of the SAPS. This compounded emasculation echoes that experienced by African men in the colonial and apartheid eras. Separated from home and family, and emasculated by exploitative labour and socio-economic inequities, many asserted their masculinity and sought to reclaim their self-esteem through violence (Morrell 1998; Breckenridge 1998). It seems that some of these patterns continue in the SAPS. Some police seek respect and self-esteem through violence at work, against a backdrop of inequality, precarity, unmet expectations, emasculation, and liminality.

This is not to say that many officers are not proud of their occupation and organisation, or that only shame motivates police violence. Violence in South Africa is endemic. It has been normalised over many decades, by state and family, home, and the school. What I have suggested here, however, is that there is a link between the tens of thousands of officers whose middle-class aspirations have been left unmet, and the violence some deploy during their duties. Despite their relatively good incomes, the weight of the country's history holds them back. This manifests most clearly in their responsibilities to disempowered social networks. In an organisation with a long history of violence and secrecy, the SAPS provides these officers a stage on which to enact performances that remind them that there is little more manly than beating another man into submission. Ironically, they are performances strikingly similar to those through which Cape Town's gang members strive to secure their own dignity (Jensen 2008; Pinnock 2016).

There can be little doubt that South Africa's crime and violence are closely related to the country's inability to provide most people, particularly young men, with respectable employment and livelihoods. It is a society that shames people for things over which they have little control, and the shame feeds a culture of violence. Police recruits are often the victims and perpetrators of violence before they join the SAPS, including the invisible. Some continue to use violence in their private lives many years after becoming police officers.

Joining the SAPS does not immediately wash away the shame with which elements of South African society paint its aspirant poor. For some officers, shame takes new forms but remains part of their personal narratives. They must carry out dirty work for an organisation they once looked down upon, and must re-author their personal narratives if they are to make themselves clean. In these new narratives, shame might spark a violence resembling that of the young men against whom officers believe they are pitted, men whose personal narratives and histories are not dissimilar from their own before they joined the SAPS.

Police in democratic societies are given the authority to use reasonable force to maintain order, and to keep people and property safe. But their ability to use force also means they pose a threat to the safety of people and property (Bittner 1970; Young 1991; Loader & Walker 2007; Manning 2010). If extra-legal force is normalised in the SAPS, if violence becomes a tool through which the shamed build self-esteem against those similarly shamed, then the SAPS will continue to struggle to win the respect of the South African public. This lack of respect will in turn shape the personal narratives of its officers.

*

I spent the afternoon of 28 March 2013 hanging around the Gompo station chatting to a group of constables. The radio was on in the background and the news was being read in Xhosa. I heard the word, *amapolisa*[8] and the name *Andries Tatane*. The constables cheered.

Tatane was a teacher, community leader, and protestor who died at a service delivery protest in Ficksburg in February 2011, following a beating by SAPS officers. The beating was captured by television cameras and seven police officers were charged with his murder. More than two years later a news reader was announcing the outcome of their trial. The constables told me the police had been found not guilty, and that was why they were celebrating.

I struggled to understand why they were happy. A father and teacher who believed his community deserved better access to water had lost his life, and the SAPS image had been tarnished, yet again. But Constable Mbelani was grinning broadly, 'There was no evidence those police did anything,' he told me.

Perhaps I shouldn't have been surprised. The event was an international and national embarrassment to the SAPS. In the eyes of the constables, the organisation, and, by association, themselves, had been shamed by it. That afternoon, they believed, they had been vindicated.

I walked outside and looked up the news on my smart phone to see what else I could learn. The officers had not simply been found 'not guilty' as the constables had claimed. Rather, they had been acquitted after what appeared to be lies and false testimony from police, and poor prosecution by the state (Gilmore 2013). But Constable Mbelani and his colleagues were on a roll; they had moved on to talk about Marikana, 'I can tell you those police will get off, too, Andrew. They were allowed to shoot. Just you wait and see. I'll call you the day they get off and tell you so.'

When, after 18 months of hearings the Farlam Commission released its report on the massacre, its findings were not dissimilar to those of the Tatane trial. The Commission found that SAPS officers, including top management, conspired and lied to protect officers and the SAPS image and so save themselves further shame. By early 2017 no officers had been criminally charged for the events at Marikana. Rather, the SAPS continued to use Twitter and Facebook to present itself as a rational, evidence-based, professional police service, carrying out common-sense tasks to make South Africa safe.

## Notes

1　Earlier versions of this chapter appeared in the June 2013 edition of *South African Crime Quarterly* (no.44, pp. 5–14) under the title 'Fighting for respect: violence, masculinity and legitimacy in the SAPS', and as a book chapter in J. Beek et al., 2017, *Police in Africa: the street level view*, Hurst: London.

2　While there appears to have been an attempt by police management to avoid such rhetoric since Marikana, on April 16, 2014 it was once again reported that a senior politician had called on police to 'shoot to kill'. According to a major news channel the Premier of KwaZulu-Natal, Senzo Mchunu, told a gathering of Richmond community members that 'Anyone who will turn their guns against the police we are saying police will be left with no alternative. They will have to shoot them; shoot at such criminals dead. That's how we need to fight crime in South Africa' (ENCA 2014).

3　Shut your mouth, you cunt!

4　A little later, when Constable Botile stopped the car to flirt with an unwilling woman walking in the street, Cethe again joked, 'Andrew, you must not see these things.'

5　No.

6　Hits, slaps, punches.

7　Homosexuals in Zulu.

8　Police.

## References

Abrahams, N., Mathews, S., Jewkes, R., Martin, L.J., & Lombard, C., 2012. Research Brief: Every eight hours: Intimate femicide in South Africa 10 years later! Available at: www.mrc.ac.za/policybriefs/everyeighthours.pdf.

Abrahams, N., Jewkes, R., Martin, L.J., Mathews, S., Vetten, L., & Lombard, C., 2009. Mortality of Women From Intimate Partner Violence in South Africa: A National Epidemiological Study. *Violence and Victims*, 24(4), pp. 546–556.

Afrobarometer, 2013. *Summary of Results: Afrobarometer Round 5 Survey in South Africa*, Cape Town, South Africa. Available at: http://afrobarometer.org/sites/default/files/publications/Summary of results/saf_r5_sor.pdf.

Afrobarometer, 2016. *Summary of Results: Afrobarometer Round 6 Survey in South Africa, 2015*, Johannesburg, South Africa. Available at: http://afrobarometer.org/sites/default/files/publications/Summary of results/saf-r6-sor.pdf.

Artz, L., Burton, P., Ward, C., Leoschut, L., Phyfer, J., Loyd, S., & Kassanjee, R., 2016. *Research Bulletin: The Optimus Study on Child Abuse, Violence and Neglect in South Africa*, Cape Town: Centre for Justice and Crime Prevention. Available at: www.cjcp.org.za/uploads/2/7/8/4/27845461/cjcp_ubs_proof_18.pdf.

Bittner, E., 1970. *The Functions of the Police in Modern Society: A Review of Background Factors, Current Practices, and Possible Role Models*, Rockville, MD: National Institute of Mental Health, Center for Studies of Crime and Delinquency.

Bottoms, A. & Tankebe, J., 2012. Crimilogy Beyond Procedural Justice: A Dialogic Approach to Legitimacy. *The Journal of Criminal Law & Criminology*, 102(1), pp. 119–170.

Bradford, B., Murphy, K. & Jackson, J., 2014. Officers as Mirrors. *British Journal of Criminology*, 54(4), pp. 527–550.

Bradford, B., Huq, A., Jackson, J., & Roberts, B., 2013. What Price Fairness When Security Is at Stake? Antecedents of Police Legitimacy in South Africa. *Regulation and Governance*, 8, pp. 246–268.

Breckenridge, K., 1998. The Allure of Violence: Men, Race and Masculinity on the South African Goldmines, 1900–1950. *Journal of Southern African Studies*, 24(4), pp. 669–693.

Bruce, D., 2006. Racism, Self-esteem and Violence in SA: Gaps in the NCPS' explanation? *South African Crime Quarterly*, 14, pp. 34–35.

Burton, P. & Leoschut, L., 2013. *Results of the 2012 National School Violence Study*, Cape Town. Available at: www.cjcp.org.za/uploads/2/7/8/4/27845461/monograph12-school-violence-in-south_africa.pdf.

Carlisle, A., 2013. Rights Groups Take On Education MEC. *Dispatch Live*. Available at: www.dispatchlive.co.za/news/2013/03/14/rights-groups-take-on-education-mec/.

Cockcroft, T., 2013. *Police Culture: Themes and Concepts*, New York and London: Routledge.

Collins, A., 2013. Violence Is Not a Crime: A Broader View of Interventions for Social Safety. *South African Crime Quarterly*, 43, pp. 29–37.

Connell, R.W. & Messerschmidt, J.W., 2005. Hegemonic Masculinity: Rethinking the Concept. *Gender & Society*, 19(6), pp. 829–859.

CSVR, 2010. Why South Africa Is So Violent and What Should Be Done About It: Statement by the Centre for the Study of Violence and Reconciliation. *Centre for the Study of Violence and Reconciliation*. Available at: www.issafrica.org/crimehub/uploads/CSVRstatement091110.pdf.

de Haas, M., 2016. The Killing Fields of KZN. *SA Crime Quarterly*, (57), pp. 43–53.

ENCA, 2014. Premier Tells Police to Shoot to Kill. *eNCA*. Available at: www.enca.com/south-africa/premier-tells-police-shoot-kill.

Equal Education, 2016. Of 'Loose Papers and Vague Allegations': A Social Audit of the Safety and Sanitation Crisis in Western Cape Schools. Available at: https://equaleducation.org.za/wp-content/uploads/2016/09/Executive-Summary-Western-Cape-Schools-Safety-and-Sanitation-Social-Audit-Report.pdf.

Faull, A., 2007. Corruption and the South African Police Service. A review and its implications. *Institute for Security Studies Papers*, (150), p. 20. Available at: http://reference.sabinet.co.za/webx/access/electronic%7B_%7Djournals/ispaper/ispaper%7B_%7Dn150.pdf.

Faull, A., 2010. *Behind the Badge: The Untold Stories of South Africa's Police Service Members*. Cape Town: Zebra Press.

Faull, A., 2011. *Civilian Perceptions and Experiences of Corruption and the South African Police Service*, Pretoria. Available at: https://issafrica.s3.amazonaws.com/site/uploads/Paper226.pdf.

Faull, A., 2013. Policing Taverns and Shebeens: Observation, Experience and Discourse. *South African Crime Quarterly*, 46, pp. 35–48.

Faull, A. & Rose, B., 2012. *Professionalism and the South African Police Service*, Pretoria. Available at: https://issafrica.s3.amazonaws.com/site/uploads/Paper240.pdf.

Giddens, A., 1991. *Modernity and Self-Identity: Self and Society in the Late Modern Age*, Cambridge: Polity Press.

Gilligan, J., 1996. *Violence: Our Deadly Epidemic and its Causes*, New York: GP Putman's & Sons.

Gilligan, J., 2000. *Violence: Reflections on our Deadliest Epidemic*, London: Jessica Kingsley.

Gilmore, I., 2013. Police Brutality, and the Mass Amnesia that Threatens to Obscure it. *Daily Maverick* (22 July). Available at: www.dailymaverick.co.za/article/2013-07-22-police-brutality-and-the-mass-amnesia-that-threatens-to-obscure-it%7B#%7D. WADVyeB97IU.

Gould, C., 2015. *Beaten Bad: The Life Stories of Violent Offenders*, Pretoria: Institute for Security Studies.

Henkeman, S., 2016. *Basic Guide to a 'Deeper And Longer' Analysis of Violence*. Available at: www.academia.edu/22684176/Basic_guide_to_a_deeper_and_longer_analysis_of_violence.

Holdaway, S., 1983. *Inside the British Police*, Oxford: Blackwell.

Hornberger, J., 2011. *Policing and Human Rights: The Meaning of Violence and Justice in the Everyday Policing of Johannesburg*, Abingdon: Routledge.

Hough, M., Jackson, J., Bradford, B., Myhill, A., & Quinton, P., 2010. Procedural Justice, Trust, and Institutional Legitimacy. *Policing*, 4(3), pp. 203–210. Available at: http://policing.oxfordjournals.org/cgi/doi/10.1093/police/paq027.

Jenkins, R., 2008. *Social Identity*, 3rd edn, London and New York: Routledge.

Jensen, S., 2008. *Gangs, Politics & Dignity in Cape Town*, Chicago, IL: University of Chicago Press.

Jewkes, R.K., Sikweyiya, Y., Morrell, R., & Dunkle, K., 2010. Why, When and How Men Rape. *South African Crime Quarterly*, (34), pp. 25–31.

John, V., 2013. E Cape Minister's Quotes 'Taken Out of Context'. *Mail & Guardian* (13 March). Available at: http://mg.co.za/article/2013-03-13-ec-education-ministers-quotes-taken-out-of-context.

Kriegler, A. & Shaw, M., 2016. *A Citizen's Guide to Crime Statistics in South Africa*, Johannesburg and Cape Town: Jonathan Ball.

Letsela, L. & Ratele, K., 2009. *Masculinity and Perceptions of Risk: Factors to Premature Male Mortality in South Africa*. Available at: www.brothersforlife.org/sites/default/files/docs/Men_and_their_perceptions_of_Risks.pdf.

Loader, I., 2006. Policing, Recognition, and Belonging. *The Annals of the American Academy of Political and Social Science*, 605(Democracy, Crime, and Justice), pp. 202–221. Available at: www.jstor.org/stable/25097805?seq=1#page_scan_tab_contents.

Loader, I. & Walker, N., 2007. *Civilizing Security*, Cambridge: Cambridge University Press.

Loftus, B., 2010. Police Occupational Culture: Classic Themes, Altered Times. *Policing and Society*, 20(1), pp. 1–20.

Manning, P.K., 1978. The Police: Mandate, Strategies, and Appearances. *Policing: A View from the Street*. Culver City: Goodyear Publishing Company.

Manning, P.K., 2010. *Democratic Policing in a Changing World*, Boulder, CO: Paradigm.

Mathews, S. Abrahams, N., Martin, L.J.,Vetten, L., Van der Merwe, L., & Jewkes, R., 2004. *Every Six Hours a Woman is Killed by her Intimate Partner: A National Study of Female Homicide in South Africa*, Cape Town: Medical Research Council. Available at: www.mrc.ac.za/policybriefs/woman.pdf.

Mathews, S., Martin, L.J., Coetzee, D., Scott, C., Naidoo, T., Brijmohun, Y., & Quarrie, K., 2016. The South African Child Death Review Pilot: A Multiagency Approach to Strengthen Healthcare and Protection for Children. *South African Medical Journal*, 106(9), pp. 895–899.

Meinck, F., Cluver, L.D., Boyes, M.E., & Ndhlovu, L.D., 2015. Risk and Protective Factors for Physical and Emotional Abuse Victimisation amongst Vulnerable Children in South Africa. *Child Abuse Review*, 24(3), pp. 182–197.

Mmotlane, R., Struwig, J., & Roberts, B., 2010. *The Glue That Binds or Divides: Social Trust in South Africa*, HSRC Social Attitudes Survey. Available at: www.hsrc.ac.za/uploads/pageContent/1607/Social%20Trust%20in%20South%20Africa.pdf.

Morrell, R., 1998. Of Boys and Men: Masculinity and Gender in Southern African Studies. *Journal of Southern African Studies*, 24(4), pp. 605–630.

Morrell, R., Jewkes, R., Lindegger, G., & Hamlall, V., 2013. Hegemonic Masculinity: Reviewing the Gendered Analysis of Men's Power in South Africa. *South African Review of Sociology*, 44(1), pp. 3–21.

Muntingh, L., 2009. Sentencing. In C. Gould, ed. *Criminal (In)Justice in South Africa: a Civil Society Perspective*. Pretoria: Institute for Security Studies.

National Minimum Wage Panel, 2016. *A National Minimum Wage for South Africa: Recommendations on Policy and Implementation. National Minimum Wage Panel Report To The Deputy President*. Available at: www.treasury.gov.za/publications/other/NMW Report Draft CoP final.pdf.

Pinnock, D., 2016. *Gang Town*, Cape Town: Tafelberg.

Ratele, K., 2008. Masculinity and Male Mortality in South Africa. *African Safety Promotion: A Journal of Injury and Violence Prevention*, 6(2), pp. 19–41.

Reiner, R., 2010. *The Politics of the Police*, 4th edn, Oxford: Oxford University Press.

SAPA, 2006. Zuma Invokes Gay Wrath. *News 24*. Available at: www.news24.com/SouthAfrica/News/Zuma-invokes-gay-wrath-20060926.

SAPA, 2013a. Bring Back Death Penalty: Survey. *Times Live* (22 February). Available at: www.timeslive.co.za/local/2013/02/22/Bring-back-death-penalty-survey1.

SAPA, 2013b. South Africa is Not Violent, Says Zuma. *Mail & Guardian* (7 March). Available at: http://mg.co.za/article/2013-03-07-south-africa-not-a-violent-country-says-zuma.

SAPS, 2013. *Annual Report 2012/13*, Pretoria. Available at: www.saps.gov.za/about/stratframework/annual_report/2012_2013/ar2013_00_front_content.pdf.

SAPS, 2016a. *Employee Helath and Wellness (EHW)*, Pretoria.

SAPS, 2016b. *Risk Management Strategies to Reduce Police Deaths*, Pretoria.

SAPS, 2016c. *South African Police Service Annual Report 2015/16*, Pretoria. Available at: www.saps.gov.za/about/stratframework/annual_report/2015_2016/saps_annual_report_2015_2016.pdf.

Schiff, K.-G., 2010. *Discourses of Workplace Violence: Painting a Picture of the South African Police Service*, Pretoria: University of South Africa. Available at: http://hdl.handle.net/10500/4844.

Seedat, M.,, Van Niekerk, A., Jewkes, R., Suffla, S., & Ratele, K., 2009. Violence and Injuries in South Africa: Prioritising an Agenda for Prevention. *The Lancet*, 374(9694), pp. 1011–1022.

SSSBC, 2011. *Agreement No.2/2011: Agreement on the South African Police Service Rank Structure, Revised Rank Structure and Matters Relating Thereto*. Centurion: Safety and Security Sectoral Bargaining Council. Available at: www.sssbc.org.za/ClientFiles/Documents/agreements/2011/Agreement%202%20of%202011.pdf.

Stanko, B., Jackson, J., Bradford, B., & Hohl, K., 2012. A Golden Thread, a Presence Amongst Uniforms, and a Good Deal of Data: Studying Public Confidence in the London Metropolitan Police. *Policing and Society*, 22(3), pp. 317–331.

StatsSA, 2014. *Transforming the Distributional Regime: Poverty Trends in South Africa: An Examination of Absolute Poverty Between 2006 and 2011*, Pretoria. Available at: http://beta2.statssa.gov.za/publications/Report-03-10-06/Report-03-10-06March2014.pdf.

StatsSA, 2015. *Exploration of Selected Contact Crimes in South Africa: In-Depth Analysis of the Victims of Crime Survey Data*, Pretoria. Available at: www.statssa.gov.za/publications/Report-03-40-03/Report-03-40-032014.pdf.

Steinberg, J., 2008. *Thin Blue: The Unwritten Rules of Policing South Africa*, Jeppestown: Jonathan Ball.

Steinberg, J., 2012. Establishing Police Authority and Civilian Compliance in Post-Apartheid Johannesburg: An Argument from the Work of Egon Bittner. *Policing and Society*, 22(4), pp. 481–495.

Sunshine, J. & Tyler, T.R., 2003. The Role of Procedural Justice and Legitimacy in Shaping Public Support for Policing. *Law and Society Review*, 37(3), pp. 513–548.

Super, G., 2013. *Governing through Crime in South Africa: The Politics of Race and Class in Neoliberalizing Regimes*, Oxford: Routledge.

Tabane, R., 2011. Don't Hold Your Breath for Action on Cele findings. *Mail & Guardian* (11 March). Available at: http://mg.co.za/article/2011-03-11-dont-hold-your-breath-for-action-on-cele-findings.

Tyler, T.R., 2004. Enhancing Police Legitimacy. *The Annals of the American Academy of Political and Social Science*, 593(1), pp. 84–99. Available at: http://ann.sagepub.com/cgi/doi/10.1177/0002716203262627.

UNODC, 2014. *Global Study of Homicide 2013: Trends, Contexts, Data*, Vienna. Available at: www.unodc.org/documents/data-and-analysis/statistics/GSH2013/2014_GLOBAL_HOMICIDE_BOOK_web.pdf.

Vetten, L., 2014. *Rape and Other Forms of Sexual Violence in South Africa*. Available at: https://issafrica.s3.amazonaws.com/site/uploads/PolBrief72.pdf.

Visagie, J., 2013. *Who are the Middle Class in South Africa? Does It Matter For Policy?* Available at: www.econ3x3.org/article/who-are-middle-class-south-africa-does-it-matter-policy.

Visagie, J. & Posel, D., 2013. A Reconsideration of What and Who Is Middle Class in South Africa. *Development Southern Africa*, 30(2), pp. 149–167. Available at: www.tandfonline.com/doi/abs/10.1080/0376835X.2013.797224.

von Holdt, K., 2010. Nationalism, Bureaucracy and the Developmental State: The South African Case. *South African Review of Sociology*, 41(1), pp. 4–27. Available at: www.tandfonline.com/doi/abs/10.1080/21528581003676010.

Walker, N., 2002. Policing and the Supranational. *Policing and Society*, 12(4), pp. 307–321.

Whitehead, A., 2005. Man to Man Violence: How Masculinity May Work as a Dynamic Risk Factor. *The Howard Journal of Criminal Justice*, 44(4), pp. 411–422. Available at: http://doi.wiley.com/10.1111/j.1468-2311.2005.00385.x.

World Prison Brief, 2016. *Prison Population Rate*. Available at: www.prisonstudies.org/highest-to-lowest/prison_population_rate?field_region_taxonomy_tid=All.

Young, J., 1999. *The Exclusive Society*, London: Sage.

Young, J., 2007. *The Vertigo of Late Modernity*, London: Sage.

Young, M., 1991. *An Inside Job: Policing and Police Culture in Britain*, Oxford: Oxford University Press.

# Chapter 6

# Individualism, transgression, coercion, and hope

## Intricate legacies

The South African state wants citizens to view SAPS officers as law enforcers, crime fighters, and people who lead by example.[1] But South African police are first and foremost private citizens in pursuit of ontological security. Like other South Africans, they navigate the laws of the land, and adapt their habits so their lives are most tolerable, stable, and enjoyable, with the least threat of sanction (e.g. Manning 1997). This, in part, is why officers are happy to support SAPS front stage performances. It makes their lives easier.

This chapter focuses on select behaviours enacted by officers on and off duty, with a focus on their misdemeanours. I suggest that officers are more respectful of rules and order where these are already established in the affluent city, and actively negate rules and order where they are weak, in the township and rural town. They show respect to those above them in the income-class hierarchy, and contempt of those below them. Put another way, they lack restraint, only tempering certain behaviours when coerced to do so by affluent environments.

I link this relationship with coercion to the way South Africa was governed and policed during apartheid. I suggest that by inserting itself into the intimacies of people's lives (their right to work, movement, education, sex and marriage) the apartheid state shaped a society accustomed to coercive governance. The informal providers of security, and the general anti-state rebellion that emerged in the late seventies and eighties (Steinberg 2008, 2012; Shaw 2002; Super 2013), combined with the many unmet expectations promised by democracy, has left many South Africans, including police, open to rule breaking where personal comfort or gain is more likely than sanction.

However, not all is bleak. I then explore some of the ways off-duty officers try to improve their home communities. I suggest that these acts – the positive and negative – prefigure officers' desire for upward mobility in a precarious society, and that they reveal a cognitive dissonance. Officers long for stability and security for themselves, their children, and those close to them. They are told that their work should help South Africans, including those close to them, achieve such stability and security, but quickly realise that they lack the tools to bring this about. As such, where they can, they retreat to the backstage actions with which they are more comfortable (Hornberger 2011), such as speeding, littering, eating fast food, and violence. These acts, and related talk, disproportionately enacted and uttered outside of middle-class space, become the culture-making acts and words that shape South African society.

This chapter pulls together two themes introduced earlier. First, a job in the SAPS serves a primarily instrumental purpose – it is about survival and upward mobility in an opportunity- and wealth-skewed society. Against these aspirations the *doing* of police work is secondary. Perhaps this is not surprising. Large public bureaucracies the world over are staffed by people trying to balance their obligations to their employer with their personal desires and needs (Lipsky 2010). This can lead to corners being cut, or time stolen, on the job (Vigneswaran & Hornberger 2009) but also to employee fulfilment. Such practices take on a special irony in the police environment where they contradict the state-promoted image of police professionalism, dedication, and efficiency. This is especially true where police transgressions break the law.

Second, coercion in South African life shapes individuals and society. There is a strong sense among SAPS officers that without them the country would descend into violent anarchy. Linked to this is a belief that without coercive deterrence, young, usually poor, Black men will inevitably commit crime. SAPS officers see themselves as a deterrent threat to such men, not only delivered through frequent surveillance, engagement (or harassment), and assault, but also through the provision of *advice*, such as the example offered by Warrant Officer Skrikker in Chapter 1, and by Constable Nzo in Chapter 5.

When I first began researching the SAPS and working as a police reservist in 2004, the frequency of officers' minor abuses of power, actions for personal gain, and open contravention of codes of conduct, ethics, and law astounded me. This remained true of my 2012/13 field work. I have come to believe that SAPS officers feel able to break certain rules for four main reasons : (1) they are broken by many, perhaps most, South Africans at a time in the country's history when individual rights and freedoms, including the freedoms to strive and consume in a patently unjust society, are celebrated; (2) there is little to compel or coerce them not to; (3) a weakness of organisational accountability and sanction has created environments in which minor transgressions are regularly ignored; and (4) South Africans (including police) feel that, if there is no immediate or likely penalty for rule breaking, they are free to break rules. In this chapter I use vignettes to illustrate why I believe this to be true.

## Minor transgressions

Following the parade one morning, Yorkton detective Constable Qoboza invited me to accompany her to court where she needed to deliver dockets. Entering the building, Qoboza walked through the security gate with a confidence that dissuaded security staff from stopping her. By the time she realised that I was not with her she was 10 metres down the corridor. She turned to catch security scanning me with a metal-detecting wand and called out, 'Oh, I forgot that people get searched here. I just walk through.'

The court's corridor was wide, the floor shone with the sparkle of a recent mopping, and the air was cleaning-agent fresh. But the scene was very different behind the closed door of the docket delivery room. While Qoboza exchanged pleasantries and paperwork with the court officer, I tried to compose myself amidst the stench of smoke that hung in the air, both fresh and stale. A uniformed police officer leant against a wall with a cigarette hanging from his lips. The court clerk behind the desk was also smoking.

It was a mundane but paradoxical sight. We were in a court of law, with officers entrusted with enforcing and administrating the law breaking the law. Of course, the law being broken was not criminal, but the acts were contradictory nonetheless. More importantly, these contradictions are indicative of attitudes and behaviours widespread throughout the SAPS. For instance, Mthonjeni's SAPS toilet and urinals were regularly clogged with cigarette butts, evidence of officers who lacked the motivation to leave the building to smoke (as required by law), or to find a rubbish bin. Butts were also left in pot plants in the station's hallway presumably placed there to beautify the otherwise drab environment, but scuppered by the mustard-yellow filters poking from the dark soil. Mthonjeni's detectives also smoked in their offices. All these examples are illegal under the country's Tobacco Products Control Act but were tacitly accepted at the station.

Throughout this book I have described incidents of mundane but unlawful police behaviour, either enacted in my presence or recounted to me. These include:

1   Constable Hendricks choosing to drive a police van without headlights, and ignoring traffic laws while driving it; Yorkton detectives' Snake of Power, which sped across the Cape Flats, ignoring road rules. Both examples are contraventions of the Road Traffic Act.
2   Constable Bhele's story about being robbed by police, in which he claimed to have been so drunk that he failed to notice the police trying to pull him over – contravening the Road Traffic Act and punishable by up to six years in jail or a fine of up to R120,000 (£6,586). It is also an offence the SAPS is tasked with policing.
3   The litter discarded by community outreach patrollers in Mthonjeni when they dropped wads of papers onto the road and into private yards, contravening the City of Cape Town's Dumping and Littering By-Law, and punishable by a fine or up to 60 days in prison.

While two of these infringements are relatively minor, they are still noteworthy. As the most visible representatives of the state on the street, officers' actions shape the spaces and communities in which police work, and so shape the nation.

## Police creating (dis)order: driving and traffic infractions

South African cities spread out across vast distances, the apartheid state having designed them to separate 'population groups' (Mabin & Smit 2010). As a result, it is far more common to see a police car than a police officer on foot. Almost all SAPS patrols are vehicle based. Patrol officers drive white vehicles marked with fluorescent yellow and blue stripes, while detectives drive unmarked, usually white cars. In my experience, the moment an officer enters one of these vehicles, certain road rules become irrelevant. Stop signs and traffic lights are overlooked (particularly in townships); speed limits are almost always exceeded; lane changes take place without indicating; cars are overtaken on the left;[2] safe following distances are ignored; cell phones are answered and text messages typed; and never, ever is a seatbelt worn. I have found this to be true across all ranks and roles, whether responding to a call for assistance, heading to a meeting, or driving to a shop to buy lunch.

If SAPS officers are at their most visible when driving, and if they regularly ignore road rules, one can infer that their actions may encourage similar rule breaking by others. More importantly, however, officers who speed, do not wear safety belts, and disregard road rules place themselves and others in danger. When I asked officers why they did not wear safety belts they told me they needed to be able to leap from vehicles when in danger. They appealed to that dramatic, myth-like and rarely occurring fraction of the police occupation that is privileged over almost all others, skewing expectations placed on police and hiding the mundaneness of their work (e.g. Moskos 2008; Manning 2005).

South African police are some of the greatest contributors to the often panic-laden national discourse on violent crime and the state's response to it. It is through their language, their authority to name and make pronouncements about the state of the country, that officers give life to labels and categories, popularising fear and risk (Loader 1997). In the face of a public perceived as disrespectful, recourse to risk- and fear-laden language validates SAPS officers' views, actions, identities, and place in society.

There were 16,259 murders in South Africa in 2012/13, or 31.3 for every 100,000 residents. SAPS officers summon such figures to emphasise that the country has a serious crime problem, the solutions to which require investment in, and support and respect for police. But where police name and give life to one category of crime or person, they silence others. The scarcity of SAPS officers' acknowledgment of the dangers of South Africa's roads is a clear example: as many people die on the country's roads each year as are murdered. In fact, South Africa has among the highest recorded rates of both murder and road deaths, globally (WHO 2013; World Bank 2016; UNODC 2014). In 2011, 32 South Africans died on the country's roads for every 100,000 residents (WHO 2010). As with murder, one can assume that behind this figure lie thousands more non-fatal injuries. And yet, outside peak holiday periods, road safety does not receive nearly as much public or media attention as crime. This is important.

SAPS officers' disregard for traffic laws is not necessarily linked to the view that their occupation is crime rather than safety focused. But their behaviour is indicative of South African norms and values more broadly. I illustrated this in Chapter 3 when I described the inaction of SAPS and Provincial Traffic officers in the face of dozens of unbuckled safety belts at a road block and various Vehicle Check Points. In that example, ritual behaviour and target chasing replaced simple actions that could have saved lives.

I noted in Chapter 2 that more SAPS officers die in car accidents each year (102 in 2014/15) than are murdered on and off duty (86). And yet far more attention is given to the murders than to the accidents. While there is good reason for this, not least that murder implies intent while accident does not, it hides a major threat to officers' lives. That so many police deaths are the result of traffic accidents should not be surprising to anyone who has spent time in a SAPS vehicle. Anecdotally, yet notably, a Yorkton detective assigned to investigate reckless and negligent driving cases, told me that 30 percent of his investigations involved police. During my time at Mthonjeni and Gompo, brand new vehicles were badly damaged in accidents, which did not involve other vehicles or result from high-speed pursuits. It is likely, then, that these accidents resulted from reckless driving.

Finally, the stickers that held licence discs in place in some SAPS cars read, 'Integrated crime policing road safety strategy. Always wear seat-belts and child restraints!' While the text was intended for those inside the car, its message appeared lost to officers. It was an *internal deception*; an institutional performance ignored by its intended audience. The same was true of 'road safety' posters on the walls of police stations. They espoused the wearing of safety belts and abiding by speed limits, both of which were rare in practice. It is deeply ironic that a police organisation must remind its officers to desist from the most basic and publicly visible offences. But SAPS officers do not only break rules in defence of rules (Brodeur's [2010] summary of the police mandate), some simply break them because they do not believe anybody will care.

## Aspiration and police work across space and place

Upward mobility in a stratified society requires the presentation of social performances that highlight the aspirant individual's familiarity with the values of those to whom they aspire, and downplay their familiarity with those they hope to leave (Goffman 1959; Pinker 2011). The stickers in SAPS vehicles were such a performance; an institutional appeal to middle-class values. But if SAPS officers aspired to be middle class, why was their behaviour at times so incongruent with this desire? Once again, it helps to explore how officers' behaviour changed across space.

Mthonjeni and Yorkton's officers had very different relationships with road rules. In the Mthonjeni policing area, almost no police abided by traffic lights (at least certain lights) or stop streets. Sometimes civilian drivers broke road rules right in front of the police car I was in, suggesting they knew that police did the same and would not act against them. But such actions also communicated disrespect for the SAPS. Despite many officers longing to be shown respect, it seemed not to occur to them that this may be achieved by following and enforcing basic road rules themselves.

When I asked Mthonjeni police why they ignored traffic rules in the area, I was always given the same answer: 'It's the Republic of Mthonjeni; there are no rules.' They did not seem to consider their own agency, let alone their mandate to challenge these practices and shape them differently. Instead they settled into routines that replicated the established disorder of the area.

Ignoring road rules is also about power. Speed and aggressive driving were at times deployed in what appeared to be a show of force, such as the Snake of Power described in Chapter 2 – the convoy of unmarked detective vehicles that swept through the Cape Flats at a terrifying pace. Without police identifiers, the speed and recklessness of the convoy communicated to onlookers that its occupants were entitled, angry, and ready for a fight. When the convoy stopped and armed detectives leapt from cars to push young men up against walls, their actions screamed: '*We know these neighbourhoods and their violence; we live in them, too. But tonight, we are here as The Police. We have risen above our personal struggles. Now we drive nice cars, and drive them as we deem fit. We deploy violence with the backing of the state. We are here to shape your young men into something better.*'

Officers' reckless driving endangered themselves, other road users, and suspects detained along the way. During tracing operations, arrested people would be made to sit on the back seats of detective cars without seatbelts. Men arrested by Yorkton detectives almost always had their hands cuffed behind their backs. Some sat for hours this way, hands trapped, struggling to maintain their balance as the detectives sped and weaved their way through the streets.

The backs of marked police vans are also precarious spaces. With hard metal sides and ceiling, and smooth metal benches without safety belts or hand rails, they are spaces in which bodies are tossed about at the will of the driver. At times, police purposefully drove recklessly so that those detained might be hurt by the combination of speed, inertia, and metal.

While Yorkton's detectives spread disorder across the Cape Flats, Yorkton's patrol officers were significantly more law-abiding on the roads of their precinct; not that stop streets, red lights, and speed limits were never ignored – they were, but not nearly as often as in Mthonjeni. In the Yorkton precinct, officers adapted to the general order and affluence of the area, and to the behaviour of the area's residents, who were significantly more affluent than police.

In the predominantly rural Patterson and Gompo policing areas, road use was understandably different. Most roads were unpaved with few intersections or traffic lights, and very little traffic. Where these existed in Patterson, they were largely ignored. Outside the town and villages, police almost always ignored speed limits. When they came across cattle or animals standing in the middle of the two busiest paved roads in the area, they did not stop to usher them to safety.

Instead, they drove around them. The same was true when the bodies of dead animals, already hit by cars, were found lying in the road. They were ignored. These are examples of how officers did not consider it their role to promote road safety, a great irony when as many people die on South African roads as are murdered.

Across the four types of police space outlined in this book, officers navigated public space in different but consistent ways. When travelling from one type of space to another, they sped. When navigating urban townships or the rural town, they ignored road rules. It was only affluent space that tempered their recklessness, which re-emerged upon return to the Cape Flats and rural villages. Their performances were intended for different audiences, the rich and the poor. To the rich they said '*Look, we can adapt and be like you. Accept us, please.*' To the poor they said, '*We acknowledge the disorder from which we all come. We are part of you, including your struggle. Because we understand you, we will ignore some transgressions, as you will ignore some of ours. But because we understand you, when we need to be hard, we will be very hard.*'

## Creating (dis)order through language

When police officers speed, litter, and drive while drunk, they foster disorder. Their actions pollute the police image and the order which law and policy intends them to shape. But, in addition to shaping order through action, officers shape the social world through the language with which they describe it. Through words, police generate and reinforce the status quo (Loader 2006; Loader & Mulcahy 2003). Whether responding to calls for service; recording witness statements; giving testimony in court; or sharing anecdotes with colleagues, police talk manufactures meaning. This is clearest in the ways officers delineate the socially taboo *skollie* from the respectful, older civilian.

Police talk reveals officers' understandings of their world and work. It divides people into manageable categories, such as *Cape Borners* and *gangster*, and links these to informal rules that guide action (Van Maanen 1979; Holdaway 1983; Fassin 2013). For those deemed unfavourable, actions might include expressions of control and authority, but also (the threat of) violence. Officers draw on these logics to justify their actions and avoid ontologically threatening moral dilemmas (Young 1991; Waddington 1999), while effectively policing the poor and marginalised in defence of the wealthy and powerful.

In Mthonjeni, more than other stations, officers referred to gay men as *moffies*; to White people as *umlungus*; and to people from other African countries as *foreigners, makwere,*[3] *Mogadishu,* or *Somali*. Most *spaza* shops in Mthonjeni were owned and staffed by Somali or Eritrean men. Mthonjeni's CPU patrollers would call out to them from their patrol cars, 'Hey Mogadishu! Hey Somali!' when they wanted to get their attention. When I challenged them on the appropriateness of their language they acknowledged that *makwere* was not a kind word but found no fault in the others. While ostensibly on good terms with shop owners, officers blamed them for their own routine victimisation. Spaza shops which stayed open until 10 or 11 at night, were regularly targeted by armed robbers (e.g. Gastrow 2013; Steinberg 2014). To Mthonjeni's officers, these shops thus threatened to disrupt the good shift, by inviting attack.

In 2008, in another example of the embeddedness of violence and its relationship to precarity in South Africa, pockets of township residents across the country attacked their foreign-born neighbours, killing 62 and forcing hundreds of others to flee their homes. Steinberg has suggested the South Africans were 'finishing a piece of business that the police had begun' years earlier (2011:346), that 'the language used by those who started the violence was one of security and was borrowed from state institutions' (2011:347). Steinberg was referring to the regular police harassment of non-South African Africans as part of the state's efforts to clamp down on illegal immigration, a project which frames foreign Africans as a threat to the livelihoods of poor South Africans. Thus framed, their removal (or attack) is more easily justified.[4]

South Africa deports thousands of 'illegal foreigners' each year: 312,733 in 2007/08; 75,336 in 2011/12; and 131,907 in 2013/14 (DHA 2008, 2013, 2014).[5] 'Taking [such large numbers of] people off the streets in front of an audience of the urban poor begins to carry meaning,' writes Steinberg (2011:355). The meaning is a 'misrecognition' (Loader 2006) of African foreign nationals as legitimate members of the South African community. Every time the officers I shadowed shouted 'Hey Mogadishu!' they reminded all within ear shot that the person they were calling to was different.

I do not believe that when Mthonjeni's officers called to shop owners they intended to disrespect them, but they did. Their words, spoken with smiles, became the curses spat African foreign nationals in Yorkton's police cells. Similarly, talk of *umlungus* and *moffies* revealed a conscious prejudice, and an unconscious ignorance of the power of words in shaping the social world, especially when uttered by highly- visible representatives of the state. They are words that remind listeners of what is new – openly gay men in township streets – and what is old – the relative absence of White people in townships. Their utterance reinforces old divisions and practices, keeping at bay the vision of the *new* country described in South Africa's constitution.

## Individual and occupational worlds

Sometimes officers spoke and acted in ways that marked people as outsiders to the South African community. As with so much else in Yorkton, officers' interactions with African foreign nationals were more tempered than in the township, at least in public. The Yorkton precinct bustles with a diversity of African nationalities and the Yorkton cells were often full of people arrested for being in the country illegally.

African foreign nationals in the Yorkton cells were spoken to by some officers in ways that made clear they were not welcome. Officials from the Department of Home Affairs (DHA) would visit the station to collect residency violators.

When the arrestees complained that their cell phones were missing from their police-confiscated property they were told to check the police stores – something they could not do in the custody of Home Affairs officials, who shouted and swore at them. Police officers joked: 'They are sending you home: you won't need [your missing cell phone] anyway'; 'Come, come, Home Affairs want to send you back to your home countries. They have transport for you'; and 'Going, going, like a Boeing. Don't come back to Cape Town!' While a Home Affairs officer joked with a police officer, 'You must keep this one in the cells. You must kick him. He talks too much,' and to the arrestee 'Fuck you! Shut up! You can stay here.' In these performances, men from one state agency performed for those from another, and for vulnerable non-South African men, whom they sought to belittle. In disrupting the ontology of others, they made their own more secure.

But at other times they participated in events that drew people together. The police *braai* (barbecue) was such an event. On a hot summer's day, I joined officers from one of the stations for a *braai* in an access-controlled public area at Monwabisi beach on the outskirts of Cape Town. It was school holidays and the beach was bustling. The only road into the area was lined with a heavy Metro Police and Law Enforcement presence. All cars entering the area were searched for alcohol, while drivers leaving were checked for sobriety. The message from the City was clear: there would be no drinking at the beach. But of course, there was and it was carried out by the police officers I was meeting.

In contrast to the busy public beach, the access-controlled picnic area chosen by the officers was secluded and empty. Entrance required the payment of a small fee, while beach access was free. As a result, two picnickers and a Law Enforcement car were the only signs of life in the fenced-off area, other than the off-duty SAPS officers and me.

While we *braaied* our meat and drank the alcohol which officers had smuggled in, the Law Enforcement car circled the picnic area's ring road, passing us every 20 minutes. Each time they passed, we hurriedly hid our bottles and glasses.

Two hours into the festivities, the Law Enforcement car, together with a Metro Police car which had entered the area, stopped near our group. Five officers disembarked and approached us. While hurried attempts were made to hide our drinks, it was clear that they knew what was going on, so a new tactic was adopted. Most senior among the City officers was a sergeant. Recognising him as a former SAPS officer, two of our group greeted him jovially, while others in our group began piling meat and salad onto paper plates. Amidst small talk and nervous laughter, the plates were handed over to the City officers together with a large bottle of Coke. With food in hand and stories exchanged, the City Officers returned to their vehicles. As a parting gift the City's sergeant said that if we had any trouble passing the police check point on our way out (as drunk drivers), we should give him a call.

While the City officers ate on the opposite end of the picnic area, the SAPS officers turned their discussion to their brush with the law. The gist of this was that '*All that is required is for one to show them respect. If one respects them they will not take action against you.*' It was respect which the officers I shadowed longed for, and so respect which they so explicitly exhibited when confronted with *The Law* themselves. Respect was central to who officers thought they were, and to how they worked. Its pursuit, however, did not always align with the rules and laws police were tasked with enforcing

As I chewed on my sausage, I noticed the Law Enforcement officers – the people tasked with enforcing the City's litter by-laws, throw their trash over the picnic area's boundary fence into the protected nature reserve on the other side. How easily they, like SAPS officers, traversed the boundary between their personal and occupational lives. Officers of both agencies shifted their performances between compliance with, and defence of rules, to defiance and turning a blind eye to their contravention. In that empty picnic area, the absence of coercive oversight left them free to embrace the agency they acquired through state employment in a starkly unequal democracy.

## Coercion, democracy, and an overflow of power

In Chapter 5, I recounted some of the stories officers shared with me about their use of violence outside work. On occasion, they also shared stories about other criminal activity which they had been involved in, some of which I have already mentioned. These were shared without a sense of guilt, suggesting that they sat comfortably within officers' sense of self.

One such tale was shared by Mthonjeni's Constable Ndungwane while on patrol with two other CPU officers. He first told the story in Xhosa, so the performance was primarily for his colleagues, but he retold it in English once done. He said he had spent the previous rest day with his brother, a tow-truck driver. A Somali man had crashed his *bakkie* into a church wall and died in Khayelitsha, and Ndungwane and his brother had attended the accident scene in the tow truck. In Ndungwane's words:

> I said to my brother, "These Somalis never travel without cash, let's search the car." We found R3,500 (£192) under the mat. We decided that we couldn't keep it because the ancestors would be angry with us, so we had to eat it straight away.

He said they had gone to a tavern and spent the money on expensive alcohol. The moral of the story was only that he was very hung over. Everyone laughed. Nobody commented on the theft.

On another occasion, Ndungwane was lingering outside the station's administration block and ambled over to where I was sitting with Constable Deyi in a patrol car. Leaning through the window he told us he was waiting to see the station's firearms control officer. He said his father-in-law, a taxi driver who owned a firearm, had recently died. Ndungwane wanted to check whether the firearm was registered (legal) so that he could know what to do with it. I asked him if it was not a bit late, as a police officer, to be wondering whether his father-in-law's firearm was legal or not. He laughed my question off and headed inside. A few minutes later he returned to report that the firearm was registered to the government of the former Transkei:

> Only Head Office in Pretoria can deal with it now. I'm not going to worry about that Pretoria stuff though. I'm going to take it to my kraal in the Eastern Cape where I will use it to protect my sheep.

I asked him what would happen if he killed someone using an illegal firearm. Again, he laughed, 'If you kill someone they will become an 'unknown' [a body which police cannot identify].' It was an extraordinary statement to make to a researcher and police colleague. While his bravado was probably exaggerated, his claim to be in possession of an illegal firearm, which he planned to keep, seemed genuine, yet he had no problem speaking to us about it.

Ndungwane's story, like my experience at the *braai*, highlights the blurred boundary between officers' personal and occupational lives. It seemed some thought it okay to break the law, as long as the risk of sanction was slim. If correct, I believe this perception, which is relatively common among both SAPS officers and the broader South African public, has its origins in the apartheid era, and in the transition to democracy. To illustrate my point, a brief review of key historical developments, some touched on in earlier chapters is helpful.

*

Between 1950 and 1960 South Africa's urban African population increased by half, to 27 percent of the total African population (Lee 2011). New laws were introduced requiring Africans to carry pass books proving their right to be in cities. In 1952, the ANC and the South African Indian Congress (SAIC) launched a campaign to defy apartheid's race laws. Eight thousand protestors were arrested. In 1960 an anti-pass march resulted in police killing 69 protestors and wounding 180 at Sharpville. In the aftermath, the ANC and Pan African Congress (PAC) were banned. In response, the movements replaced peaceful disobedience with armed struggle. In subsequent years, coercive violence was increasingly deployed by the state to ensure adherence to the law. But while the SAP coerced compliance in White urban space, it largely left Black townships unregulated, violent and lawless (Posel 2009). Thus, the state signalled to Black South Africans that they could do as they pleased if it did not impact White South Africa. In the absence of police, other providers of coercive force emerged across the country's townships (Steinberg 2008; Shaw 2002). In effect, the state had taught South Africans that order was achieved through force, and that whoever controlled force, controlled space.

By 1983, academics at the University of Cape Town speculated that (Black) Cape Town was one of the most violent cities in the Western world. More recent research supports this claim (Kriegler & Shaw 2016), and shows that, nationally, violence began to increase rapidly in the mid-seventies, peaking in 1993. It began when a generation of young people rebelled against their parents, whom they believed were too subservient to the racist state. This lead to the 1976 Soweto massacre, and a surge in subsequent violent resistance to, and defence of, apartheid. As a result, violence was further normalised in both Black and White communities. Beginning in 1967, all White men between the ages of 17 and 65 had to serve nine months in the South African Defence Force (SADF). In 1972, this was extended to one year, and in 1977 to two years. SADF members and police were deployed in townships, and in Angola and South-West Africa (Namibia). One effect of this conscription was to teach White men that ideologies could be enforced or punished through force.

In the mid-1980s, official crime statistics (representing mostly White urban space) revealed a sharp increase in murder, robbery, housebreaking, and other crimes (Super 2013). This probably resulted in part from calls for civil disobedience and law breaking promoted by the anti-apartheid movement. Either that, or crime and violence in general became more ideologically justifiable. While crime increased in White areas, it was in Black communities that violence became endemic.

When the ANC came to power, it believed that to stem the violence and crime that had taken root in the previous decades, South Africans simply needed a democratically elected government and accountable criminal justice system (Steinberg 2012; Shaw 2002; Super 2013). But a detective service that had previously focused on political crime, and crime in White areas, and which liberally used torture, was woefully unsuitable. Crime spread from the townships into suburbs and onto farms. And while murder numbers halved between 1993 and 2013, millions of young men (and women) who had in the early nineties pegged their hopes to the *better life* promised by the *new* South Africa, found its delivery slow, while the market excluded them.

South Africa in the early twenty-first century is the product of this past; of systems that actively restricted and shamed the Black population and generated an anger that fed rebellion and crime, unchecked by the White state. Though the above review is limited, it shows that the social attitudes generated in South Africa's past, shape: (1) South Africans' attitudes towards law and law enforcement; (2) the way police see South African society; (3) the way police perceive themselves and their personal identities in society; and (4) how they practise police work. In all instances, both police and public views are coloured by an understanding of the world based on relative personal freedom in the absence of coercion. This sense of freedom has been amplified by the shift in language and law that accompanied the democratic transition. Put another way, apartheid taught South Africans that society was not fair and that breaking the law in pursuit of justice (whether dictatorial or democratic) or ease of living, could be justified. In contrast, democracy has taught South Africans that they have a right to aspire, but that their aspirations will be difficult to attain within the bounds a highly unequal economy. It has also shown them that they are at risk of violent attack, and that the state cannot protect them. For many this has produced a retreat from engagement with police and a turn to private, gang- and vigilante-based security, and a weakening of respect for the law and police (O'Regan & Pikoli 2014; Super 2016). These same forces shape police officers' understanding of South Africa, themselves, and their work. They further encourage minor abuses by police, such as speeding and littering, and more serious offences, such as Ndungwane's alleged theft from an accident scene.

Brodeur (2010) defines police as agents authorised to use diverse means prohibited to others to maintain order; or to break rules to enforce rules. But, he suggests, police are more self-regulated than they are law-regulated. As such, only a thin line separates legitimate and illegitimate police action. Considered in this light, two further points should be noted in relation to the officers I shadowed in 2012/13. First, they were aware of the illegality and rule-breaking of their actions but did not think them important in relation to their crime-prevention mandate, despite interpreting that mandate literally. Second, believing their best means to reduce crime was the provision of a coercive deterrent, they were unconcerned about their own petty offences like speeding, littering, or labelling language. This was especially true in the absence of effective (coercive) organisational oversight. When the officers I shadowed broke the law, it was generally not in defence of other laws. Rather, it was indicative of a quiet overflow of their occupational privilege, and a celebration of the power that comes with policing a fragile, emerging democracy. And yet, seemingly unbeknown to the officers, these acts threatened to undo the order many expected them to shape.

## On personal freedom

In Chapter 3, I discussed attitudes towards sick leave, and described the lengths to which SAPS managers sometimes go to check that officers are ill when they call in sick. The logic is that if officers know management might call on them when they report being sick, they will be less likely to abuse sick leave. But in 2013, 80 percent of SAPS employees took an average of 10 sick days (SAPS 2014) – exactly a third of their three-year allocation, suggesting that the SAPS coercive sick-leave management strategy did not work.

There were other, less obvious ways in which coercion, or the absence thereof, shaped officers' personal and occupational lives. At three of the four stations, I met officers who had suffered health complications due to the overconsumption of soft drinks, two of whom were hospitalised. One told me she had drunk so much Coke because her husband had worked for Coca-Cola and received a free quota every month. She said the company had had to provide employees with free Coke to prevent them from stealing it, suggesting that without such a disincentive theft would have been natural.

She had since stopped drinking Coke because of the damage it caused to her stomach, but others I met resumed their habits after medical intervention.

Officers routinely consumed soft drinks, *vetkoek*, and fast food on duty, little of which was healthy. They knew the food was bad for them, but seemed set on pushing their bodies to the brink before changing their habits. In 2013, 8 percent of discharges from the SAPS were due to ill health (SAPS 2014).

Like attitudes towards sick leave and food, the absence of coercion shaped some officers' sex lives. At one of the stations it was assumed that (heterosexual) male officers, most of whom were married or had long-term partners, had one or more lovers in the precinct. Officers there repeatedly encouraged me to participate in what they joked was *police culture*, to take a lover in the area.

On two occasions while on patrol with Warrant Jiyana, he found humour in members of the public who had fallen out with their partners after being caught with another lover. His advice to them was 'not to cheat so close to home'. After stopping to talk to a group of women who were beating a man in the streets, Jiyana laughed:

> It is right that they are beating him in the street. He cheated too close to home. You must respect your wife. When you cheat, you must not cheat close to home.

The fact that Jiyana and colleagues used the word 'cheat' implied that they believed having sex with someone other than their wife or primary partner was, at least in some contexts, socially unacceptable. However, they also believed that *cheating* was part of being a man. As such, it was a man's fault if his wife caught him out. Like the Law Enforcement officers who littered at the beach, men should only *cheat* when nobody is watching.

Some threats to an officer's infidelity are invisible. Telling me about his sex life, one constable told me: 'I don't use condoms with my girlfriend; only with the other women.' He told me there had been only one occasion that he had not used a condom with a lover, and that afterwards he had panicked that he might have contracted HIV. More than 11 percent of South Africans are believed to be HIV positive, rising to 19 percent among women (StatsSA 2015), and 14 percent within the SAPS (SAPS 2016). The officer told me that the six week wait before he could accurately ascertain his HIV status was excruciating, and that, as a result, he would not have unprotected sex again. The coercive threat of HIV had changed his behaviour.

The logic of coercive control that animated the ways officers worked, spilled into their self-narratives and so shaped their private lives.

## Shaping a hopeful future

On a Saturday morning in my final weeks at Yorkton, I cycled into the station to meet with Sergeant Jonker. He had said I could accompany him on an investigation. But when I arrived I found his mentee, Student Constable Carelse, sitting at his desk instead. In contrast to her more formal week-day attire, she was dressed casually in blue jeans and a purple tank top. At about 24, the casual look accentuated her youth and conjured a lightness that seemed out of place among the weight of the docket-filled desk.

Sitting next to Carelse was a girl of about four, whom Carelse introduced as her daughter. Carelse greeted me with a smile but her daughter avoided my gaze. Carelse told me Jonker had postponed the planned investigation. Disappointed, I said I would head home, but first I tried again to connect with her daughter. Dropping down to my knees I asked her a number of questions, which she ignored. But when I asked her whether she wanted to be a police officer like her mom, Carelse immediately replied on her behalf, 'No! She's going to study!' Like so many SAPS officers, Carelse saw *study* and *police work* as incongruent. It seemed she too understood her place in the organisation as the result of her inability to access tertiary education. She did not want the same for her daughter.

Carelse was preparing to leave the office so I hung around to walk out with her. As we made our way down the empty corridor, she pointed out that the door to her captain's office was ajar and whispered, 'He is here every Saturday and Sunday, working, working, working. It's not right. You have to have time for yourself, too.' And yet she was also working on a Saturday morning, her young daughter in tow. The SAPS was shaping her life, but to some extent, she was pushing back and shaping it in return. She would work hard when the organisation asked her to, but would also ensure she had time for herself and to shape her daughter's future.

My exposure to officers' private lives was limited to what they chose to share with me. These were glimpses of lives in flux in a changing society. Ultimately, some of the most important shaping work SAPS officers do is at home, with their children, families, friends, and neighbours.

## Snippets of a world beyond police work

The younger officers I shadowed usually referred to cars as something that could be purchased with savings and a bank loan; a sign of accomplishment. But not everyone thought a new car worth the money. I spent a significant amount of time with Warrant Jiyana visiting scrap yards and road-side mechanics in search of spare parts for his *cockroach*. It was something he was really invested in; something through which he could see his efforts shape a machine and so shape his life.

He told me he called his car a 'cockroach' because he had bought it used, could not afford a new one, and that it was always a work in progress. Still, he said he would buy a brand-new car for the first of his children to finish university. There was no greater gift they could give him than getting a degree, he told me, and he would overextend himself financially to mark such an accomplishment. This was the man who had woken his 11-year-old daughter in the middle of the night so that she could watch him forcefully reclaim her stolen phone from a house that he had entered illegally (Chapter 5). In his life, as in that of so many officers, coercion could be deployed in the form of both carrots and sticks.

Similarly, Constable Mxenge, an Mthonjeni murder detective whom I once watched rob and slap teenaged boys in the holding cells, spent his weekends coaching a youth football team in his neighbourhood. He told me he did it to keep them away from crime. He routinely appealed to me – someone he saw as part of a more privileged world – to help him with sponsorship of team kit. He wanted to instil a sense of pride in the teens, to occupy their time and deter them from conflict with the law. Yes, in his capacity as a SAPS detective he used violence to punish young men, but he also volunteered his time so that others might avoid the violence meted out by him and his colleagues.

Another officer at the station was known in the area as *Skip*, short for *Skipper*, because of the lead he took coaching teen football when off duty. 'It's not easy without the support of my family,' he told me:

> These things cost money and you have to do it out of your own pocket. Then at about the age of 15 the kids start to drop out and become gangsters. It's peer pressure. They turn to crime; they become tempted.

While Mxenge told himself he could divert teens away from crime, Skip saw his efforts as delaying the inevitable. Still, he remained invested, as if not to do so would be to give up hope that life could be better for him and the others walking the streets in which he lived.

During my time in Gompo, officers organised a two-day sporting weekend for youth from the villages in the area. It was an energy- and resource-intensive feat intended to deter young people from crime. Independently, Gompo's Constable Magona told me he wanted to get village youth involved in golf to keep them away from crime. He had worked as a private security guard before joining the SAPS, but also as a professional caddy at a golf club in an affluent nearby coastal town. He thought that young men would benefit from the skills he could pass on to them, both the caddying and the playing of golf.

In these examples, officers were invested in shaping the lives of young men and women, both their own children and relative strangers, in ways they hoped would steer them away from conflict with the law. These investments acknowledged that the risk that pervades South African society, from the criminal to the financial and ontological, is a risk shared by most South Africans. Like a coercive intervention in parallel to the violence meted out by Yorkton's detectives on the Cape Flats, they were actions that said: '*We are like you. We see ourselves in you. We know the dangers of your path. We are trying to make things better for you, and so for all of us.*'

## Dancing to a different tune

While some of who SAPS officers think they are, and how they practise police work, mirrors negative stereotypes about them, there is a fair amount which remains hidden from public view. The few occasions that I socialised with officers exposed me to things that seemed to contradict their occupational mandate, and that challenged the idea that the SAPS is the 'same as the apartheid police,' as some allege.

Social events organised for Yorkton and Mthonjeni staff, which I attended, are good examples. At the Mthonjeni event, station staff and their partners came together to eat, drink, and dance the night away. To some degree at least, rank, class, and culture evaporated in these spaces and South Africans from different backgrounds came together in celebration. DJs played music from Brenda Fassie and Mafikizolo, to Kurt Darren, artists singing in different languages and styles, but celebrated by SAPS staff as if they were the products and inheritance of all. Old and young, Afrikaans and Xhosa, they *langarmed*[6] and line danced, sang and laughed together as if there were little to divide them, and plenty to unite them.

Similarly, team-building games played at a Yorkton event encouraged station staff to unleash their inner child. Members of the notorious ghost squad cheered on two of their colleagues in a three-legged race, hopping along as if their lives depended on it, their lips stretched wide with smiles. The previous week they had been accused of killing a man, yet there they shouted and cheered, giddy with laughter. In that moment, they were just South African men, quite probably raised and still living in relatively difficult and violent environments, but securely employed in the SAPS and enjoying a few hours in the sun.

When one of Yorkton's senior officers who had helped organise the event asked me what I thought of it, I told him I was impressed. 'This is how I do a *braai*,' he replied:

> Those other police *braais* are just booze fests. I don't do that. This is about team building. At the beginning of the year I told my members that we were on a bus and that the destination we were heading to was that of crime reduction. I told them that the bus was not going to stop until we had reached that destination, but that we might need to pull over for a service at some point. This is our service today. This evening the bus will pull off again and carry on heading for its destination. I believe that at the end of the day we will all go to God. Some of us will go before others but we will all go in the end.

He took a drag on his cigarette and turned away. He was trying to shape his officers' worlds. To be sure, he wanted their focus to be *crime reduction*, but he recognised that they needed some time out. Ultimately, death and God were the only constants for him, as for so many in the SAPS. What happened in between depended on what could be coerced; achieved with a combination of carrots and sticks.

## When the day is over

In Chapter 2, I suggested that it was in the morning meetings and parades, when officers and detectives gathered before moving to their offices and cars, that I saw the most joy in those I shadowed. But I did not always hang around for end-of-day meetings and parades; they were usually brief and uneventful. The truth is that those that I did attend were also joy-filled. Yes, police were tired after a day of work, but there was a lightness that returned to them in those meetings, too. At times one did not need to search for it: it was right on the surface, bubbling up through the jokes and cheeky exchanges shared before meetings began, and once they had been released for the day. And, in a sense, that is exactly how it felt: that they were being *released*. They were being allowed to return to the stories they told themselves about themselves outside their occupation; to their lives without coercive commanders and the constraints of bureaucracy to direct their social performances and to shape who they should be. It was as if in the mornings they surrendered a part of themselves to the organisation, claiming it back only when the work day was officially over.

In 2008/09, I conducted a series of in-depth interviews with SAPS officers, exploring their lives as police (Faull 2010). I ended the interviews by asking what they would want to tell South Africans, were they given the opportunity. Most responses conveyed a longing to be recognised as *human* and for South Africans to realise that as police officers they were limited in what they could achieve. They did not want to be blamed for matters that were beyond their control. They craved gratitude and understanding. Viewed in relation to the officers I shadowed in 2012/13, these desires made more sense to me. It is as if the officers I interviewed in 2008/09 were asking to be recognised for what I saw in the morning meetings and afternoon parades in 2012/13 – spaces that remain invisible to the public. They wanted to be seen as people whose investments, challenges, and joys were unexpectedly found within the SAPS, but were in more abundance outside the organisation. Outside station walls and working hours they could cast off their occupation's stigma and impossible mandate, connect with their children and friends, and free themselves from a *liminality* born of great expectations hindered by precarity and bureaucracy. Perhaps they hoped that if the public could see them in this way they would more easily secure the ontological security that remained so elu   sive.

In this chapter I have highlighted behaviour incongruent with the imagined ideals of an exemplary police service. By stripping away the organisational façade, I have exposed some of the informally patterned cultural and shaping work carried out by discretion-empowered officers. I have highlighted the minor infringements more common to township and rural spaces than to the affluent inner city with which most police are less familiar. I have suggested that this is because where officers feel more comfortable (where coercion is absent) they are more likely to behave like many South Africans, disregarding traffic laws, littering, speaking their prejudice, and resorting to violence to solve conflicts among peers. Their turning to such behaviour, like the crime and violence they are tasked with tackling, has its roots in the disparate ways the apartheid state governed Black and White space, and the opposition to state law and authority this fostered. Extended into the democratic era, disorderly space encourages disorderly police conduct, while order encourages police compliance with the ideals of objective, professional policing.

I have contrasted these infringements with exercises in positive coercion or engagement, such as officers volunteering to coach sports teams, or rewarding their children who succeeded at school. These acts typify police' aspirations in a precarious social and economic environment. Officers long for simpler lives, but have limited means through which to realise them. Instead, some retreat to speeding, littering, and violence, which, disproportionately enacted outside affluent space, sustains South Africa's inequalities.

## Notes

1 For example, addressing police women on August 21, 2007, then Deputy-President Phumzile Mlambo-Ngcuka told them, 'We expect you to lead by example and good deeds that must impress your peers and make those of your peers who fail society to re-commit to noble values of the SAPS.'
2 Like the UK, South Africans drive on the left of the road. As such, drivers are encouraged to 'keep left, pass right' to avoid accidents.
3 Short for 'Makwere-kwere', a derogatory term for non-South African Africans.
4 Numerous other outbreaks of violence against foreign-born Africans have occurred since 2008.
5 In 2014/15 only 54,169 people were deported from the country, marking a major shift in the established trend (DHA 2015).
6 Long-arm – a kind of ballroom dancing most commonly associated with Afrikaners.

## References

Brodeur, J.-P., 2010. *The Policing Web*, Oxford: Oxford University Press.

DHA, 2008. *Annual Report: Building the New Home Affairs 2007/2008*, Pretoria.

DHA, 2013. *Annual Report 2012/2013*, Pretoria. Available at: www.home-affairs.gov.za/files/Annual Reports/Annual_Report_2012-2013.pdf.

DHA, 2014. *Annual Report 2013/2014*, Pretoria. Available at: www.home-affairs.gov.za/files/Annual Reports/Annual_Report_2013_14ss.pdf.

DHA, 2015. *Annual Report 2014/15*, Pretoria. Available at: www.home-affairs.gov.za/files/Annual%20Reports/Annual_Report_2014_15.pdf.

Fassin, D., 2013. *Enforcing Order: An Ethnography of Urban Policing*, Cambridge: Polity Press.

Faull, A., 2010. *Behind the Badge: The Untold Stories of South Africa's Police Service Members*. Cape Town: Zebra Press.

Gastrow, V., 2013. Business Robbery, the Foreign Trader and the Small Shop: How Business Robberies Affect Somali Traders in the Western Cape. *South African Crime Quarterly*, (43), pp. 5–15.

Goffman, E., 1959. *The Presentation of Self in Everyday Life*, New York: Doubleday.

Holdaway, S., 1983. *Inside the British Police*, Oxford: Blackwell.

Hornberger, J., 2011. *Policing and Human Rights: The Meaning of Violence and Justice in the Everyday Policing of Johannesburg*, Abingdon: Routledge.

Kriegler, A. & Shaw, M., 2016. *A Citizen's Guide to Crime Statistics in South Africa*, Johannesburg and Cape Town: Jonathan Ball.

Lee, R., 2011. Death 'On the Move': Funerals, Entrepreneurs and the Rural–Urban Nexus in South Africa. *Africa: The Journal of the International African Institute*, 81(2), pp. 226–247.

Lipsky, M., 2010. *Street-Level Bureaucracy: Dilemmas of the Individual in Public Services*, New York: Russell Sage Foundation.

Loader, I., 1997. Policing and the Social: Questions of Symbolic Power. *The British Journal of Sociology*, 48(1), pp. 1–18.

Loader, I., 2006. Policing, Recognition, and Belonging. *The Annals of the American Academy of Political and Social Science*, 605 (Democracy, Crime, and Justice), pp. 202–221.

Loader, I. & Mulcahy, A., 2003. *Policing and the Condition of England: Memory, Politics and Culture*, Oxford: Oxford University Press.

Mabin, A. & Smit, D., 2010. Reconstructing South Africa's cities? The Making of Urban Planning 1900–2000. *Planning Perspectives*, 12(2), pp. 193–223.

Manning, P.K., 1997. *Police Work: The Social Organization of Policing*, Prospect Heights, IL: Waveland Press.

Manning, P.K., 2005. The Police: Mandate, Strategies and Appearances. Reprinted in T. Newburn, ed. *Policing: Key Readings*. Cullompton: Willan Publishing, pp. 191–214.

Moskos, P., 2008. *Cop in the Hood: My Year Policing Baltimore's Eastern District*, Princeton, NJ: Princeton University Press.

O'Regan, J.C. & Pikoli, A.V., 2014. *Towards a Safer Khayelithsa: Report of the Commission of Inquiry into Allegations of Police Inefficiency and a Breakdown in Relations Between SAPS and the Community of Khayelitsha*, Cape Town: Khayelitsha Commission of Inquiry.

Pinker, S., 2011. *The Better Angels of Our Nature*, New York: Penguin Books.

Posel, D., 2009. The Apartheid Project, 1948–1970. In R. Ross, A.-K. Mager, & B. Nasson, eds. *The Cambridge History of South Africa – Vol 2*, Cambridge: Cambridge University Press, pp. 319–368.

SAPS, 2014. *Annual Report 2013/14*, Pretoria. Available at: www.gov.za/sites/www.gov.za/files/SAPS%257B_%257DAnnual%257B_%257DReport%257B_%257D20132014.pdf.

SAPS, 2016. *Employee Helath and Wellness (EHW)*, Pretoria: SAPS.

Shaw, M., 2002. *Crime and Policing in Post-Apartheid South Africa: Transforming Under Fire*, Bloomington, IN: Indiana University Press.

StatsSA, 2015. *Statistical Release P0302 Mid-Year Population Estimates*. Available at: www.statssa.gov.za/publications/P0302/P03022015.pdf.

Steinberg, J., 2008. *Thin Blue: The Unwritten Rules of Policing South Africa*, Cape Town: Jonathan Ball.

Steinberg, J., 2011. Security and Disappointment: Policing, Freedom and Xenophobia in South Africa. *British Journal of Criminology*, 52(2), pp. 345–360.

Steinberg, J., 2012. Establishing Police Authority and Civilian Compliance in Post-Apartheid Johannesburg: An Argument from the Work of Egon Bittner. *Policing and Society*, 22(4), pp. 481–495.

Steinberg, J., 2014. *A Man of Good Hope*, Jeppestown, South Africa: Jonathan Ball.

Super, G.J., 2013. *Governing Through Crime in South Africa: The Politics of Race and Class in Neoliberalizing Regimes*, Oxford: Routledge.

Super, G.J., 2016. Punishment, Violence, and Grassroots Democracy in South Africa – The Politics of Populist Punitiveness. *Punishment & Society*, 18(3), pp. 325–345. Available at: http://pun.sagepub.com/cgi/doi/10.1177/1462474516645685 [Accessed October 31, 2016].

UNODC, 2014. *Global Study of Homicide 2013: Trends, Contexts, Data*, Vienna. Available at: www.unodc.org/documents/data-and-analysis/statistics/GSH2013/2014_GLOBAL_HOMICIDE_BOOK_web.pdf.

Van Maanen, J., 1979. The Fact of Fiction in Organizational Ethnography. *Administrative Science Quarterly*, 24(4), pp. 539–550.

Vigneswaran, D.V. & Hornberger, J., 2009. *Beyong 'Good Cop'/'Bad Cop': Understanding Informality and Police Corruption in South Africa*, Johannesburg: Forced Migration Studies Programme, University of the Witwatersrand.

Waddington, P.A.J., 1999. Police (Canteen) Cub-Culture: An Appreciation. *British Journal of Criminology*, 39(2), pp. 287–309.

WHO, 2010. *Estimated Road Traffic Death Rate (per 100,000 Population), 2010*, Geneva. Available at: www.who.int/gho/road_safety/mortality/rate_text/en/index.html.

WHO, 2013. *Global Status Report on Road Safety 2013: Supporting a Decade of Action.* Available at: http://data.worldbank.org/indicator/VC.IHR.PSRC.P5?order=wbapi_data_value_2012+wbapi_data_value+wbapi_data_value-last&sort=desc.

World Bank, 2016. Intentional homicides (per 100,000 people). Available at: http://data.worldbank.org/indicator/VC.IHR.PSRC.P5?end=2014%257B&%257Dorder=wbapi%257B_%257Ddata%257B_%257Dvalue%257B_%257D2012+wbapi%257B_%257Ddata%257B_%257Dvalue+wbapi%257B_%257Ddata%257B_%257Dvalue-last%257B&%257Dsort=desc%257B&%257Dstart=2012.

Young, M., 1991. *An Inside Job: Policing and Police Culture in Britain*, Oxford: Oxford University Press.

# Chapter 7

# Accidental occupations in the post-colony

## The last entry

On a Sunday afternoon in April 2013, I sat at a desk in the house I was renting in a village 15 kilometres from Gompo, about to type up my notes from a shift with the Patterson CPU the night before. I always began my diary entries by noting my mood, to give myself a sense of how my emotions may have shaped the way I recorded my observations. 'I feel strange,' I wrote that afternoon, 'I guess the strangeness comes from the feeling that this was probably my last shift, and yet that so much remains unresolved.'

I had set out to answer the question, *Who do South African police officers think they are and how does this shape police practice?*, spent eight months shadowing officers, and amassed a 700,000-word diary. And yet, the answer to my question was not obvious.

Five pages into my entry I received a call from Gompo's Constable Booi. He told me he was in the area with a friend and wanted to swing by for a drink. I had accompanied him to a Patterson tavern the previous Friday night and we had established that we shared a taste for Savanna cider.

Booi was in his late 20s, fit and wiry. He had grown up in the city of Port Elizabeth where, on finishing high school, he had completed three years of a four-year business degree before dropping out. He had signed up with the SAPS and been posted at Gompo, which he found dull after city life. He was friendly and confident and we got on well.

Booi arrived shortly after hanging up, driven by a friend in a gold VW Golf – a sign of real wealth amidst the poverty of the area. His friend introduced himself as Andile. 'I'm a tenderpreneur,' he beamed through silvery eyes. He was hopelessly drunk. In South Africa, a *tenderpreneur* is a pejorative term describing people who get rich through nepotism and government tenders. I had never heard anybody describe themselves using the term, let alone with pride. But Constable Booi did not think his friend's behaviour odd, neither his introduction nor his intoxication.

Walking into the house Booi told me they had driven from East London, 100 kilometres away. I fetched Booi a cider from the fridge, but told Andile I wasn't comfortable giving him more to drink with such a long drive ahead. Instead I offered coffee or tea. Both men protested. Annoyed and still tired from the long night, I responded unkindly, 'I should probably call the cops when I see someone as drunk as you driving, but I see there's already a cop here.' I immediately regretted my words, but neither man seemed offended.

Andile told me about the R30,000 *lobola* he had paid to his fiancé's family, and about the two tenders he was managing. While he talked, Booi quickly finished his drink and led us back to the car. He said he needed to be at work in 90 minutes but would visit again that night. Approaching the car, I noticed a young woman passed out on the back seat, and asked Booi who she was. 'I don't know, probably one of his girlfriends,' he replied. Andile emptied his bladder next to the road and climbed into the driver's seat. Within ten minutes of their arrival they were gone.

Constable Booi visited me again at 10:40 that evening. This time he was on duty, in uniform and a marked police car, together with his colleague, Constable Kani. I welcomed the two inside and offered them tea, coffee, or Coke. Kani said he'd like some Coke, but Booi said he wanted a cider. I thought he was joking and was about to pour him a glass of Coke when he repeated his request. I asked if he was serious, 'Yes, it's night shift,' he responded, 'there's no Captain Dlamini,' referring to Gompo's station commander. I told him I could not support his drinking on duty. Kani withdrew from the conversation, taking out his phone to play a game. To change subject I asked Booi about a woman he had met during our night out together. He said he had gone home with her but that he had met someone new the following day, 'I'm young,' he grinned, 'I must have fun.' Half an hour later the two left.

*

When Booi visited me mid-diary entry, I was frustrated. I was tired from the night shift, wanted to get the long entry down, and felt anxious about how the mass of data I had collected would help me answer my research question. But, like every other SAPS officer who allowed me to glimpse their sense of self, I owe Constable Booi a great gratitude. I was too selfish and self-righteous to see it at the time, but he had brought me the answer to my question.

When, eight months earlier, Warrant Officer Skrikker had taken me to his house, it was to show me what he had made of his life. Similarly, when Booi took me to his favourite tavern, and when he and Andile visited me at home, he allowed me a glimpse of the life he was building outside of the SAPS, showing me a piece of the story he told himself about himself, which he believed to be true. It was a life of friends with connections (including a researcher from Cape Town), drinking, dancing, women, and fast cars that could carry him from the former White city to the former Black homeland, with speed and comfort. It was a life in which his status as a securely employed young South African man allowed him to taste the promises of the *new* South Africa. It was these elements of his life, he signalled to me, that informed his sense of being far more than the uniform he put on when he went to work. Yes, he was a police officer, but he was first and foremost a young man making his way from the precarious periphery to the more stable centre of a deeply unequal society. For the moment, the SAPS was simply the vessel through which he journeyed in pursuit of ontological security. That was Constable Booi's narrative, and it is the central narrative of this book.

## South Africa, precarity, and police work

South Africa in the early twenty-first century is a place of minority wealth and widespread poverty, social and economic precarity, and violent crime. It is home to one of the world's most unequal societies and possibly one of the more violent. It has been shaped by centuries of race- and gender-based oppression in which the state ascribed descriptive, identity-shaping labels to people, and through them distributed rights, resources, and opportunities. It relegated vast swathes of the population to ethnic homelands and tied hundreds of thousands of Africans to a White-owned economy. Established to serve the White population, the SAP carried out limited crime prevention and investigation work in townships. In their absence, community and vigilante groups, and gangs, competed to monopolise force. Outside townships, SAP officers habitually stopped Africans to request passes that proved their right to be in White South Africa, and returned those without authority to rural homelands. This ebb and flow of mostly men for most of the twentieth century introduced rural Africans to new identities, religions, cash, markets, goods, and practices which they carried back to villages. The migrant labour system simultaneously emasculated and taught violence to its oppressed workers, and spurned generations of men and women with identities and social networks split between the cities in which they worked and the countryside they called *home*.

In the face of growing and increasingly militant resistance from the 1970s, apartheid waned, then collapsed. In the aftermath, the country was enveloped in both great expectation and violence. The new government's vision was to 'Improve the quality of life of all citizens and free the potential of each person' in a South Africa that 'belongs to all who live in it, united in our diversity' (Republic of South Africa 1996:2). But, despite the significant provision of houses, basic services, and welfare since 1994, most South Africans remain poor.

In the early nineties, the democratically elected government moved to refashion the SAP from a politically captured, rights-abusing *force* to a human rights-respecting, community-oriented *service*. Reforms included the replacement of military ranks with civilian titles. The South African Police Service (SAPS) assumed a key role in the country, both as government's most visible response to violent crime and one of the country's biggest employers. But, in 2010, in the face a crime-fatigued nation, the SAPS and government abandoned the language of *service* and returned to apartheid's signifier of *force*. Civilian titles were replaced with the military ranks of old and political rhetoric on crime became increasingly militant. Police and political leaders hoped this shift would bring discipline and respect to both police and the public, but subsequent scandals suggest this has not occurred. In 2010 the former National Commissioner, Jackie Selebi, was convicted of corruption, and in 2012 the Marikana massacre took place, and Khayelitsha Commission of Inquiry into allegations of police inefficiency and a breakdown in relations between the community and the police was instituted. Considered in relation to the narratives described in this book, it is apparent that the personal and organisational are indeed entangled, each shaping the other.

## Selebi, Khayelitsha, and Marikana: the SAPS in three acts

### Selebi

Former National Commissioner, Jackie Selebi's crimes not only tarnished the image of the SAPS, but those of all associated with it. As a political appointee, his corruption was an embarrassment to government, too. When in January 2000 the Minister of Safety and Security, Steve Tshwete, had introduced Selebi as the country's first African commissioner, it was with great celebration. His appointment was about much more than a single man. It was about justice and redress, and a competent government peacefully reforming an institution that had once tortured and killed its members. It was about the *new* country and its promise of a brighter future. But, in 2012/13 Selebi remained a figure of derision and embarrassment for many of the officers I shadowed.

Selebi's fall laid bare the frailty of power and aspiration in contexts of great inequality and historical precarity. Despite having devoted his life to the anti-apartheid struggle, and being one the best remunerated civil servants in a generously paid public service, he was still corrupted, including through gifts of clothing and shoes. Considering the deprivation and abuse to which apartheid had subjected Selebi and his generation, perhaps such materialism is unsurprising. It is, however, notable. It highlights the power of inequality, and how easily personal aspiration and consumption can disrupt and undo an institution and legacy. It shows that the SAPS is as much a police organisation as it is a means to an end for tens of thousands of people struggling to secure ontological security in a context, and against an historical backdrop, of deprivation, precarity, and risk.

### Khayelitsha

If Selebi's scandal reveals something about aspiration and power amidst precarity and inequality, the Khayelitsha commission peeled away the SAPS façade to reveal the disparate ways in which South Africa's rich and poor are policed.

The Commission described Khayelitsha, like Mthonjeni, as a product of apartheid: a township where half the residents lived in informal dwellings, where most adults were migrants from the (rural) Eastern Cape, and where 50 percent of working-aged young men were unemployed. It chronicled pervasive violence and crime, including frequent street justice and murder of the criminally accused. It portrayed SAPS officers as homophobic, xenophobic, ill-disciplined, absent from work, and mistrusted by residents, some of whom still associated them with apartheid. But the Commission also documented the challenges police there faced. These included low morale, especially among officers who had migrated to the city for work, and who wanted to return home – a belief among police that they were vulnerable to attack; that informal settlements were nearly impossible to police; that apartheid stigma made recruitment of informers very difficult; and that witnesses were too scared to share information with police for fear of violent reprisal from the criminally accused. In short, the Commission found that policing in Khayelitsha is shaped by a complex combination of precarity, aspiration, and risk. And yet, despite the Commission's detailed report, it can be difficult to connect to the humanity of police officers behind the damning claims it chronicled. It is here that this book complements the Commission's work.

The Commission began its work when I began mine in Mthonjeni. In a morning meeting at the time, the head of detectives told his members to hope the Commissioners did not visit their station next. He was an extremely impressive, dedicated police officer, but he knew he and his colleagues were failing to meet Mthonjeni residents' expectations or needs. In this book, I have shown the risk and effect of SAPS officers reinforcing inequality by reproducing (dis)order, rather than enforcing it, thus neglecting spaces like Mthonjeni and Khayelitsha. But I have also sought to communicate this in a way that the Commission could not, by incorporating officers' personal histories and self-narratives into those generated in the front stage of the SAPS, and thus how officers' personal identities, forged of South Africa's precarity, shape police practice.

### Marikana

Officers' personal identities are similarly helpful in understanding the police killing of 34 striking mine workers at Marikana in 2012. While significant attention has been paid to the plight and poverty of the miners, the same has (understandably) not been afforded the police involved. If one applies the narrative of this book to that of Marikana, both the protesting miners and police deployed to disperse them died and killed for the dream of a better life promised by the new South Africa.

Constable Faizyl Moilwa was deployed to Marikana in the days after the shooting. I never met Moilwa, but I read about him in a 2015 newspaper article. In it his family recounted how he had used his first SAPS pay cheque to buy his aunt a cell phone, and later had renovated his mother's house, bought clothes for the family, and a new television for his grandmother. He was a fortunate and generous young man who lived with precarity and shared with those around him.

But once deployed to Marikana, Moilwa phoned his family each day and cried about the violence and death. He collapsed in shock and was sent home when a colleague's arm was chopped off. Two days later he shot himself on his grandmother's veranda. As he bled out she remembers asking him, 'My child, why did you do this? What will become of me? What will I tell your mother?' (Davids 2015). They were the words of a woman whose life had been moored to that of a young police officer who, with the squeeze of a trigger, had set her and the family adrift. According to the article, Constable Moilwa's family wanted:

> The country to know that most of the officers deployed to Marikana were not 'monsters', not the enemy. They hope his death will help South Africa realise that behind every badge is an ordinary man or woman.

And yet, like Selebi's conviction, and the chronicles of Khayelitsha, Marikana remains a scar on the face of the SAPS and its officers. The Farlam Commission's Marikana report, released in June 2015, was an indictment of a SAPS leadership prone to political interference and lies. The report presents a narrative of global, national, and political elites – the mine company's management, and senior police and politicians – treading on the lives of disempowered miners, security staff, and police officers, whom they had pitted against one another in a struggle for dignity, in a deeply unequal and precarious society, itself born of an indefensibly skewed distribution of global wealth and opportunity. Until that is addressed, SAPS officers, like police elsewhere, may struggle to do more than reproduce the general (dis)order in which they work.

## Personal identity and policing

As police navigate the spaces between what society and their leaders expect of them, what the law allows and requires of them, and what they understand of their occupation (including its relationship to their understanding of themselves), particular ways of doing police work manifest (Manning 1978; Newburn & Reiner 2007). The traditional view contends that the socialising power of a police agency's organisational culture guides police practice (Manning 1978), and that related narratives must be considered if organisational reform is to be effective (Holdaway 1983; Crank 1998). This book has shifted the lens from the police organisation to the lives of its officers, thus giving their personal narratives primacy over that of the organisation. Drawing on a cluster of concepts, I have sought to explore the overlap and entanglement of personal, organisational, and national narratives related to policing, and to explore how they shape police practice.

The popular archetype of a police officer is a crime-fighting hero, threatened but committed to the noble cause of keeping the vulnerable safe (Manning 1997). And yet, little of what patrol police do in the course of a shift involves crime. This is as true of American (Manning 1997) and Canadian police (Brodeur 2010) as it is of French (Fassin 2013) and South African (Steinberg 2008; Altbeker 2005; Hornberger 2011; Vigneswaran & Hornberger 2009). In the absence of the police mythology manifesting on the streets police patrol, officers appeal to an organisational narrative to secure their occupational identity. They apply labels to, and tell stories about, people and places, then give them life through performances that reinforce a narrow vision of the police mandate. In so doing, they act as magicians conjuring an illusion that justice will be done (Manning 2010).

But there is something far more obvious, mundane, but central to being a police officer, which is not sufficiently acknowledged: it is a job. The twentieth century was a period in which employment became the locus for inclusion in global capitalism, and so central to identity and ontological security. This was true in South Africa, where work held particular importance for men, their aspirations, self-esteem and sense of self. It provided income and security, a means to survive, and a title through which one might choose to be defined. But the notion that occupations should be identity-shaping vocations, that money is earned through activities which people voluntarily pursue, is a myth of capital and markets, and of the elites whose privilege allows them to describe their activities as *work*. The workplace, and the income and opportunities it provides, certainly shape who people become, but not because workers welcome it. Rather, work intrudes on sense of self. Like Yorkton's Student Constable Carelse who disapproved of her captain working all weekend, every weekend, individuals push back against the occupational forces that vie to mould them into people they may never have imagined being.

Among the officers I shadowed, it was in the spaces where they gathered before the work began and once it was over that they seemed most at ease. There, it seemed, they could shrug off the organisational forces that intruded upon their sense of self, and return to being the people they thought themselves to be.

*

Perhaps for the first time in police sociology, this book has asked what policing looks like when understood, foremost, as motivated by individuals' pursuit of ontological security. In so doing it makes a claim that being a police officer is 'just a job', even accidental, and that the overriding motivation for SAPS officers is the search for ontological security in a society where pervasive precarity makes such a pursuit extremely challenging. The book positions the individual as central in shaping police behaviours and practices – a shift away from the police cultural lens, which has dominated much of the policing literature. In so doing, it proposes an approach to understanding policing in South Africa that considers SAPS officers' personal identities, and the ways in which they overlap and become entangled in the social, political, and wider cultural contexts where policing takes place.

But this book also presents empirical support for existing themes in policing literature generated elsewhere. Most notably, these themes include: suspicion, the search for respect, and a flexible – if not outright instrumental – relationship with laws, rules, and procedures. However, this book extends these in the South African context, exploring their relationship to violence, distrust *among* police officers, and by linking expectations for respect (and examples of disrespect) to their authority and order shaping work.

Set in the fragile, transitional, relatively new democracy of South Africa, the book adds a fresh perspective from the Global South, and one that could readily and valuably be duplicated in other jurisdictions.

## Conclusion: accidental police officers

Born and raised in the poverty-stained shadow of South Africa's minority wealth, most officers I met found themselves in the SAPS after original aspirations had slipped out of reach. Some had actively disliked, or been in conflict with, the SAPS and law before signing up. Yet once inside, given a gun and uniform, and asked to carry out the dirty work of the fragile democracy, they found themselves re-writing their self-narratives, reconsidering who they thought they were. They told themselves the SAPS was not ideal, but that it was also not bad. It offered them job security, a reasonable income, and a diversity of opportunities.

Officers' personal narratives shaped the way they thought about place and space. Most African officers I met considered the rural Eastern Cape *home*. They remembered it as a place of authority and respect. Outside of affluent pockets, cities were viewed as places of danger and risk. In the urban township and rural town, officers sought to stop, search, and label men – young, Black, and poor – whose lives were often too like their own for comfort, while in the affluent city they worked to protect its order and please its middle-class residents.

In the rural town and village, officers selectively borrowed from national narratives on urban crime, inserting them into the quiet countryside in ways that helped them make sense of the threats to its tranquillity, and to bring purpose to days of boredom.

In the township, affluent city, and rural town and villages, the violence officers believed poor, Black, young men capable of threatened their notion of success as police officers. It also threatened the vision of security they longed for in their communities, and the future they wished to provide for their children, i.e. their ontological security. Through their work, they sought to claim this back. They did so through actions that reinforced their sense of self and their right to project that sense of self into their vision of the future.

A job in the SAPS is primarily just that, a job – a means to strive and survive. The meaning and income it brings to officers' lives is usually more important to them than the work they carry out. Consequently, they seek first to please their institutional overseers, and so to ease the pressure of the work. They enact institutional performances that promote the myth that the SAPS is a rational, effective, evidence-based, and rule-bound organisation consisting of well-trained officers performing common-sense crime prevention tasks, while hiding the grimy by-products of police work. Through official reports and statements, and carefully choreographed public performances, the SAPS and its officers present a strategically crafted façade behind which individual officers cocoon themselves and hone their sense of self.

Because officers are aware that the SAPS' front is part-fiction, and because of a general mistrust between South Africans, many officers seek to detach their sense of self from the organisation. Instead, they present themselves as what might be thought of as 'accidental police officers', and as deserving far more respect, more dignity, than the South African public gives them. But, with prospects of comparable financial remuneration and stability outside the SAPS unlikely for most, officers simultaneously and contradictorily invest in and protect the SAPS image. This is achieved through *public performance deceptions; data performance deceptions;* and *internal* and *external deceptions*, which contribute to a *culture of suspicion*.

While officers aspired to live in big houses and drive shiny cars, few had the money to do so. Instead they deferred their dreams to their children, investing in their education, while sharing what little remained with networks of precarious kin. Some officers invested in more than their immediate relatives. They volunteered their time and money to support youth who they believed were at risk. Like the *skollies* they hunted at work, the teens reminded officers of themselves. By investing in them, officers hoped they could deflect them from the violence of the criminal justice system. In a sense, they offered the teens carrots so that they might avoid becoming the objects of the violence through which some officers asserted their masculinity and right to respect.

Like most South Africans, SAPS officers are accustomed to coercive governance, including assemblages of informal and non-state security and force provision. This familiarity, together with their intimate experiences of crime as private citizens and officers, justifies many officers' belief that coercive policing of poor, young men is necessary. However, attitudes to coercion also inform their behaviour on and off duty. Where officers sense an absence of order or coercion, some revert to who they think they are – *free* South Africans with 'rights' to do as they please, including breaking laws. In so doing they contradict the SAPS' official front. Put another way, they feel entitled to leverage the freedoms of a fragile democracy in which they are intimately familiar with the state's law enforcement limitations. They reproduce both order and disorder, thus shaping, and being shaped by, South Africa in the early twenty-first century.

*Who do SAPS officers think they are and how does it shape police practice?* Like Skrikker and Booi, they are men and women born and raised on the periphery, chasing a vision of a more prosperous future. At times proud, at times shamed by the work they do, they are nourished by the knowledge that, while they may not be able to make South Africa safe, they can provide themselves and those they care for with a better life than the one they were born into. In the meantime, they do what they must do to get through the day, hold fast to the story they tell themselves about themselves, and with that secured, strive to colonise the future with a vision that is golden.

## Afterward: accidental academics

To describe another's occupation as 'accidental' may be thought disparaging. This is not my intent. Indeed, my occupation is in many ways as accidental as those of the police about whom I write.

At some point in my first weeks at Mthonjeni, Warrant Officer Skrikker and I had an impassioned debate about the death penalty. He told me he believed in an eye for an eye and that rapists should be executed. When I suggested that capital punishment in democracies did not reduce crime, he retorted with anger:

> Andrew, you don't know anything because you grew up in the nice areas with the White people. You had role models all around you, Springboks walking past you in the street, Raymond Ackerman as your neighbour.[1]

In South Africa, Skrikker didn't need to know the details of my life to make such a statement, he could see it in my skin and hear it in my language and accent. As for his upbringing, he continued:

> We growing up on the Cape Flats, Gugulethu, Mitchells Plain, we only had the gangsters. Our role models were the gangsters. You're never going to change it. It will be the same a hundred years from now, it will always be the same for Blacks and Coloureds. It's a thug's life.

It was rare to hear Skrikker so pessimistically fatalist. He usually extolled the promise of the *new* South Africa. The stories he told of himself were of escaping the 'thug's life', getting out, getting into the SAPS and building something better for himself and his family. But even Skrikker's optimism was rattled at times.

Of course, Skrikker had a point. In South Africa, apartheid's race labels still predict life outcomes, with those born White likely to be better educated, earn more money, and live longer than others. This book is the product of such facts. My life has been no more precarious than it would had I been born in Western Europe or North America.

Of course, knowledge is not neutral. The concepts and texts from which I have borrowed in this book were predominantly produced in wealthy countries, written by White men, about developed societies' police organisations and criminal justice systems. Similarly, where I have cited South Africans academics, they, like me, have mostly been White. It is equally obvious but noteworthy that the subjects of this book are Black. Some may think I've belaboured this point, but I have good reason.

From 2015 to 2017, as I prepared this manuscript for publication, protests broke out across South African universities.[2] Employing a range of strategies, from the peaceful and negotiated to the violent and destructive, students forced universities to close, at first in objection to increased fees, and subsequently to demand *free, quality, decolonised tertiary education*.

Through their protest action, Black protestors made clear that they did not feel welcome at universities. The languages of instruction were not African, the theories taught were not African, and, while most teaching staff were *South African*, they were predominantly White, they did not *look* African. Students from low-resource high schools, who had beaten the odds to qualify for university and funding, struggled to navigate the wealth and whiteness of their new institutions. Moreover, university fees were more than many could afford, so that they either took on unreasonable debt, or had to drop out of their programmes, when, as for so many of the police I met in 2012/13, 'the money ran out'. In some sense, through their protests, students were saying, '*We don't want to be accidental police officers*'.

Some protestors called Nelson Mandela a 'sell-out', accusing him of letting South Africans down by not redistributing White-wealth in the mid-nineties. Others called for their 'Marikana moment', saying they were willing to die for their cause. In so doing, they laid bare the invisible violence – the symbolic, structural, and psychological – that remains central to the lives of millions, perhaps most, South Africans (Henkeman 2016). Life in the *new* South Africa, the students made clear, was not meant to be so difficult. They had been sold lies.

This book is, and can only be, a product of who I am, of whiteness in the post-colony. I take no pleasure in the inequality of the country and its universities, but acknowledge that, in many ways, *all* the pleasures of my life are its products. I wanted to be a cop when I finished high school, but was dissuaded from it by the adults in my life who, like the police officers I met in 2012/13, thought it better that a young person be 'educated' than join the SAPS. An undergraduate degree led to a graduate degree, which, many years later, led to a funded doctorate at the University of Oxford. I had no great aspiration to be an academic, but was seduced by its offerings of skill, status, and adventure. This book is based on that doctorate, as was the post offered to me at the University of Cape Town to write it. While the result of privilege rather than precarity, my occupation is also an unplanned product of South Africa's inequality, an inequality long-shaped, in part, by its police whose ranks are filled by those whose dreams have been deferred. Between these accidental occupations, the academic's and the officer's, justice is elusive.

I have written this book for the police who gave me their time, for the funders who financed it, and for those for whom it may be useful. To not add it to the record, even if only as an artefact of an unequal era, would be unethical. My personal identity is, clearly, also the product of overlap and entanglement, which bind my future to those with whom I work, live, and play. Our narratives shape each other's. But I have also written this book for myself, to secure my own interests and ontology. If the story I tell myself about myself is that I am an accidental academic, then this book is an example of how that narrative shapes my work.

## Notes

1 The 'Springboks' are South Africa's national rugby team. Raymond Ackerman is one of the country's wealthiest business people.
2 University students had protested for many years before 2015, but not at the country's biggest universities, and thus without equivalent visibility or power.

## References

Altbeker, A., 2005. *The Dirty Work of Democracy: A Year on the Streets with the SAPS*, Johannesburg and Cape Town: Jonathan Ball.

Brodeur, J.P., 2010. *The Policing Web*, Oxford: Oxford University Press.

Crank, J.P., 1998. *Understanding Police Culture*, Cincinatti, OH: Anderson Publishing.

Davids, N., 2015. Tears for a Cop Whose Dream Died at Marikana. *Sunday Times* (19 July). Available at: www.timeslive.co.za/sundaytimes/stnews/2015/07/19/Tears-for-a-cop-whose-dream-died-at-Marikana.

Fassin, D., 2013. *Enforcing Order: An Ethnography of Urban Policing*, Cambridge: Polity Press.

Henkeman, S., 2016. *Basic Guide to a "Deeper And Longer" Analysis of Violence*. Available at: www.academia.edu/22684176/Basic_guide_to_a_deeper_and_longer_analysis_of_violence.

Holdaway, S., 1983. *Inside the British Police*, Oxford: Basil Blackwell Publishers.

Hornberger, J., 2011. *Policing and Human Rights: The Meaning of Violence and Justice in the Everyday Policing of Johannesburg*, Abingdon: Routledge.

Manning, P.K., 1978. The Police: Mandate, Strategies, and Appearances. *Policing: A View from the Street*. Culver City: Goodyear Publishing Company.

Manning, P.K., 1997. *Police Work: The Social Organization of Policing*, Prospect Heights, IL: Waveland Press.

Manning, P.K., 2010. *Democratic Policing in a Changing World*. Abingdon and New York: Routledge.

Newburn, T. & Reiner, R., 2007. Policing and the Police. In M. Maguire, R. Morgan, & R. Reiner, eds. *Oxford Handbook of Criminology*, Oxford: Oxford University Press.

Republic of South Africa, 1996. Constitution of the Republic of South Africa. Available at: www.thehda.co.za/uploads/images/unpan005172.pdf.

Steinberg, J., 2008. *Thin Blue: The Unwritten Rules of Policing South Africa*, Cape Town: Jonathan Ball.

Vigneswaran, D.V. & Hornberger, J., 2009. *Beyond 'Good Cop'/'Bad Cop': Understanding Informality and Police Corruption in South Africa*, Johannesburg: Forced Migration Studies Programme, University of the Witwatersrand.

# Index

Printed in Great Britain
by Amazon

40689471R00133